A Place to Stand

Also by Samuel Hall:

Daughter of the Cimarron

"*A Place to Stand* is a well-told story that captures the mid-20th century challenges facing a young farm widow on the Oklahoma plains. Highly recommended. Readers will relate to this woman who persevered against overwhelming odds when others expected her to quit."

> **PAULINE HODGES, PH.D.**, College professor & public school teacher; acknowledged historian; editor/author for five largest public school textbook companies in the USA; edited and compiled seven books on the history of the Oklahoma Panhandle; researcher interviewed by Ken Burns for his documentary, "The Dust Bowl."

"Samuel Hall deserves an Oscar for *A Place to Stand*. It's a good read for those interested in the true story of a woman determined to leave a legacy for her sons after her husband dies. She never quite overcame the pain of grief, but moved beyond despair when tribulations stripped her of all but faith in the God who created all things."

> **MARION DUCKWORTH**, Author of 16 books, including *Naked on God's Doorstep* and *The Greening of Mrs. Duckworth*.

Praise for *Daughter of the Cimarron*

"As a consummate crafter of words and characters, Sam Hall weaves an engaging story of one woman's search for herself and her God."

> **BILL MYERS**, Author of 184 books on Goodreads, including Eli.

"Sam Hall writes the kind of narrative I love most, the search for self amidst the search for faith."

> **GINA OCHSNER**, Author of *The Necessary Grace to Fall* (Winner of Flannery O'Connor Award) and *People I Wanted to Be* (Winner of Oregon Book Award).

"*Daughter of the Cimarron* grips the reader's heart while at the same time illuminating the historical period in which the story is set. Author Samuel Hall hits all the right notes in this compelling debut novel. Recommended!"

> **ANN SHOREY**, Author of the *At Home in Beldon Grove* and *Sisters at Heart* series.

Published 2022 by Reify Press Inc.

Printed in the United States of America.

A memoir.

Scripture references are from the King James Version and are in the public domain.

ISBN 978-1-949638-07-3

A Place to Stand

by

Samuel Hall

Published by Reify Stories, an imprint of Reify Press, Aurora, Oregon.

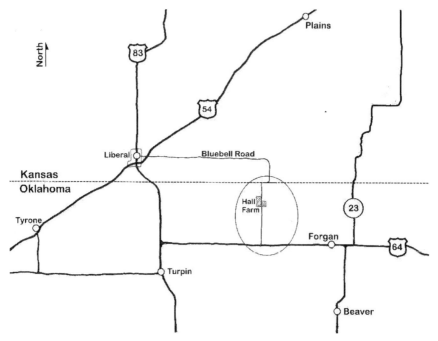

Hall Farm, in the Oklahoma Panhandle.

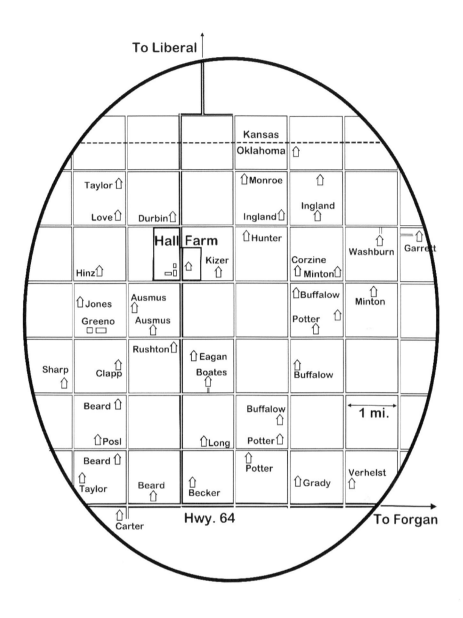

Detail map

Dedication

For my brothers Richard (Dick) Hall & Jerry Hall,
who lived this story with me

Chapters

1   The Gathering Place

August 1950

Claire

Waiting occupied the space between not knowing and knowing. I felt safer not knowing, as if innocence and ignorance could protect us. What we'd learned had come in fragments, pieces of truth pried loose from reality.

I'd always thought I could depend on truth, that it would eventually be safe because God was truth. I'd learned—accepted, even—that I could depend on God, and his truth.

There was just one problem. The more we knew, the worse things seemed to be.

But time doesn't stand still. During the week of waiting for the lab report to be sent to the Medical Arts Clinic, my faith faltered. I believed God cared for us but had no idea if he'd deliver us.

Each night, questions. Sleep came like a barely wound clock. Sometimes not at all. Was it faith to believe God cared, regardless of how he answered? Answers would bring promise or peril, overcoming or being overcome. Somewhere in between lay the sliver of hope that my husband would be all right.

We were at the Medical Arts Clinic in Liberal, waiting again for results from a laboratory report. Three weeks previous, in late August 1950, our family had been intact and unthreatened.

The five of us had trooped outside to sit on the sandy hillock north of the milk house and the big pear tree. On calm summer evenings past mosquito season, we'd slipped into an occasional after-supper ritual with Jerry, Dickie Lee, and Sammy. Ages six, eight, and ten respectively, they prized those special times with Mom and Dad, intended mostly for them.

We'd barely settled on the blanket I spread on the ground when Jerry pointed overhead. "Lookit that bird, Mom."

"Don't you know it's a nighthawk?" Dickie said. We watched

the streamlined creature flit and dive for insects, white flashes on wings, throat, and tail making it easily identifiable. It swooped toward the barn, a silhouette across the road.

A bat darted overhead. The boys giggled and Elmer snorted as I grabbed a shawl to cover my hair. Jerry flung his small body over me. "I'll protect you, Mama."

Dickie pushed him away and put his arms around me. "No, I'll protect you. That bat will gobble Jerry up, like a juicy bug."

Sammy ignored their pushing and shoving, concentrating on the nighthawk's flight. Elmer told the boys to settle down, and we all grew quiet as the dimming sunlight pulled the curtain of night over the rolling prairie.

In all directions, the shortgrass plains of the Oklahoma Panhandle stretched outward where they met the sapphire sky. I envisioned the heavens as an upside-down plate turned over our farm. Known as the Eagan place, it sheltered our little world where we built upon the dreams tethered to our daily lives.

Scarcely more than a whisper, the parched voice of the wind brought with it the aroma of sage from our pasture north of the barn. Such blissful quiet, only in the country. I could never want for more.

As usual, the boys insisted on a story, which meant my stories growing up on Pop's farm in western Kansas. No Mother Goose or once-upon-a-time tales for them. They wanted to hear about chasing badgers and catching tadpoles, discovering wild bird nests, and foot races at Rosedale School. They loved to hear about the time my friend Helen Schweitzer and I ambushed a bully—the biggest kid at school. We pounded him good, and he never tormented another schoolmate again. Mama had a fit when she saw my skinned knees and clothes a mess, but Pop just laughed.

Other favorite stories were about the big cities back east where Elmer and I worked on a traveling sales crew twenty years previous. He would light his pipe and pretend not to be too interested, but I could tell he enjoyed hearing them too.

I glanced at him. Unusually silent, he hadn't started to smoke.

"You want me to get your pipe?" I asked.

"Not tonight. Mouth is sore. Corral gate caught my pipe and jammed the stem up into the roof of my mouth."

I glanced over Dickie's head at Elmer, trying to catch his expression through the gloom. Skinned knuckles, a splinter under a fingernail, or a bovine hoof planted atop his instep, Elmer seldom complained about the bruises and cuts of working with animals or around machinery.

Before I could ask further, he pointed to the southeast, where a thunderhead rose like a giant's fist, catching the last rays of sunlight. "Look there, boys. Might get rain by morning. Could be a toad-strangler." Of course, how could a farmer not consider the weather? He again broke his silence to point out Orion's Belt and correct Sammy's misidentification of Venus as a star.

I always marveled at the night sky, so profound as to be unknowable. Countless points of light studded the deep blue expanse, confirming a divine presence, though Elmer claimed he didn't believe a divine anything. Pop's reminder from scripture countered that: For the invisible things of him from the creation of the world are clearly seen, being understood by the things that are made, even his eternal power and Godhead . . .

Our boys chirped about the day's events, sharing surprises and discoveries peculiar to growing up on a farm, with the ever-present possibility of exploration. We discussed what-ifs and maybes. The new and unusual added variety to our evening ritual.

My heart overflowed each time we ended those sandhill sessions. How blessed we were, having each other.

Elmer grimaced at he sipped his morning cup of hot coffee. Setting the cup down, he arose from the table as I plunged breakfast dishes into steaming dishwater. He shouldered into his khaki shirt. "The road might be slick from the shower last night. But the way Taylor came flying past here this morning, it should be dry enough to get into town without any trouble."

I shot him a look. "What town? We don't need groceries."

Casual like, he said, "Liberal. Too wet to work in the field, so figured I'd go see Hilbig this morning. Have him take a look at this sore in my mouth. It'll just be a quick there and back."

"Nothing doing. If you're seeing Doctor Hilbig about anything above your kneecaps, I'm coming with you, big boy."

"For crying out loud, Claire, those nurses will think I'm a milquetoast."

I reached up and pinched a quarter pound of his cheek. "I'm concerned about those nurses, too. They got awfully friendly with my man the last time you visited that clinic." I pulled his head down and kissed him on the mouth.

His lips lingered, like he wanted more of me. Why did men always feel they had to play that game—be a tough guy; don't show your emotions?

споре

Dr. Albert Hilbig squinted one eye as my husband pointed to the skinned area above his tongue. "So—it won't heal? How'd you do that?"

"Corral gate banged my pipe—nearly drove the stem up through the top of my head. It's plenty sore—"

"And this happened when?"

"Last of August."

"Two weeks ago . . . Tilt your head back, please." He thrust a tongue depressor into Elmer's mouth. "Mmmh. Nurse, hold the light down a bit more, please . . . Pretty sore, is it?"

"Gnngh! Yecgg!"

"I thought so." The doctor placed his right hand on Elmer's shoulder. "I believe it'd be best if we take a biopsy."

Elmer only blinked. Just like him. Show no fear, whether he felt it or not. Sometimes I wondered if he feared anything.

I did. My lower lip began to tremble. I blurted, "Biopsy? What's that?" Without waiting for an answer, I said, "Doctor Hilbig, is this serious?"

He turned to me, his face as expressive as that of a contented cow. "A biopsy is a tissue sample taken from the afflicted area. It's always a concern when a sore doesn't heal, and two weeks is more than enough time. He's experiencing discomfort and a lab test—a biopsy— will tell us why. We'll send the sample to the pathologist in Hutchinson. Results will be back in five to six days . . ."

My heart felt like it was going to fly out of my chest. Despite the doctor's casual manner, I sensed an urgency beneath his words. I had questions, but couldn't speak them.

"Marie will schedule Elmer back here a week from today. You should probably come too, Claire. Any other questions? If not, you can take this young man home with you."

споре

We parked in front of the clinic, across from Epworth Hospital, where I had given birth to each of our three sons. Elmer and I sat in a small waiting room back of the reception desk, waiting to hear truth at this place I did not want to be. Nothing had changed since we'd been in that room the week before. The solitary window looked out onto the same gravel parking lot between the clinic and North McKinley Street. Opposite the parking lot was a dry cleaner, a shoe repair shop, a weed-covered vacant lot, and a beer joint, the Dew Drop Inn.

I turned from staring out at the purposeful parade of men ambling into the Dew Drop Inn. Elmer seemed preoccupied, showing little concern about the pathologist's findings. My head pounded, not having slept much the previous night.

Footsteps in the hallway. About time. Dr. Hilbig entered, mumbling that he'd just come from the hospital and was sorry he'd been delayed. . . . He didn't fool me, and wisely kept his eyes focused on the folder in his hands.

The doctor looked up, took a breath, and spoke to Elmer. "And how are we today?"

Neither of us spoke. I felt a twitch work its way up my back and settle into the base of my skull.

He opened his folder and began. "Well, we received the pathology report yesterday. Not what I was hoping for. It confirms . . . a problem." He stopped, his gaze moving from Elmer to me. "The biopsy shows you have a malignancy in the roof of your mouth, Elmer."

"No! It can't be." My voice must have scraped the ceiling. "Dr. Hilbig, by malignancy, you mean cancer, don't you? That's been a death sentence—for every person we know who's had it." My eyes sought Elmer's.

I wanted to howl. I wished we were someplace else—living in that tiny apartment in Kansas City . . . at a dance in Brownie McNabb's barn . . . back on the road with Deluxe—anywhere but at this fated place, facing an invisible destroyer that threatened my beloved.

Dr. Hilbig's voice continued, a basso profundo in a junkyard, outlining procedures, tests, a specialist in Wichita, . . .

I must have been wrenching Elmer's hand. He grunted but didn't pull away. I could only think how our lives that were once so full seemed about to be swept asunder. Tares had been planted in our garden of Eden while we slept.

5

2 Through a Glass Darkly

Claire

As if by mutual agreement, Elmer and I sat in silence at the kitchen table, listening to the wind—Pop called it the farmer's harbinger of hope or despair. Elmer's mother and the boys were asleep. I brewed a pot of tea and opened a jar of amber honey that Lew Buffalow brought us from Pond Creek. In comparison, what we faced at that moment shriveled anything the wind could bring.

Elmer's voice broke the pall. "Within a day, that wind will change to the northwest. Cousin Ray said *The Farmer's Almanac* forecast a hard winter. We're in good shape, though. Got plenty of feed for the cattle." He grasped his pipe but stopped, letting it clatter to the table. "Better put that away. Hilbig said it's probably what caused all this . . ."

I couldn't speak, fearing I'd dissolve in a flood of tears. Elmer, please tell me we'll get through this. He seemed about to say something, but stopped, a far-off look in his eyes. His movements stiff and deliberate, he hadn't let his eyes engage mine in the casual, playful way that delighted me. I wondered if his own doubts had driven him into himself.

"Got the boys taken care of?"

I'd bunched up a dish towel in my right hand. Carefully smoothing it out on the table, I took a deep breath. "Honey, I told you already. Ray and Edith will stay here until his sister Amy gets in from Denver. We can depend on them. They care more about us than your own blood. And your mother won't have to do a thing."

"Amy's a fine woman. Reminds me of Maggie." He turned businesslike. "We'll leave for Wichita around seven Monday morning. Should be there by mid-afternoon. Give me time to check into the hospital by four o'clock. I'll get you settled first. Hilbig said there's several decent hotels close by. One's across the street from Wesley Hospital."

I hurried to say my part, as if such plans would generate control over our situation. "I'll register at a hotel, but I'm not leaving you to check into that hospital by yourself, buster. I've been by your side for twenty years, and I'm not going to fall in the ditch at a time like this . . . Hilbig never mentioned how long we'd have to be at the hospital . . ."

"Depends on how surgery turns out. He said it was pretty straightforward, but carving into the top of my mouth, well—"

"Elmer, you're going to have everyone in my church praying for you. Not to mention Myrrl and Grace, and my sisters. Ethel and Pearl wouldn't let us go through this all by ourselves. That's what they'll do . . ." Saying those words seemed to dampen the terror which threatened to swarm my thoughts. I pulled him to me, wrapping my arms around his right arm. "But I'm afraid, Elmer. We've never been through anything like this."

Formless fear and my fragile faith disturbed me. Soldiering on, I whispered, "Can't let this destroy us. Ever since Hilbig gave us the results of that lab report, I felt like the floor had dropped out from under me. Not his fault. It's . . ." I couldn't say it aloud. Cancer. The beast, the enemy. "I don't want to think it, but I'm afraid. . . . We're not in the driver's seat now. It's running our lives."

Elmer rubbed the back of his neck. His words rapping like a metronome, he said, "It'll try to take control. But it's not in charge yet." Amazing. My unbelieving husband speaks with confidence, and I'm a wet mop. Can't let fear rule me. Elmer drummed his fingers on the table. "Hilbig speaks highly of this specialist, Melancamp. We'll get through it all right, honey." He patted my hand. "There'll be checkups after we come home. Except for the soreness, I'm feeling good. I'll be okay."

With the sudden realization of one trying to cross a river, but forgetting their canoe, I hurried into the bedroom and returned with my Bible. "Elmer, I'd like to read something—for both of us— some words of encouragement. You want to listen?"

He sucked in his breath and let out a long sigh. He unbuttoned and redid the top three buttons on his shirt. "Won't hurt."

I fanned the pages, finally opening the volume and tracing my finger down until I found the passage I wanted. "Psalm 18. I'll just read the first few verses. It's true, every word . . ."

> *I will love thee, O LORD, my strength.*
> *The LORD is my rock, and my fortress, and my*
> *deliverer; my God, my strength, in whom I will trust;*

7

*my buckler, and the horn of my salvation, and my high
tower . . .*

*In my distress I called upon the LORD, and cried
unto my God: he heard my voice out of his temple, and
my cry came before him, even into his ears. . . .*

I raised my eyes to detect his mood. Elmer had never before
shown the slightest interest in God's Word, disparaging it when I
talked about God's blessings. Concerned I might've offended him,
I asked, "Isn't that an encouragement? Did you . . . doesn't that
make you think there's hope, Elmer?"

"I, uh, maybe so. I can trust strength." A sigh. "I like being
heard . . ." He pulled out his gold-plated Bulova watch, stood, and
stretched. "It's late. Think I'll turn in."

"Those words have lifted my spirits so many times. I wanted
you to have that treasure, too." My eyes followed him as he
stepped outside, into the darkness. After he returned and went
into the bedroom, I wilted. On one knee beside the bentwood
chair, I pressed my face into my arms. "Oh, Father . . ."

Wichita sparked memories of earlier times in similar bustling
cities—the years with Deluxe before we eventually re-started our
lives in Oklahoma. Traveling sales during the twenties felt like an
ongoing adventure, the fancy hotels and bright lights. Except the
dancing. For me, that was liberation—the Charleston, shimmy,
even the tango. Could've done without the nightclubs. Mama
would've been scandalized by the drinking crowd, but I made sure
she didn't know. Since Elmer liked the bangtails, we went to more
horse races than concerts.

I'd forgotten the noise of the city—impatient traffic, bells and
clanking of streetcars, sirens wailing from both directions, and a
distant locomotive whistle. How could healing and treatment exist
in such a place? I was offended that our doctor would send us
here, so far from the calming quiet of the country.

I wondered if the crowds on the sidewalks had ever heard the
sweet piercing call of a meadowlark. That thought calmed me,
fresh as spring rain. Hard as life on the plains could be, I realized I
could hardly wait to return—as soon as the contamination of
cancer was removed from my man.

We knew our way around Wichita. Had been there plenty
times before, back with Deluxe. Elmer liked the city; said it gave

him a feeling of being in touch with what was happening.

This time, I could do with nothing happening.

ॐ

Back from Wichita, I shadowed Elmer every place he went, alert to misstep or stumble. We went to Liberal for his biweekly checkups, but Christmas came as just another date on the calendar.

The hoped-for healing wasn't happening. Sleeplessness and pain were constant. He didn't complain but anyone could tell he was suffering.

The weight of managing the household and running the farm slid downward onto my shoulders. Thank God, Elmer was able to advise me on important decisions. He prepped me for talking to the banker about how much to borrow to keep the farm running, if and when to sell livestock, and planning for the next crop year. I would've been overwhelmed, had I been alone. That would all end, once Elmer got well. Medical bills for Elmer's care and medicines came every month, and I dutifully filed them in the top drawer of the buffet. Someday, we'd be able to mark them all Paid.

ॐ

After New Year's, I went to Liberal to see Chet Naylor at People's National Bank. I liked Naylor. He treated me as an equal. The desperateness of Elmer's condition made me push aside any qualms about my status or capabilities.

"Have a seat, Claire. Elmer didn't feel like joining you today?"

"He's just not doing well, Mr. Naylor. We have to go back to Wichita for a second surgery. Dr. Hilbig called yesterday to get us in as soon as they have an opening. I guess they're awfully busy."

"Best cancer treatment center between Denver and Kansas City, from what I hear."

"But it's not cheap. You have to pay up when you check out." I sighed. "I'll need another two thousand to cover the medical—both here and Wichita, and about three hundred for farm expenses—gasoline, cottonseed cake, fuel and machinery maintenance, seed for spring crops. I'll have to hire some of the work done. Elmer's not strong enough, and the boys are too young to help very much. My oldest is only ten, and I can't ask them to do more . . ."

"I understand, Claire, you've got to take care of your boys and Elmer, especially at a time like this." He drew in a deep breath.

9

"Now, what we have to do . . . Better put a note on the farm. I could get the loan committee to stretch an extra five hundred onto your existing principal, based on just your signature. But for twenty-three hundred, we'll need collateral. Maybe after Elmer's condition improves, we could modify the conditions—"

"No, I understand. We have a long road ahead, and I don't want to worry about the financing part . . ."

"I'll have Eleanor contact the title company and prepare the loan agreement. Come by after you finish your shopping, and the initial papers will be ready so you can sign before our notary. We'll put the rest of it in the mail to save you another trip."

"I'll stop in when we see Dr. Hilbig, before we go back to Wichita."

Naylor told me to give his best to Elmer—that he knew he would pull through. Such a nice, caring man. Certainly not the image of moneylenders we'd had during the thirties.

Talking as we were about how to revitalize two major concerns—my husband and the farm—I almost blurted out to the banker all that was on my heart. Silent messages of can't and won't, should and should-not seemed to shout my incompetency and fears. Yeah, and the fact I was a woman trying to do a man's job.

I hadn't shared the emotional weight of the previous four months with anyone, only asking Myrrl, Ethel, and Pearl to pray with their families . . . for Elmer's healing. Not for me. I had to—

I had to tell someone. Better that I tell Jesus. I hoped he was listening.

3   The Gathering Storm

January 1951

Claire

If there's life, there's hope. I'd always believed that.

Buoyed by prayers of those at home and Doctor Melancamp's assertion that Elmer's operation involved minimal risk, I tried to be optimistic.

It bothered me that this was his second surgery. Which meant that either the first operation wasn't successful, or Doctor Melancamp's diagnosis was incorrect. Maybe both.

I tried not to think of such, hoping faith would prevail where human effort failed. Hollow hope or fragile faith. Brother Caywood might say neither was sufficient, but that was all I had.

Two days after Elmer's second operation, Doctor Melancamp met with us. A tall man with shaggy eyebrows and thatch, his eyes and face flashed an impish grin that belied his serious station in life. He pulled a chair beside Elmer's bed and sat, looking at him. The once virile man had been altered into a thing. He looked more like a mummy, his neck and jaw encased in gauze and tape. He couldn't speak, and thankfully, wasn't able to see himself. I wanted to cry. Instead, I slid a chair beside Elmer's shoulder and drew my arm above his head, turning to face the surgeon.

Doctor Melancamp gave a similar speech to what we'd heard after the initial surgery. He talked about the need for confidence in dealing with a difficult adversary, that he and his team had exercised all diligence despite limitations in the rapidly changing field of oncology. He said, "We believe we've successfully removed all malignant cells in the lymph glands and surrounding areas about your neck and face." He paused to raise his hand and touch Elmer, almost with reverence, it seemed.

I wondered what he must have felt as he wielded his cutting tools upon the skin and sinews of this man I loved so much.

The doctor continued, "Other than massive excision that might permanently affect your quality of life, Elmer, there is one other option. We could use radiation to—"

"Absolutely not." I jerked my hand up. "We will not consider that. I . . . we do not have good reports about that procedure."

The doctor waited for me to run down, his face mournful. "I understand, Mrs. Hall. We respect your feelings in this matter. Radiation can be problematic, despite its successes."

"So where does that leave us?" A spider of doubt crawled up my back. I shook my head, as if to dislodge it. With a great effort at control, I shivered to a forced stillness.

The doctor drew his hands together, almost prayer-like. "I understand your concerns." He drew in his breath. "While we've made every effort to remove all malignancy, we want to be certain, and recommend that Elmer go directly from here to your local hospital for two weeks—in Liberal, I believe? They will monitor his condition every day and report back to us. He can be released day after tomorrow, assuming his condition remains stable."

Doctor Albert Hilbig came to Elmer's room shortly after he was admitted to Epworth Hospital. In his trademark racehorse stride, Hilbig careened through the door, almost causing an aide to drop a bedpan. His usual jovial self, he proclaimed, "Elmer, Melancamp surprised us. We thought you were going straight home. But he wants you here under our careful eye to assure you're healing. More probing and poking, samples and swabs. Now, how do you feel, my good man?"

Elmer liked Hilbig; called him Big Hill on other days, tapping the doc's substantial gut. "Not do-nn-ng worta d-mm . . . T'me mm gonn lib." He waved his hand limply. I thrust a towel, dabbing drool from his chin.

Hilbig threw up both hands, his eyes wide and mouth agape. "Sure, you're gonna live, you ol' coyote. You're too . . . too mean to die." Turning to Dorothy Glover, my favorite nurse, he said, "Get his vitals." And to Imogene Briles, leaning in the door to wave at Elmer, he said, "Get this boy something to eat. Something he doesn't have to chew and that has taste."

I began to relax. Home folks—people I knew—how special they were.

Within days I knew, and I think Elmer did, too. He wasn't

feeling any better, and none of the tests performed by the medical staff at the hospital showed improvement.

Then the doctor said he wanted to talk to me. Something was up. I managed to speak. "Whatever it is, you might as well tell both of us. Elmer has never been a coward, and he's not going to be one now." I turned and headed to Elmer's room.

Ray's sister Amy and her gentleman friend, Henry Amen, had come in to see Elmer. They took one look at my tear-stained face and arose to gather their coats. Amy, dear Amy, fighting back tears, embraced me on their way out.

Standing there beside Elmer's bed, I listened as Dr. Hilbig told us they'd done all they could. I wondered how many times he'd had to give such bad news to other families. For Elmer, he said three or four months, which meant April or May.

Much as I tried not to, I could only weep, gasping out a prayer. *Oh, Heavenly Father, minister to us. Help us. We need you so much. We need your mercy.*

The doctor had a printed protocol for home care situations; plus, he'd drive the eighteen miles to the farm as many times as we wanted or was necessary to attend to Elmer's needs.

Brother Caywood once said we serve a merciful God, but he doesn't always show his mercy in the way we expect or want. I didn't see how that could be mercy, but there had been other things in the Bible I didn't understand.

Sammy

It was two days before Fathers' Day, after I'd finished fifth grade. We'd just gotten up, and Mama gathered us three boys to her. She was crying, but she started talking anyway.

Dizzy with alarm, I pulled away to run to Daddy's bedroom. He wasn't on his sickbed. When I returned to the living room, Mama told us that the night before—right after they took us in to see him—Daddy had passed away.

Passed away. I tried to comprehend the swirl of meaning in those two words as Mama's voice wavered in the background, a flag in the wind . . . While we slept, an ambulance had taken Daddy to the mortuary in Liberal.

Jerry and Dickie were already crying. We three crowded around Mama, wetting her dress with our tears. Daddy truly was gone. I didn't want to hear it, couldn't believe it. Surely it was a mistake. I expected Mama to stand, arms outstretched, and proclaim it wasn't true. Eleven-year-olds didn't lose their daddies. Dickie and Jerry, younger than me . . . how could we go on without Daddy? All our lives, he had been with us, and then he wasn't.

Mama went to the wall phone, cranking for the operator to call relatives and old friends from far away. One of the first was Daddy's older son, Durward, down in Texas—the one we called our big brother. Then she called her kinfolks up in Kansas and back in Ohio. Same message, time after time, all of Daddy's brothers and people we'd heard them talk about. Part way through Mama's calling list, someone cut into her monologue—really made her upset. Said they didn't know why Daddy had lasted beyond the first day of spring, as if he shouldn't have extended the pain of their suspense. I wanted to yell at them.

Dickie and Jerry stayed in the kitchen with Mama, but after hearing her tell people the same thing, I went outside. The more I heard, the worse it seemed. I headed to my private place—two big spreading locust trees southeast of the house.

I sat under a low sweeping branch that almost touched the ground, where no one could see me—from the road or the house. A rising breeze brushed leafy twigs against my face, a gentle hand of comfort. Again, the realization—we were alone—and I cried awhile. No one else I knew had lost their daddy. Losing him meant we'd lost almost everything. All Daddy had been to us, and how he would've been there to watch me and my brothers grow up, being our defender. Would Mama be our protector? She wasn't nearly as strong as Daddy.

I began thinking what Daddy had been. First, a farmer, which automatically made him a weatherman. Since we couldn't afford new tractors and combines every other year, he had to be a fixer of things big and small. Besides that, he was an animal doctor, horse trader, pig seller, salesman, and cattleman. When he took time off from farming, he was a pond fisherman, bird hunter, and sometime beer drinker. Mama didn't like that; I could tell drinking made her scared. She said smoking a pipe all those years is why he got sick. We boys knew he was a great storyteller and Mama said he was always pulling pranks when they were on the road.

I choked up when I thought of Daddy being a talker. We'd never hear his voice again.

Mama said when he was sales boss with Deluxe, no one could

put deals together like Elmer. Before he and Mama had us kids, he'd been a traveler, scout, salesman, and sales crew boss. I remembered a school meeting. Everyone quieted down when he stood to say his piece.

Daddy told us you had to be a man of ideals and convictions; that I'd learn more what that meant as I got older. More than once Daddy said someone had to stand up for the little man.

He upset some folks when he spoke out against people using county equipment for their relatives. When I let on that such talk made me anxious at school, he said it wasn't always easy to do the right thing. Daddy embarrassed people when he called them out, so they didn't like him.

Right then, I didn't care. How could we live without Daddy?

Claire

Grief is a hard taskmaster, but I couldn't let it keep me from watching out for my boys. All the days, weeks, and months I'd devoted to caring for Elmer . . . Now everything was for my sons. They were all I had, and I was all they had.

Ethel came down from Dodge the next day. I couldn't have done without her. She helped get the boys' clothes ready for the services at Forgan Baptist Church—shoes polished, and shirts ironed. Even laid out an extra shirt for each, knowing about accidents and spills from raising her four boys and three girls.

Somehow, we got through the funeral, the hardest day of my life. Through tears, I saw a vast throng of caring friends waiting out in the parking lot when my boys and I descended the church steps that day. That gave me strength, knowing they had come that day to honor Elmer's life—and to show their support for us. Blanche said folks had driven from all over the Panhandle, besides the relatives. I guess all of his brothers came, except Bud, the youngest. No one knew where he was. Elmer had been the bright star of that family, the one who'd made something of himself. With him gone, I wondered when I'd see the others again. Family ties are never what we expect them to be.

Myrrl and Grace were our only overnight guests after we returned from the cemetery. Their kids had gone back to Ness City with my sister Pearl. Exhausted as I was, I wanted Myrrl and Grace to stay and never leave us, knowing that was impossible.

The following morning, Ray and Edith Hunter pulled in beside Myrrl's blue Ford. Edith, her sunburned face wreathed in a smile, carried a small basket as they entered. Rather surprising, as she never went to much trouble cooking. After I introduced everyone, Edith said, "Got a clutch of eggs from our bantams, Claire. Bet you never had such eggs. Since they're smaller, they got a higher percentage of yolk—makes great omelets."

"Oh. My boys have never eaten an omelet—"

"I'll fix those boys an omelet." Grace had been listening. "That will be fine. In fact, I'll make breakfast for everyone."

"Nah," Ray spoke up. "Edith wanted to help out a little, so we just brung these little eggs." He looked my direction. "Claire, you let us know anytime you need anything." With that, he turned and Edith followed him out, waving at the boys.

The omelet was a success. Grace knew what she was doing. After the boys went outside to play, I poured a round of coffee and sat at the kitchen table with those two favorite people in my life.

Myrrl cleared his throat. Twice. I looked at him, waiting. Finally, he said, "Well, little sister, what are your plans?"

Blanche and Henry came by to collect her dishes and a roasting pan just as Myrrl and Grace were leaving. They hurried in and out, apologizing for interrupting. As I watched both couples leave, I realized how much I wanted someone to stay. Loneliness and grief, like giant pillows pressing down, seemed about to suffocate me.

Grace had cautioned me about the blues. The boys and I would be alone; probably why Myrrl questioned our staying on the farm. But there we were, just the four of us. Our house, quiet after the hubbub of activity and voices, seemed bleak and lonely, so I took the boys outside to our special place north of the house. Jerry held my hand all the way.

Once we got settled, he said, "Are we going to watch the stars, Mama?"

The older two laughed. Dickie said, "There's no stars in the middle of the afternoon, silly." He looked to me. "We're here so we can talk. This is our talking place, ain't it, Mama?"

By then, all three had crouched in a semicircle around me, looking up expectantly into my face. I almost broke down, looking into their trusting eyes. Tears coming again, I ducked my head. At that moment, I had to be strong. "Yes, this will always be our talking place, just like when Daddy was here."

Their questions ascended, rising like the morning glory vine climbing the trellis Elmer built back of the house. Each blossom as fragile as my hope. They didn't expect answers; my little soldiers simply wanted to hear me say everything would be okay. Reassurance. My heart swelled, a growing confidence within me. God whispering affirmation of my leadership.

The throaty sound of a '38 Ford turned our attention to the driveway. We trooped back to the house.

Durward and his new wife Wilma emerged from a blue coupe. They had visited his mother in Elkhart, but he'd promised they'd stop and see us before they returned to Borger and there they were. I was so glad. Brawny arms outstretched, he engulfed me with a hug. Wilma, a striking redhead, was new to us. I fell into the lattice of their arms as she patted my back.

Breathless, I said, "It's so good to see you. Won't you stay for supper?"

Durward leaned down, drawing his cheek next to mine. "I'm sorry, Claire. We can't stay long. Gotta be out on the rig at six tomorrow morning, ready to go." He released me and leaned against the front fender, a breeze riffling his dark wavy hair. "We didn't get to talk much before the funeral, but I wanted to see what you plan to do, now . . ."

My antenna up, I said, "What have you been hearing . . . about what I plan to do?"

A sheepish grin. "Can't catch you unawares, can I?" His right hand fumbled in his shirt pocket for a pack of Chesterfields. Idly spanking it against the palm of his other hand and withdrawing a cigarette, he said, "John's crowd—and some of the others on Dad's side—said they ain't no way you're gonna make it out here on this little plot of ground."

I stared at him as he lit up. "Do you believe that?" My throat felt dry.

"Claire, I know you. Shoot no, I don't believe that. You're a strong woman."

"Well, why throw salt in my eyes with rumors?"

"That ain't all they said . . . but I wanted to put an end to their gossip. 'Cause I think what they're saying is bull . . ."

"And what else are they saying?" By that time, my breathing was shallow, agitated.

"They're saying . . . that you plan to farm the boys out—to different relatives—so you can go work in—"

"That's a lie!" I hissed. "A stinking lie. I wouldn't split up my

17

boys. . . . What kind of mother would do that?" I wanted to yell.

Wilma put an arm around me. I heard Durward's voice. "That's what I thought you'd say, Claire. Anybody tells me different, I'll cram it down their throat."

Durward stood behind Wilma, wrapping his arm around both of us. "We're not that far away, Claire. It might seem like it, but if you need us or want to talk, you call—anytime."

I knew he'd come if I called one lonely, terrifying night. He was a stalwart, like his father. But I also knew in the end, I'd have to depend on God.

Behind it all, my brother Myrrl's question still haunted me: What are your plans?

My plans? That's easy. To finish what Elmer and I had started. To build a home, a foundation, a legacy, nest, den, mooring, whatever we might call it—a secure place for us to grow old together and for the boys to launch their lives.

That's what every responsible parent wanted for their kids. Myrrl knew that; he wanted the same heritage for his own. Actually, I knew that wasn't really what he was asking. He questioned if our debt-ridden little farm would withstand the storms of life.

Such a question. I didn't know if we could survive on the place. But what choice did I have? Elmer said you have to play the cards you're dealt or get out of the game. The farm, such as it was, was all we had. We had to make it go . . . or quit.

Couldn't quit. But the odds of making it on that dryland spread looked mighty thin.

My mind went back ten years to when Elmer and I believed we were going to make it. The drought and dust storms had ceased. Of course, on the Great Plains, nothing was ever certain, but we'd survived the worst the prairie wind could deliver. We felt we could hold on. But we didn't know then what we knew now.

4   The Farm on the Prairie

Spring 1944

Claire

In our purely imperfect way, Elmer and I clawed and worked and endured through the thirties and forties to possess our promised land. Four hundred acres was small for a dryland farm in the Panhandle. But with adequate rain, we'd have enough to wire the house and install indoor plumbing.

After those first rough years, three wet seasons had turned our fortunes around. Wheat and milo harvests had brought in enough to anchor us in the caliche bottoms and sandhills of western Oklahoma, pulling us up from survival to fulfillment. It made me want to sing, which I did with increasing regularity, whether peeling potatoes or scrubbing overalls. Sitting at my upright piano, I would sometimes play arrangements from simpler days gone by.

However, a dissonant note interrupted my song of satisfaction. We had struggled with the capricious plains weather so hard and so long, I hadn't paused to look in a mirror to ponder the image staring back at me. If pressed, I might've summed up who I was by pointing to our three little boys and saying, "for them." They were, indeed, much of my personal identity. Mother and wife.

I knew there was more to me, but I only began to recognize it when the stirrings of the hardest day appeared on the first of many days of uncertainty. Without that event—a slow-moving rockslide that swelled into an avalanche—I wouldn't have perceived God's hand, leading me to perform tasks far beyond what I ever thought I could do.

Certainly, I wanted to express my originality and uniqueness to any who might doubt my goodness and abilities. But had I known the cost, I wouldn't have touched the key, much less opened the door to that journey of self-discovery.

I read my Bible most days and even took our boys to a little community church nearly every Sunday. My husband never shared my religious convictions—that God's word is true, that He is good, and that He created everybody and everything. In fact, Elmer didn't believe in any higher power beyond working hard, provide for your own, and respect as you are respected.

For my part, I believed the farm had tumbled into our hopeful hands because God wanted us to have it. Small and ordinary, the house still hoped for a coat of paint from the day we bought the place eight years before, in September of '36.

One afternoon, having returned from the ice plant in Liberal and to see Elmer's sister Maggie, I let slip a word of thanks for God's blessings. While Elmer unloaded the blocks of ice and put them in the icebox, I began supper, singing "Amazing Grace" half under my breath. Aware Elmer was frowning at me, I said, "What?"

He banged his pipe on the ceramic coffee mug he'd taken from the Waldorf-Astoria when we were on the road. "Claire, you give the Almighty credit for everything good that happens to us. If he's responsible for the good things, why doesn't he protect us from the bad? We lost our jobs and everything but the shirts on our backs during the thirties. If God was around, he didn't show me he cared." He stood and grabbed his hat. "Once we started farming, we didn't get a drop of rain for months. Months! It looked like the whole creation was going to blow away. So don't give me that God nonsense . . ."

His emotion almost buried me before I parsed his words. The potato I'd just peeled slid out of my hand onto the breadboard. I began cutting, each slice a blessing from the Holy One.

Did he just refer to this land as creation? Does he realize what he's saying? That's just a step from confessing the Creator's existence. I stifled a chuckle and tried to manufacture an answer. Usually, Elmer clammed up or went outside whenever the name of Jesus was spoken respectfully. But there he was, loosing a tirade against the nature of God—like dumping sour milk over a vase of roses.

This wasn't merely a phase. Maggie told me Elmer had gotten cranked up when she said, "Thank God." She just let him roar, which surprised me. I'd expected her to tell me she'd grabbed his overalls by the suspenders and had given him a shake. I snorted, amused by my imagined picture of such a thing.

Elmer whirled like he'd been snake-bit. "What's so funny?"

"Oh, er, nothing. . . . Just thinking of something . . . that Maggie said."

His quick stare told me he suspected otherwise. Not surprisingly, he was offended.

"I'm sorry, Elmer. I'm not making fun of you. Believe me. I really was thinking of something about Maggie."

Mumbling about checking on the pigs, he barged outside, shutting the front door none too gently.

I stewed over that exchange for a day or two but didn't try to talk it out with my husband. Wouldn't have done any good. For one thing, I wasn't sure how to go about it. Elmer already knew how Maggie and I felt about God. He would've gotten his back up if I'd pushed further exploration of believing anything about God.

Our families and most people I knew who would talk about religion had elevated evasion to a fine art. Avoid conflict at all costs. We would have discounted the problem—if there really was a problem—with the expectation that it would all go away. Or not matter.

I wondered how long before an incident or casual conversation would push our differences about the meaning and purpose of life under our noses again. Worldview was the issue, according to Reverend Holder. So aggravating. At times, I felt the primitive impulse to go screaming out into our cow pasture . . . in the middle of some August night . . . clothes and hair askew . . . simply to relieve my frustration at such lack of engagement.

In the meantime, I accepted that my husband would never discuss politics or religion calmly. He could only disagree or attack. No in-between, so I chose not to dwell upon it.

Elmer didn't object to my reading the Bible as long as he didn't have to listen. He seemed indifferent to my taking the boys to Bethel, the neighborhood church, as long as Sunday dinner still appeared on the table—on time.

Niggling doubts demanded that he acknowledge our differences peacefully, if for no other reason than to confirm his caring for me, and my love and respect of him. At times, he seemed driven to show his way was better than mine—like a competition between us.

Actually, he didn't have a way. Elmer had no faith, except in himself. He depended on his quick mind and ability to outsmart or outwork anyone else. Rather than let me be, it seemed he needed to prevent what I had from rising up against him. As Pop once said, perhaps it was evidence that God's Spirit was contending with his spirit.

Elmer probably saw my willingness to cast my cares upon the Lord as naïve, and possibly a put-down of him. No way could he express such a commitment, when he saw it mocking his cupful of himself.

When my brother Myrrl met Elmer, he quietly told me he believed Elmer had a complaint against God. Not something I wanted to hear. I couldn't bear to hear such speculation about the man I planned to marry, even from my favorite brother, and told him to put a lid on it. Nevertheless, hadn't Myrrl's insight been confirmed by our conflict, and my frustration with Elmer's hard-headedness?

Having been married to Elmer fourteen years, and never seeing any softening in his attitudes toward religion or God, I had to face how appalled Mama and Pop must've been that I hadn't married a man of faith.

But not married to Elmer? I loved him, so much, and couldn't imagine life without him. He had given me something I never quite expected, a feeling of legitimacy. I felt like a queen, knowing that this tall man with the hazel eyes and chiseled profile had chosen me out of any number of other women. Yet I felt stuck, wed to someone who couldn't understand who Jesus is, let alone begin to see why He meant so much to me.

5   Losses

Claire

I called to Elmer as he went to the front door, "Is something wrong?"

"I'm going out to the pasture. That two-year-old whiteface is due, and I haven't seen her in two days. Ray said he'd come over this week to check her out, but I'm not waiting any longer." He opened the door, which brought Ring to his feet for an excited dash around the yard.

"Can we go, Daddy?" Sammy and Dickie both ran for the door.

I reached out and snatched one by the suspenders and the other by his arm. "Hold it. You boys stay inside with the baby." Joining Elmer out on the stoop, I said, "Why don't you wait, Elmer? That wind is out of the southeast. Those clouds are coming with it. Look at the lightning!"

"It better not storm. We've got a decent looking wheat crop, but . . ." He paused. "I need to see about that heifer."

The wind suddenly quieted. Together, we edged away from the house, which blocked our view of the threatening sky. Clouds frothed over Lew and Kate Buffalow's place, two miles east. "Look at that sky, Elmer. You go now and you'll get soaked. There's sure to be more lightning, too." As if in answer, thunder grumbled overhead and the leaves of the big cottonwood chattered in a nervous frenzy.

Two small faces peered out from the house. At a bark from me, the boys hastily closed the door. Wind again rattled the cottonwood. Raindrops, big as dimes, lashed the house and trees, like a giant flinging liquid stones.

Elmer had seen enough. "Awright, let's get inside." Yet he stood, looking up. I grabbed his arm and pulled him to the front door. Indoors, we watched from the kitchen window as the wind rose, as if borne by the thunder. To the north, the pasture and fields lay bathed in an unnatural light, but roiling clouds soon choked off sunlight. A sudden clatter on the roof drew Elmer back to the window. He cursed. "Look at that—hail!"

Marble-sized pebbles of ice dotted the yard, quickly mounding into small dunes of white before the whipping wind. Elmer swore again and paced from one side of the kitchen window to the other. "If hail hits the wheat field, we'll lose it all. It'll cut the stalks like a scythe, now that it's headed out."

Half a beat later, all around us sounded as if we were inside a drum. I wanted to cry, wishing I could conjure a way to stop the catastrophe. Not only for myself, but for my man. An arm around his waist, I groped for positive words. Exhortation seldom penetrated Elmer's stone veneer. I could only be with him.

Four-year-old Sammy piped up, "Mama, Mama! There's Ray!"

I turned to see Elmer's cousin lurching from his old Chevy toward the house, one hand clamped on his Stetson. Elmer flung the door open. As Ray skidded in, the boys stared in awe at the pair of scuffed Acme boots that propelled him into the house in a dozen bounds.

Gasping for breath, he removed his drenched vest and hat and tossed them beside the door. "Boy, oh boy! It's raining pitchforks and kangaroos. About the time I got to Kizer's, that caliche turned slick as glass. I was all over that road and could hardly see besides—"

A jarring clap of thunder shook the house. The baby wailed from the back room. I scooped up the two boys and stumbled to the crib. To the east, lightning jittered across the curdled sky. I hovered over little Jerry, clutching the boys. Seconds later, another mighty boom echoed above the wheat field to the east.

An acrid smell penetrated the charged air. I cried, "Elmer!"

A chair hit the floor and I felt him beside me.

"That was just outside the window," I whispered. I put down the boys, who quickly clutched my legs. Picking up the baby, I leaned into Elmer's chest.

"The hail's quit, Elmer." Ray called from outside the bedroom.

Elmer squinted and leaned toward the window. "Yeah, after it did its damage."

The wind continued for another half hour, whipping rain sideways against the lap siding. Nervous jumps of light marched northwest across the pasture. Sage-colored hills bled white. Finally, the rain quieted to a mist. Our front yard looked like a phantom sea.

I opened the kitchen window. The rolling pasture hills gleamed in the afternoon light, and the prairie lay quiet, its magical smell after rain like that of new-cut clover. All was silent but the patter of rain dripping from trees.

Ray coughed twice, which meant he had something to say. "I told Edith this is the craziest country to live in—dry as a bone for months at a time, then we get half a year's rain in four hours."

I tucked the blankets around the baby, trying to recall snatches of encouragement Pop had given me as a girl, when I was despondent or afraid. "I'll fix supper, Elmer." No response. I motioned to Ray. "Why not stay and eat with us? Cornbread and beans."

Elmer had spoken little once the hail began. I tried to think of something else to say. The previous year's bumper wheat crop had raised our expectations high—maybe too high. No greenbugs, grasshopper plague, or hard freeze, leaving the elegant stems of wheat to wave in the wind. Now that same wind brought life-giving rain, but turned it into a destroyer, as if ruin was its true nature.

Elmer's frustration spread a contagion of tension among us. The boys spoke in whispers or not at all. Ray coughed, almost comical in his effort to keep conversation going. He muttered that the Buffalows might miss the card party Saturday. Lew had told him Kate had jabbed a nail in her hand the day before and it was paining her considerable.

Elmer glanced up, his face grim. "At least the rain won't hurt the pig crop. . . . Makes no difference, anyway. Hog prices are at beggar's level. I'll have the most pigs ever, but you can bet we'll make less money than last year."

Ray's hesitant cough introduced another opinion. "It's a sorry market, Elmer. But look at the bright side—the war's almost over. If it was to go much longer, Roosevelt would call up us farmers. Then you and me'd be off to the South Pacific, fightin' the Japs. Those fanatics never knowed when to quit, even when they was beat."

I shuddered. No. Elmer couldn't leave me and the boys. The thought of him going off to war sent chills up my back. I needed to affirm the positive. "Ethel and Pearl and Gar all have sons in uniform. Eight of their boys—and they're all safe."

"I suppose so." Elmer seemed distracted. "That storm was a blow below the belt. Let's go look for that cow . . . and see if I have any wheat left."

Ray followed him outside. A flash of sunlight glinted across the saturated field. As Elmer climbed into Ray's pickup, I asked God to lift his spirits.

৽৽৶

They were gone a long three hours before I heard that old pickup, slogging up the road.

Elmer didn't raise his head when he got out of the Chevy. Usually a sign things hadn't gone well. Ray came in first, waving one hand. "We found that Hereford the other side of the pond. A stillborn—nice little bull calf, looked like."

"That ain't all—" Elmer's voice had an edge to it, and he almost never said 'ain't.'"

Ray chimed in, "That big roan cow was laying over by the west fence—deader'n a doornail. Struck by lightning. Probably too close to the fence and lightning run the wires. That was it for her."

Elmer said, defeat slowing his words, "Wheat field is done. Pounded into the ground like Tojo's army had taken a hammer to it."

I pulled him to me. "We can still farm with horses, Elmer. And I don't have to have that washing machine."

Ray coughed. "You lost a good third of your wheat crop, Elmer. Just a crying shame. It was a nice stand, too." He looked over as if that might be an encouragement and coughed again. "If it ain't hail, grasshoppers, or green bugs, then it's the drought or a hard freeze. The High Plains on any given year can make you or break you. Ain't no wonder some folks just packed up and left. Me and Edith—we ain't gonna leave. We come here to stay."

Elmer had handled disappointment before, but the storm felt like tribulation. I wondered what he thought of God right then. Expecting him to curse, I squeezed his hand and motioned both men to join me at the round oak table. "Why don't I get you coffee before we have supper? There's a few cookies left, if my bandits haven't gotten into them." A quick glance toward the living room, the boys were playing cars with blocks of wood Elmer had cut for them.

Ray waved my invitation away. "Thanks Claire, but Edith will be expecting me. Doubt we got any hail, but she'll be looking for them old hens that didn't have sense enough to get outta the rain."

Elmer spoke as if he hadn't heard. "For the first time, I feel like we've been hit below the belt. Both of those dead cows—over a hundred and twenty dollars, counting the calves they were carrying. Worth more than that on the black market—"

"Ain't nothing to do but get up and keep on going, don't you reckon?" Ray said. "You probably had a few setbacks when you was on the road selling—before you got back to farming."

Elmer eyed him. "Before I started farming? Yeah, I did, but I hadn't been beat down for nine straight years before getting a decent crop last summer."

I said, "We aren't beat yet, Elmer. Not really. We always got through those hard times. And think of the wonderful people we've met—the DeBeys, Lew and Kate, Ray—you and Edith. Henry and Blanche. Most everybody in this community is salt-of-the-earth people. That's what you called them. We can depend on them. That wasn't so when we were in sales." Elmer looked like his mound of defeat was beginning to melt. "I shouldn't forget Myrrl and Grace. And you said you'd never met a man like my dad. Elmer, God has been wonderful to us. We've got our boys. . . . We could've done a lot with that wheat crop. I'm disappointed, too. But if it hadn't been for the grace of God—"

"Okay, okay. Back off. It was . . ." Elmer sighed deeply from his chest. "I thought the bad years were behind us. When we crawled out of that, I guess I figured we were on the high road, like back on the crew. Made big money; traveled lots of places. Maybe it spoiled me. Not that I think religion had anything to do with getting through it. Yeah, it hasn't been a bed of roses, but we've had good times and . . . we've met good people."

He poured more coffee and held the cup with both hands out in front of him, as if giving an offering. He lifted the cup so his eyes met mine over the rim through the rising steam. "This means we won't be able to get a place for the folks. We may have to make room for them."

My breath caught. No way would I allow them to crowd us out of our home again. My feelings must've showed, because Ray suddenly stood to go.

He slid into his vest, stuffed his kerchief and rawhide gloves in a pocket, and grabbed his hat. "Uh, I'd better get home for supper. Anyways, it can't get no worse. Don't bother with them dead cows. McCarter claimed coyotes wouldn't eat his lightning-struck cow a month ago. But if them carcasses lay out in the sun three, four days, they'll get good and ripe. Coyotes will clean 'em up in nothing flat." With that, he mashed his hat to his ears and clattered out the door.

27

It did get worse. Stucks Potter pulled in our driveway two days later. Pearl stayed in the car, her head down. For someone usually wisecracking, Stucks walked like he'd been kicked in the gut. He and Pearl had just come from Beaver Hospital, where they'd been with Lew and Kate. He said he had bad news. Shortly after Lew had brought her in, McGrew had diagnosed her with lockjaw. At that stage, nothing they could do.

I went alone out to the hill north of the house, feeling like my soul had dried up. So capricious—this act of God. The wild storm had ravaged crops across the county, but a single rusty nail in the end of a stick had infected Kate. We could always look to next year for another crop, but Kate was gone forever.

I felt like I'd lost part of myself, like when Mama died.

6   The Care of Cows and Kids

Claire

I hadn't appreciated how blessed I was to have sisters until the day I cried with Maggie.

It began as a hurry-up day. I'd started baby Jerry's bath when Sammy and Dickie burst through the front door, Dickie babbling that "Daddy has a sick cow and he wants you . . . wants you . . ."

The boys waited as patiently as five- and three-year-olds can be expected to stand still while I dried off my naked child and dusted his bottom with talcum. He squealed, expecting a game of tickle and raspberries on his tummy. "Sorry, baby boy, we've got to go see Daddy's cow."

"It's not a c-cow," Sammy shook his head. "Dickie calls everything a cow—even the old b-bull."

Emerging outside, I relished the bright May day, with only a wrinkling of clouds to the southwest. The breeze picked up, but I'd cocooned the baby against the chill. Ray Hunter's pickup was parked by the corral fence, so either he'd happened by or Elmer had driven over to fetch him, as we had no telephone. Good—Ray was the neighborhood expert on livestock ailments and cures. He saw me and waved.

Elmer had already isolated the animal, a whiteface yearling steer, in the holding pen. The boys watched wide-eyed as the men quickly got two ropes on him—a front leg and a back leg. The end of one rope went over the snubbing post at the center of the pen and the other to a stout post at the side. Taking the slack out of their ropes each time the steer lunged, they soon had him wobbling on his two free legs. Down he went and they had him where they wanted him.

I'd helped Elmer with enough livestock crises that another animal predicament seemed manageable. Elmer wanted me nearby in case they needed something right away. From snatches of conversation, I gathered the animal had a dangerous and gross condition, a cut infested with screwworms.

"Lookit them . . . maggots, Elmer. . . . They . . . eating him alive . . . Hold it!"

The yearling erupted in a frenzy of bawling and jerking against the ropes.

I barked at the boys to move back, while covering Jerry's face against the wind. We resumed our surveillance—close enough to hear a summons from Elmer but far enough away that the boys might not hear the men swearing.

Ray's operating tool was an oil-soaked rag on a stick, which he thrust at the animal's belly, the apparent site of the infestation. That started another round of bellowing and shouts about maggots and gore. Elmer leapt up to retrieve a can of kerosene. As he sluiced the kerosene on the lesion, the steer emptied his bowels.

I grimaced. I had just washed that shirt. The boys shrilled at the sight of their daddy's face. Enough. I turned to leave, pushing Sammy and Dickie ahead of me. Too late. I twisted aside and lost my breakfast.

I had little time to recover, what with the baby starting to cry and the older two babbling about Mama being sick. Elmer's voice carried against the wind, hollering something. I wiped my face with my apron, sang a few notes to the baby, and shuffled back toward the corral.

All I could see was Elmer's hat bobbing up and down. Removing a rope from an animal was often harder than getting it on, and this appeared to be one of those times. Ray bounced up, dabbed a third rope around the animal's neck and looped it over the snubbing post. More shouts. Ray yelled, "That'll take the fight out of him, Elmer."

The two men flopped on the ground, their chests heaving. Manure and muck dominated, but I saw red smears on their shirtsleeves and overalls. "You all right?"

Elmer dismissed my question with a wave. I croaked, "I'm taking the boys to the house. Come get me if you need . . ."

It was one time I was glad I wasn't a man.

ง∾ౕ

Lacking enough emulsion for additional treatments of the steer, Elmer cleaned up and prepared for a trip to Liberal. Grimacing, he showed the boys where he'd been stepped on and kicked. He suddenly sat, his hand extended. "Claire, can you give me a dollop of Bag Balm? Look at this hand. Stupid. Forgot to put on my gloves before grabbing that rope."

The boys crowded around to look. The lariat, with steer attached, had zipped through his grip, leaving a red welt across his left hand.

"Oh, Elmer! That's going to be sore for a while." He winced as I rinsed cold water over his palm and spread Bag Balm across the wound before wrapping his mitt in gauze. "You're not driving anywhere, honey. I'll get what you need from the vet."

My tough guy managed a smile. "Okay, I'll trade you the grand opportunity to do business with the horse doctor if you'll give up watching the boys for a few hours."

I almost got lockjaw from trying not to giggle and whoop. Much as I loved our boys, I also loved the few chances I got to un-cling them from my skirt. Once in the car, I did whoop as I headed to Liberal.

It had been a while since I'd been just by myself. The best part of going to town was that I'd get to stop at Maggie's while the vet mixed his potions. Still smiling, I must have talked to myself the whole eighteen miles to Liberal. Some called it the hub of southwest Kansas. Its 5,000 people made it bigger than any other town within sixty-five miles. We got our groceries there, doctored, and did our banking. Elmer made a point to drop in to Ezra Shorb's hardware store for the out-of-date and unusual, plus equipment parts the blacksmith couldn't create. He sometimes took the two older boys along if he wasn't in a hurry. I mused whether Maggie and I should venture in there sometime . . .

My reminiscing brought me to the outskirts of town. I went to the vet's office first.

Bob White's toothbrush moustache and lubricated hair reminded me of the song-and-dance men we'd often see when we were on the road. White considered himself a lady killer, which always irritated me. Thankfully, when I went in this time, he was all business, and said he'd have the emulsion ready in an hour.

Except for Elmer's brother John's four-year-old, Gary, Maggie was alone—Billy at school and Gracie working part time. She gave me a hug and showed me a new recipe she wanted to try. But I could tell she was upset; she kept shaking her head as she put on a pot of water for tea. Then the declaration: "We've got to get something permanent for the folks."

I waited for an explanation.

"Claire, you know Earl's, uh, his woman—Gertrude, I think it is?"

"Oh, yes. I thought he'd have dropped her by now. He brought her out to the farm. I learned more about her than I really cared to know. Face powdered up like she was rolled in flour."

"Yes. Well, last week, they came here, insisting I take John's girls."

"You're not serious."

"Completely. That female isn't even a member of the family, and she pipes right up, telling me how easy it would be to help John out. After all, the girls could take care of their little brother Gary—she called him Larry . . ."

"You shouldn't have to take those girls anyway, Maggie. You've had Gary—" I motioned toward the bedroom. "—all his life."

"I have no intention of taking those girls. But when John showed up last Tuesday—I remember, because I was meeting a friend later that afternoon and could hardly get him out of the house. John was all lathered up about his in-laws Weldon and Hassie. They said they were done keeping his kids. Weldon told John that Hassie was packing up the kids' stuff and he'd better come down there and get them by morning."

I shook my head. "I'll never understand a man who doesn't take care of his own."

"Makes no difference to John. They're a bother to him." Maggie looked defeated. Oddly, I was relieved. I had imagined her as super-woman, and realized I'd been comparing myself to her. She continued, "Hassie told him the girls had gotten to be a handful. She's wore out and Weldon's blood pressure is acting up. They called John and laid down the law."

"Did John take the girls back?"

Maggie rolled her eyes. "John took them across town and dumped them with the folks."

"With your folks? Not in a one-bedroom house."

"I wanted you to know. John will be after Elmer to get them in a bigger place."

I said, "And I suppose he'll expect someone else to pay for it? He only wants it so he'll have a place to flop. With those girls sleeping in the living room, he can't use it as his free hotel anytime he chooses."

"Anyway, Claire, would you ask Elmer—how much would a

two- or three-bedroom house cost . . . say, an older home?"

"You mean to buy? Elmer wouldn't go for that, Maggie. Where would we get the money?"

"Look, I'll chip in if we could get everyone else to donate. Maybe . . . maybe, my brothers would help out. Why not ask Elmer? We all have a stake in getting them somewhere permanent. It's something we should've done a long time ago—buy Mom and Dad their own home. Best would be some little town around here where Dad can have a garden, walk to the grocery store. Where they can be out of our hair, for heaven's sake!"

Exactly my sentiments. There had to be a sensible way of getting the folks on their own. It seemed like shooting at the moon, if we expected any help from her brothers. Which we'd need to pull it off.

She got up to rearrange the lilacs in her blue vase. I dug out my nail file and swiped it across the nails I'd just done that morning. Somehow, I felt we weren't looking at the root of the problem. Elmer and Maggie's brothers hadn't changed; that's how they were raised.

Maggie stood, looking out the front window. I said, "Why don't your folks have a place? Didn't they homestead?"

She turned, a hard smile forming. "Dad had his chances. Could've gotten a quarter of land in the second Oklahoma land rush. At the last day, he backed off, according to Mom. Like owning land was too much responsibility. He would never talk about it." She pulled the teapot off the range and refilled my cup. "Dad always shied away from being in charge."

"Don't I know it. He and your mother showed up on our doorstep time and again—like they were helpless in a basket with a sign saying 'Free Kittens.' I felt heartless about sending them back with Earl. After all, they are Elmer's folks. But we didn't have room for them. As a last choice, we shoehorned them into our front room—but that was before we had kids. Sometimes Elmer put them in our bedroom. I guess I've told you about that plenty of times."

Yes, Maggie had heard just about every variation of the folks settling in with one of their offspring. She started laughing, a snicker that gathered momentum to a wild snort. She shook out a lace handkerchief to wipe her eyes. "Glad it was you and not me . . . Aw, Claire, you look like you were weaned on a pickle."

Trying not to laugh, I wasn't sure how to express myself but wanted to try. Another instance where I wished I was more educated. "Maggie! Maggie, listen. With the folks always around, Elmer and I could never settle into just being us. Not that your folks are bad people, they simply aren't very, uh, aware. With them in our house for weeks at a time, I can't be a wife, a mother . . . I can't be me. You understand?"

I took a deep breath. "I can't sit across the table and simply stare at my husband, sure I can hear his heartbeat, and believe he hears mine. Know he is . . . loving me, with his eyes and, his passion." My voice had dropped to a whisper. "You don't do that when the in-laws are living with you. . . . Mary Grace, telling me what to do in my kitchen. Will, complaining about his ailments or saying what he'd do, only if . . .

"Life—as man and wife—seems likely to tip over anytime, when they're underfoot." I expected a reaction, but Maggie sat very still, each hand clasping the opposite forearm. "Thinking like that, I can't help but be anxious.

"When they lived with us, we were doing good just to get by. Sometimes it was hard to get one square meal in an entire day. If they'd kept interrupting our lives, we probably wouldn't have gotten the farm."

"Claire, you don't know what it means to have you as a sister-in-law." She shook her head slowly, several times.

"Oh, Maggie, do you know what you've done for me? You taught me to see good in myself, to be thankful for what God has given us—instead of tripping over my problems, things I can't change."

She smiled, her blue eyes connecting with mine. Then a pall came over her. "I can't remember how long it's been since I was hugged." Lips quivering, she drew her clasped hands up and dropped her head down, mouth against her knuckles.

Feeling tears coming, I moved my chair around the table as close as I could and put my arm over her shoulders. "Oh, Maggie, my dear sweet sister. Forgive me. Just talking about myself. Here you are, always comforting me, listening to my troubles. You've been by yourself all these years, ever since Maclaren left you."

Both arms around her, I felt the side of my face against her face and the salt of my tears blending with hers, dripping onto the checkerboard oil cloth on her rickety kitchen table. My voice back to a whisper, I said, "We're like doves at sunset—calling for someone to listen to us. We're just as powerless, too. So, we have to ask . . . Maggie, didn't you tell me once that we serve the God of the impossible?"

She said, "You're right, dear sister of mine. Dear Jesus . . ."

7   The End of Home

Claire

A revved engine complained above the moaning wind. I looked out the kitchen window to see a green International pickup outside— Henry and Blanche Ausmus, neighbors to the southwest. Elmer had said he didn't know anyone else in the county who used leftover house paint to re-finish a beat-up old pickup.

I dried my hands from finishing the dishes and opened the front door. Blanche, her head down, clutched her purse as if it contained state secrets.

Like wind before rain, her words preceded her before she came in the door. "Claire, you got a telephone call. A relative, she said. You got a niece, name of Vivian?"

"Yes, my sister Pearl's daughter. Did she call? Or did someone call about Vivian?"

"Vivian's who called. She insisted on talking to you personal. We'll carry you back to our place, and you can phone her back."

"She didn't say what it was about?" My throat felt constricted. I swallowed.

"Where's Elmer? If he's in the field, we can fetch him."

"Over at Ed Jones'. He had to get a piece welded for the lister. Took Sammy and Dickie with him." My heart pounded. I lost my breath and had to sit. This, whatever it was, could only be something bad. By force of will, I put one foot in front of the other. "I'll get the baby. Yes, better leave a note."

I scribbled a message and left it on the table. Henry had the International ready to roll, probably out of habit, as Blanche was never one to sit still when she could go someplace. I waited for her to scoot to the middle before I crawled in the passenger side with the baby.

"Mind the seat spring, Claire," Henry said.

Too late. "I'm afraid I found it!" Blinking back tears, I freed my dress and a piece of my skin from the protruding spring. I glanced down—my dress in one piece but not my hide.

Blanche chattered the whole two miles, which seemed to take a half hour, as Henry firmly believed that haste caused accidents and would wear out the bearings or clutch plates. I nodded with an uh-huh every minute or so. Otherwise, Blanche would repeat herself to make sure I heard every word of whatever she was sharing "in the fullest confidence."

After giving me the lowdown on speculators selling cattle on the black market, Blanche said their son and his wife were moving back to Beaver County. It'd been forever since they'd seen poor Charles. He'd finally gotten that wife of his to agree to leave her old maid aunt . . .

I stopped nodding. Blanche ratcheted her voice up a notch every time Henry revved the engine to downshift. I'd been holding my breath, absorbed with what the telephone call was about, and wishing Blanche would can it.

I re-tucked the yellow and blue blanket over baby Jerry. Kate Buffalow gave it to me when Dickie Lee was born. A muffled cry and I looked down. Poor child, I'd trussed him so tightly, he could barely breathe. "Oh baby, I'm sorry. Here, now."

Henry's pickup rolled to a stop beside the big lilac bush next to the yard fence. I put Jerry against my shoulder and was halfway through the front gate by the time Blanche thrashed her way across the front seat. A howl of indignation signaled that the wicked seat spring had ambushed her too. My telephone call was momentarily forgotten as she laid a heavy scold on Henry. No doubt he'd have that spring tied or taped down before the day was done.

I alternated between chewing my lower lip and adjusting my sweater as Blanche rang the operator, and then responded to the familiar routine for all long-distance calls. ". . . Yes, the Bill Howard residence. Ness City, Kansas."

The line finally cleared. Right away, Blanche pulled the baby from my shoulder to hers in a smooth motion born of practice. To my surprise and relief, Myrrl answered. He had come in from the farm and had gone straight to Bill and Vivian's house.

Quietly, he gave me the news. "Vivian found Pop in his garden."

"No, not on the ground . . ." I wanted to close my ears.

"No, Claire. He was sitting in that old wicker chair . . . hat flopped across his face, like he'd just gone asleep. Which was true. He must have been surprised, to wake up in heaven with all those

37

angels around."

I felt, but didn't hear, my own sobs. Henry eased a chair toward me, and I collapsed into it. The room seemed to be spinning as I struggled to breathe against a sudden pall of unbearable loneliness. Beloved Pop, my defender, was forever gone. I already felt abandoned.

His had been the solitary voice of comfort and reassurance in the dark days after my divorce from Harold. No one else in the family had consoled me in the rejection and pain which cauterized my soul like acid. Except for two others—Mama and Gar—no one in the family broached the subject, as if the divorce was such an abomination that to even speak of it was to invite God's judgment. Much later, I realized divorce was so foreign to them they had no idea what to say.

Pop knew. I once asked him why he alone made the effort to comfort me. He said, "Babe, I don't have to understand divorce to know you felt abandoned. You didn't need answers. You needed us—your family, the ones who know you, the ones you belong to." Ridges of sorrow spread across his face. "I was fifteen—I told you about this—when old Ruff came to me right after my mother gave birth to his fourth child. He said I had to go. Pushed out of my home, I learned this lesson—we can live for a few days without water, many days without food, but we can't get through a single day without hope."

He made it his mission to give me hope. If not for him, I might never have escaped the suffocating darkness of guilt and shame over losing my first marriage.

Pop had stood against Mama, not an easy thing for anyone. She had always maintained divorce was a sin in God's eyes. I could never talk to her about it. While Pop showed me the Bible teaches that God actually likes me, Mama could only see God as Judge.

I'll never forget the blighted afternoon Mama said people were already talking about the family. Pop, bless him, sat beside her and took her hand. He said, "Lillie, we know the Almighty judges sin. He does that—not us, and certainly not those people you speak of. Our Heavenly Father loves us. Right now, he wants to show his love to Claire. She made mistakes but she wasn't the one who violated the marriage vows. Jesus will show his grace to Claire, and maybe to this entire family—all in ways we can't imagine. Don't you believe that?"

Mama didn't answer. In fact, she said little more about fault, blame, or judgment after Pop gave her that lesson in humility and mercy.

In the first rush of grief over Pop, my thoughts went back to the day Mama died, exactly a year after the ceremony that made Elmer and me man and wife. The ceremony Mama didn't attend. Even in death, her judgments would ever be with me.

Her nurture of me as a child turned controlling when I began expressing my own opinions as a young woman. There was room for only one queen in that household and it wasn't me. Probably why Pearl and Ethel married early. Pop trusted me and complimented me on my independent spirit. My confidence soared.

In my own household, Elmer didn't exactly treat me as a queen, and he favored his parents over me. Against my wishes, he let them move in with us during the hard months and years after the Depression forced us to leave the Deluxe sales crew. . . . The folks crowded into our apartment in Kansas City and followed our hand-to-mouth existence in Beloit and Cawker City—barren little Kansas towns that hid their want behind the façade of silence. Pop was the only one to offer a haven of rescue when we'd almost reached the end of our rope.

Gar, of course, seldom missed an opportunity to comment how much my ill-fated marriage had cost the family in reputation and treasure. Both meant a great deal to him.

I stopped. The flood of memories had gone from inspiring to invasive.

My breathing calmed. The pall of abandonment eased. Myrrl would miss Pop as much as I. Pop had been the buffer between him and Gar. Like two cripples, we alternately wept and rejoiced over the man who had tried to teach us to fly.

Elmer

As soon as I came in the door and saw Claire's face, I knew something was wrong, terrible bad. The boys started jabbering about Ed's blacksmith shop, and she turned to quiet them. Pulling them to her, she embraced them as they told about the wonderland of fire, smoke, and clanging steel, overseen by a little man with a big hammer. Then, just like that, my wife began crying like a baby.

Sammy and Dickie Lee responded like any kid when faced with a crying adult; they tried to comfort her. I sat and watched while she hugged them and told them, "No, Mama is just sad. I'm not hurting. Thank you for being nice to Mama. . . . Yes, thank you for helping Mama. Now, can you go outside while I talk to Daddy?"

She followed the boys out the front door and waited for them to scatter before returning inside. My woman, the dauntless one, collapsed into my arms. Her tears soaked my shirt as she told me about Pop.

Pop—that's who he was, although I never called him that to his face. I respected him as much as any other man I ever knew. I relaxed with most men—personal with maybe two. My own son Durward and Sam Kanaga being the exceptions. I spoke his name only when a crowd confused his focus. At the sound of my voice, he'd give me his full attention, radiating a warmth I didn't feel I deserved. I gulped the first time that happened; wasn't ready for such total engagement. Almost from the beginning, Sam treated me like I was the crown prince. Receiving honor from someone who'd made so much out of practically nothing—that was real honor. More so because he knew my history—as much as I'd allowed anyone to know.

We were practically starving in Mitchell County, Kansas. Claire's dad came and insisted we stay with him until we got back on our feet. That was in '34—twelve years ago. Good as he was, I hated, literally hated, to take charity. We left the minute the wind brought a whiff of hope.

My dad and my four brothers—they always wanted something from me. I accommodate them if I can, but I don't offer myself to them. Not to my brothers because they don't value the sweat and sacrifice that produces what I have—and seldom to my dad— because I respect him.

I love my folks. Never told them and I don't recall them ever using that capricious, risky word with me, either. I survived well enough without it, although Claire has told me plenty of times that she loves me. I believe her, and I like hearing it. But I don't say it much a-tall. Don't want to cheapen the emotion by talking about it.

But Claire really took her dad's death hard. It was odd to think we'd never see Pop alive again. Of course, her being religious, she believed he'd be in heaven. Granted, he would be if anyone was—if there really is a heaven and a god to rule over it. I hadn't got to the point where I could swallow that. Not yet. Maybe I never would. I wished . . . I wished I would have told Sam Kanaga how much I respected and valued him. That man meant a lot to me. With the heel of my hand, I swiped away the moisture that threatened to run down my face.

Emotions should be private, anyway. If a man has to wear his emotions on his sleeve, he's advertising he needs special consideration. Maybe that he's needy or weak—a condition anathema to what I am. Claire makes me feel I'm exceptional. Sometimes, she tells me. I'm reluctant to say that about myself, as I see it as a form of bondage—having to brag up myself.

Some way, I want her to know she can spread her wings without me. Even to run this farm if anything happens to me. Don't want to lose our farm. The Depression showed me nothing is certain. Claire handled herself after she and Harold split the sheet. She could've folded her tent and gone back to western Kansas. By staying with Deluxe, she proved the naysayers wrong, including me. Pop had a lot to do with that—put steel in her spine.

She knows I can back her up, if necessary. I've always been a doer. Pop was impressed at what I'd done—making it on my own. Much as he'd done, I suspect. Having people call me Mister, running the sales crew. Just knowing how to sell—to close a deal with no funny business, whether I'm talking to a banker or a barber.

Sam Kanaga met me where I was, not where he thought I should be. Read his Bible every day without making it a big show. He was one of the few church-goers who practiced what he preached—the exception being that he didn't make his eldest son toe the mark.

Gar is a hypocrite. Gets satisfaction in seeing other people in a bind—even if he has to push them in the ditch himself. He'd like nothing better than to see us fail. No one else in the family wants to tangle with him but he knows I'll pin his ears back if it comes to that.

Claire reminds me my brothers aren't so perfect. Don't I know it? Unlike Gar, they're not mean, just lazy.

Even though I sensed Pop knew what I was made of—right to the bottom of the scariest part—he never played on my feelings to provoke me into revealing the quivering rabbit that hides in the deepest part of every man. Like I told Claire once, "Your dad never judges me, but sometimes when he looks at me, I feel like he's gazing right into my soul."

I listened to all Claire wanted to say about her dad. She talked a long time, how he was so much different from anybody else.

Most, she'd already told me. Finally, her voice whispered away and she seemed to go in to her private self. I knew only she could bear her own grief.

I pulled out my kerchief and dried her tears. I went outside and called my two little farmers. My pardners.

Claire

I needed angels but settled for Maggie. She knew the beat of my heart better than my own kin. So it was that we stopped at Maggie's trim little house en route to Ness City. She was sitting on the front step, peeling potatoes. Some angel.

Elmer took Maggie's kids and our boys and baby to Light Park—big trees, green grass! To spare him, I allowed only an hour to share my grief with Maggie. She listened as I told her about a family that wouldn't deal with conflict. Decades of misunderstandings and hurts festered, preventing healing and restoration. Maggie didn't disappoint, pointing me to several Psalms and First John, which I'd hardly even noticed.

The morning May sun spread its golden warmth, anointing her front room with a sense of wondrous peace. I felt fortified, as if strength had surged into me like molten lead Elmer poured into molds for weights on his fishing lines.

"You're not ready to go, are you?" She reached for her chipped teapot adorned with blue asters but kept her eyes on me.

"I had to tell you what I was afraid of. The manipulations, the awkwardness of not knowing how to respond to the subtle put-downs and judgmental comments."

Maggie didn't speak. She waited, her hand on the teapot. Then she said, "From everybody, or just one or two persons?"

I sighed. "Mostly one person. My oldest brother, Gar. I'm nervous . . . really nervous about going back home. Without Pop there, it's just me dealing with whatever he dredges up. Usually my divorce, in an indirect way . . . Always used it, to hold over my head.

"Elmer will be with me, of course, but he's an outsider." My voice caught. "Gar and I have never gotten along. But Pop shielded me from Gar's insults and lies. I may never know the full extent of his protection. That cover is gone now. You see, no one else in the family has had the stomach to confront Gar . . . and he's been the troublemaker in the tribe.

"You won't believe this. When Gar learned I planned to marry

Elmer, he stormed over to the house, all holy and righteous, demanding Pop disinherit me! His reasoning? Because both Elmer and I had been married before. Gar claimed by his reading of the Bible, we were both adulterers. Can you believe that?"

"My stars! Does Elmer know he said that?"

"Oh, he hit the ceiling. I debated not telling him . . ."

Maggie sighed. "You couldn't not tell Elmer. You can bet he'll be primed for your brother." She raised the teapot and poured the last of the tea into my cup, which ended with a tiny rush of sodden leaves.

I fished the leaves out, wishing I could dispense with my problems so easily. "So . . . there could be a terrible row, Elmer and Gar going at one another. And I can't head it off. If those two get into it, I won't be able to stop them."

"The Lord Jesus led you out of captivity, Claire. 'For he hath broken the gates of brass and cut the bars of iron in sunder.'" She shook her head. "With your daddy gone, you're afraid no one will back you. That they'll all be silent and let Gar humiliate you. Satan hasn't changed since he flimflammed Eve in the garden. So, you doubt if Jesus will be there for you when you really need him.

"Sis, you're wounded, vulnerable. Laid low with grief. Don't blame yourself for feeling weak—because you are. Here, look at this . . ." She flipped open her Bible, laying on the hassock.

In the short minutes before Elmer returned with the children, Maggie alternated between reading passages aloud from the Psalms and licking her finger and flicking the pages of her worn Bible. "Look here, in Psalm 18: 'I will love thee, O LORD, my strength. The LORD is my rock, and my fortress, and my deliverer; my God, my strength, in whom I will trust; my buckler, and the horn of my salvation, and my high tower.'"

I heard the car stop outside. She said, "Sometimes God delivers us from our pain. Other times we need to go through the fire. You're not in this by yourself. When you're feeling alone or scared, tell Jesus. 'Come and get me. Carry me. Help me.'"

She stood and pulled me up beside her. Her arm around my waist, we went to the door. When it opened, she stooped, arms outstretched. "Well, look at these young'uns! Ain't you something?" She looked up at Elmer. "Big brother, your boys are proof God loves you."

43

The sun low in the west, we arrived at the Ness County farm where I had learned much of how to be me. How to bake a pie, ride the pokey pony, hitch up a team of horses in full harness . . . Beyond the barn, a slant of light gleamed off the pond I waded in and built little ships to sail across. Elmer cut the ignition and looked my direction. I turned away, not wanting to share emotions with anyone. It wasn't that Pop had simply passed away but that his hopeful, encouraging voice was forever stilled. Only the tic-tic-tic of the cooling engine broke the reverent quiet. Somewhere, a turtle dove began his evening lament. Much as I wanted to simply be there, stirrings in the back seat prompted otherwise. "Elmer, could you wait with the boys a few minutes?"

"We're not going anywhere." He flung his arm over the seat back and riffled his fingers through Jerry Elmer's hair. "Boys, see the swing hanging from that big locust tree? I'll bet your mama rode that thing to the moon when she was a little girl."

Sammy laughed and pointed. "Daddy, it's just b-big enough to take her to that cloud."

I pushed through the front gate and stood in the grassy yard, the fragrance of lilacs a rush of memories. A puff of wind stirred the nearby elms I'd climbed nearly every day when I was a girl. My eyes went to the last window on the left—the downstairs bedroom where Mama and I met face-to-face the first time, August 6, 1906.

The slap of the front screen door announced Grace and Myrrl coming to embrace me. Four years older than me, his sun-darkened features carried a mix of boyish excitement and trusting warmth. He was what Jesus spoke of Nathanael, a man "in whom there is no guile." As we went inside, Grace, calm and shining compassion, bustled around her kitchen with floury hands and her face a-smiling as if she could hardly wait to bless you.

Their three youngest, Lillian, Evelyn, and Gary, lingered in the background but they quickly took charge of Sammy and Dickie Lee. Grabbing the boys' hands, they trooped out to the barn to show off a new litter of kittens. Grace hollered after them that supper would be ready in half an hour, so they'd have time to see the new calf too. A pony ride and exploring the pond would have to wait until morning.

Myrrl brought extra chairs into the dining room as the kids returned. He seemed jittery, nearly breaking one of the globes as he refilled two lamps with kerosene. Amid giggles and scuffling of small feet, we gathered around the table and Myrrl asked God's blessing over the meal. I thought of Pop—how many times had he presided over a family gathering in this same house?

The men talked grain prices, cows, the weather, and the end of war rationing. Out of the blue, Myrrl blurted, "Gar's been calling—several times. He asked—actually, demanded, that we go over there to finalize Pop's obituary tonight. I told him you'd be too tired from your trip to do anything this late. He didn't like it but that's Gar. He expects to run the show, which—"

"Yes, that's Gar," I said. "He expects to run things, and we've let him do it. Mostly because no one likes conflict. He gets his back up if anyone questions him."

Grace stood to pull two pies from the oven. "He's never been one to do things by committee. I'd be surprised if he ever asked anyone else's opinion."

Myrrl chuckled. "Gar talked about running for school board last year. You should have seen the feathers fly. Delaney threatened to resign. He said Gar would expect to be treated like the prophet Isaiah. They'd had words after Gar's milk cows waltzed through his shoddy fence and ravaged Millie's garden—twice in a month."

"We've let Gar have his way because no one wanted to upset Pop. Every time we gave in, I felt bullied," I said.

Elmer kept quiet throughout the discussion but finally arose to get his tobacco pouch and pipe. He swept his hand toward Grace and, with a nod, went outside on the front porch for his evening smoke.

Perhaps this melancholy day would awaken the belief that those in the family of Samuel Kanaga could speak—freely and respectfully—of things as they actually were.

I sighed. I knew who was least qualified but most likely to bring that about.

8 Coyotes and Codicils

Claire

Half-awake, I heard the cry again, close enough to raise the hair on the back of my neck. Elmer snored softly beside me. I slipped out of bed, put on my robe, and padded toward the lamplight from the kitchen where Grace sat, her Bible open before her.

"Oh, Claire," she whispered. "That coyote woke you, too. Myrrl has never got a clear shot at him. We've lost five pullets since the sun rises so much earlier now. Those self-willed biddies insist on roosting in the trees, then they think they can go parading out at first light."

A sudden yip-yip-ah-oo-waaaaah made both of us jump. Myrrl's old shepherd went into a spasm of barking and growls.

I caught my breath. "That howl gives me the willies. You say Myrrl has a rifle?"

"Yes, but he and Elmer stayed up to all hours talking." Her eyes widened. "Claire, your brother said you could outshoot him any old day. Why don't you take a crack at that chicken-killer?"

"Well, I guess I could." I grinned at her. "Any livestock I should watch for?"

"Just the pony. She's in next to the barn. That coyote howl came from the southw—"

Two more yips and a bark cut our voices to breathy whispers.

I hissed, "Now he's southeast. If you want me to take a crack at him, go get your gun."

"Goodie. Us women will take care of that critter." A picture of conspiracy, Grace arose and crept into the bedroom. She returned with a bolt-action .22 rifle. "I could only find six shells, what with war rationing. Myrrl's still asleep, so it's up to you, kiddo."

In the dim light, I fumbled two long rifle shells into the magazine. Whispering fiercely, we discussed tactics. Pointing the muzzle toward the floor, I inserted a round into the chamber and clicked on the safety.

Grace said her chicken delinquents would begin clucking out to the east, right at morning light. I slipped out the west door while she peered to the east. A chill breeze made me pull my cotton robe around my shoulders. It wasn't enough, and I began shivering. Elmer would snort if he saw my hunting getup. Too bad, it's not his show. I stopped to let my eyes adjust to the half-light, then scanned the southwest quadrant. Creeping south along the west wall, I fingered the safety off and slowly raised the gun barrel as I eased around the corner. Nothing nowhere.

The dog set up a racket to the north. If the varmint was near the barn, I'd have to locate the pony first. Hurry, hurry . . . My robe caught on a bush. Almost fell. Heart thudding, I crept around the southeast corner to see what provoked the dog. Grace piped out the window—couldn't understand her . . . Suddenly, a wild squawking to my right!

I turned to see a murk of tawny gray and flying feathers. The morning hush abruptly shifted into a din of cackle and squawk. The coyote fled in a half-sideways lurch toward the granary with his shocked victim. Surprised by the beast showing up at a different location from what I'd expected, I hesitated. Then I lowered the barrel and squeezed the trigger.

He stumbled as a patch of fur flew off his back. By the time I cranked in the second round, coyote and chicken had disappeared behind the granary. I dashed toward it, tripping again over that infernal robe. Chest heaving as I rounded the structure, I stopped, lungs burning and eyes tearing. By the time I blinked my vision clear, I saw—a ravine thirty yards distant had swallowed my quarry.

A babble of voices and shouts cut the morning air as I trudged back to the house. The remaining chickens cranked up a chorus of cackles. Grace was praising my efforts to the men, who were soon joined by the wide-eyed children. Myrrl's oldest, Lillian, had scooped up little Jerry, squalling for me. Grace and I told the story three or four times, and Myrrl located a clump of hair.

Elmer gave me a quick hug. "Sal, it sure looks like you winged the varmint."

I squeezed him back. "Yeah, but I didn't close the deal."

ৎ৵৶

Later that morning, I called my sister Ethel about Gar's rash of phone calls to Myrrl. I was tempted to brag about my near-kill but kept everything all business. I told her Gar was demanding that Myrrl get us three girls over to finalize the obituary.

47

Ethel said, "Demanding? Well, that's rude. Why didn't he call me or Pearl? He knows we have telephones. I'll tell you why—because the men are supposed to be running things.

"I shouldn't tar every man with the same brush, Claire. Right after we married, Ed bought five spring calves without letting me in on it. I keep our books and when I told him he'd just written a hot check, he wanted to cry. He'd forgotten how much we spent just keeping Dimple alive the first year of her life. Ed never pulled anything like that again."

"I understand so well. I'm still fighting that battle in my own household. But right now . . . how would you stop Gar's bullying?"

I waited for a reaction, a plan. Time for me to test the waters. "Why not . . . Look, here's what I think. If we're ever going to stand up to Gar, it better be now." Still no response, so I kept going. "We've never bucked Gar about anything, because it would upset Pop. Now is a new day, so we either stand against Gar, or he rolls over us. You agree?"

It sounded like Ethel was sucking in a great draught of air through her nose, something she did when she was riled. "My stars, why don't we? I'll stand with you. Let me call Pearl."

"Oh, goodie. Yes, you give Pearl the lowdown."

Ethel called back in twenty minutes. "It's all set. She wants something done. And I just now called the preacher. We're set for a private meeting with him at four in his office."

Due to Elmer's prejudice against religion, I hadn't attended the Methodist church with Pop on our infrequent trips to Ness City. I'd met Reverend Lewis twice before when we visited Pop. Tall and rangy, he looked like he'd be more comfortable astride a horse, herding cattle, rather than as a parson shepherding God's sheep.

His office, an unpretentious space in the original church structure, looked out through a single window toward two Chinese elms atwitter with sparrows and their nestlings. He dragged another chair out of a closet and motioned for us to sit in a semicircle around his desk. A ceiling fan turned overhead, burping at odd moments. Ethel wasted no time. "Pastor, you've known most of our family for as long as you've been in Ness City."

"That I have, except you, Claire." He nodded at me, his smile friendly. "Your brothers, Myrrl and Gar, they attend church elsewhere. Are we waiting for them?"

"No, it'll be us girls for now. We have a request, which involves our brothers. Thought we'd better clear the air with you first." She paused, composed and calm. I was so impressed with Ethel. Her nursing training had prepared her to handle plenty of hot potatoes, including families like ours that swept problems under the rug. Everyplace, women had been held back like tumbleweeds stacked up in the corner of a barbwire fence. It was time for a breakthrough.

She continued, "Afterward, we'll all meet with you to finalize the service. Right now, we've got a simple request, and it addresses—for the first time, I'm sad to say—issues with our brother Garwood. You may have not had direct dealings with him, but over the years, you might know a little bit of what he is—"

Reverend Lewis sat back in his chair. "What he is like? Yes, somewhat."

"Well, Gar is very careful about how things are done. That can be a good thing. Gar especially wants to be in charge, which is all right by itself. But he grabs control so he can do everything his way. Since he's the oldest son, he expects to be first in . . . well, everything." She paused again and looked directly into the pastor's eyes. He nodded, and she continued, "That's been Gar's way— putting himself in the lead and never getting an opinion from any of us afterward. It's like he thinks we don't know what to do . . .

"Reverend, he's pushed others aside—sometimes even against Pop. Over the past thirty years—fifty for some of us—we have had enough of his way."

The preacher's eyes widened. Ethel didn't miss a beat. "Pearl, Claire, and I have come to ask that our younger brother Myrrl read the obituary. It's mostly symbolic, but now that Mama and Pop are both gone, we want to establish our place as equals in this family. We never raised a ruckus when Pop was alive. He's been vulnerable since Mama died. I'm sure you know that."

"I see." Reverend Lewis paused, as if he might have indigestion. His eyes swept our semicircle. Probably wants to see if we're firm about this. He continued, "Often, the eldest son—or daughter—is chosen to read the obituary. Sometimes the family designates a close friend for that honor or they ask the pastor to handle it. And it is an honor—"

"That's why we're here." It was Pearl, who had remained silent. Leaning forward, she said, "I'm the oldest, not Gar. He's nearly two years younger, but I don't—"

49

"Gar isn't the eldest? That's not what—" The parson cut himself off in mid-sentence.

"Not what you'd been told?" Pearl drew a lace hanky from her sleeve and began smoothing it on the desktop. "That's no surprise, as I expect you heard from Gar already, him 'being the oldest and all.' Well, he's not the oldest. I am, but I don't want to be the reader of anything. We want Myrrl to read the obituary. If it comes to a vote, we outvote our brothers."

Silence in the room as we let Reverend Lewis digest this new bit of information. He finally spoke. "I understand, ladies." A deep sigh. "If there's nothing else, I'll see all of you at six this evening. Thank you for telling me your plans and for the information you've shared. . . . Have you decided who's going to announce this change to your brothers?"

Ethel and I spoke at the same time. She raised her hand. "No, Claire, you got us to show some gumption for once. I'll do it. I'll tell them that this is how we want it. No reasons needed. We voted unanimously, and that's the way we want it handled."

As we left the church, I felt a mixture of uneasiness and excitement. A hundred minutes later, we would try something we'd never attempted before—confront our overbearing brother.

Elmer wanted to sit in with Reverend Lewis, but I told him it was our party. Besides, I wanted to spend some time alone so I could pray about the meeting. Maggie had always said, "If it's a hot potato, you better let the Lord pick it up first."

Ethel and I were the last to arrive and quickly sat—in a larger semicircle across from the pastor. Gar seemed preoccupied and Myrrl and Pearl were talking about expected visitors from Ohio— probably the Tilleys, relatives of Pop's mother.

The reverend greeted us and launched into a simple prayer, in which he gave thanks for Pop's life and asked for God's comfort and strength. He closed with these words: "And Lord, bring your peace and comfort to this family as we prepare to honor the life and memory of your servant, Sam Kanaga. In the holy name of Jesus. Amen."

Peace and harmony would be nice. I tried to relax, although my heart was pounding. Didn't want Gar to suspect anything; he'd derail our train if he saw it coming down the track.

The pastor cleared his throat and glanced at Ethel. Then he

half-turned toward Gar and Myrrl, who sat on his left. "Before we get started with particulars of the service, Ethel wanted to make a comment."

One would think that siblings who'd spent years in the same household would be perfectly at ease with one another. With Pearl sixteen years older than me and Gar fourteen, they were starting their own families by the time I began school. Gar's oldest son, Val, was only five years younger than me. We often played together. Add Gar's suspicious nature to my working far from home on the traveling sales crew and I was somewhat of a stranger to him.

Ethel made it short and sweet. As expected, Gar exploded. We let him rant. No one said a word. He finally ran down, then demanded he be allowed to give the history of the family.

Myrrl, who had been silent, interrupted. "Gar, if we say more than what's in the obituary, it will raise the difficult issue of Pop's parentage. Only his mother is mentioned in the obituary but the fact of his . . ." He swallowed, then swept a kerchief from his pocket to his face. Finally, he gasped the words, ". . . of Pop's illegitimacy must die with him. Don't bring it up! This is to honor Pop, so friends and family can show their respect for the life of a wonderful godly man. It's about him. Not you or anyone else."

Every eye was on Myrrl. I knew that had been hard for him to say. I wanted to applaud.

Gar knew he stood alone and sat with a half-snarl on his face as Reverend Lewis reviewed the order of the service.

The meeting done, Gar stood, banging his chair against the wall. "You want to be in charge, you can write up the obituary yourselves. But I'll expect the finished version for my review tomorrow morning." He stared at each of us in turn. With difficulty, I held his gaze.

A carved wooden rod vibrated off the wall upon Gar's door slam. Pastor Lewis picked it up and held it out for us to see. "This is a chief's walking stick—his badge of authority. It was given me by Claude Leavitt, our missionary to Ecuador. Claude said that a cannibal chief had given it to him. He wanted to show his commitment to stop eating people—a good idea, I think." The pastor looked around the room. "I'll give this to your family—when all of you commit to be at peace with one another. And I'll tell Gar before the service tomorrow."

We all seemed struck dumb by the pastor's suggestion. But

afterward, the four of us worked on the obituary till nearly ten that night.

༄๛

Filled to capacity, the Methodist Church received mourners from all over Ness County and beyond. Elmer joined me as part of that "beyond," which caused a swish of whispers behind us. Gar had forecast that Elmer wouldn't show, given that Elmer had openly expressed his distaste for "the hypocrites." I wondered if the pastor had explained the walking stick to Gar.

After seating of the family and a medley of hymns by the organist, only the rustle of paper interrupted the quiet. Then Myrrl made his way to the pulpit and began to read.

He made no mention of Pop's parentage. Only that his mother, Lydia Ruff, had produced six half-brothers and half-sisters after her marriage to Ruff. I knew Elmer was thinking—more religious hypocrisy. Pop knew who his father was, though he'd never met him—an aristocrat back in Marion County, Ohio— nor had his mother married the man. Yet he'd taken the last name of his father. Yeah, Elmer's thinking we're pretending the man never existed.

Reverend Lewis stood and acknowledged the grief of the family. He said many things about Sam Kanaga, that he'd started the first Sunday school in Liberty Township and served thirty-seven years as superintendent. "His word was his bond. Out on his own when he was fifteen, he took on adversity and defeated it . . ."

I glanced at Elmer out of the corner of my eye. Pop was actually pushed out of the home by old Ruff. Elmer knows that, and respected Pop all the more. But he's probably thinking, more hypocrisy from the preacher.

"Sam looked after his own, honored God, and loved his family."

The preacher said that, and when he had no more to say, he nodded to Josephine Minor, pianist for the Methodist mixed quartet. My breath caught. How could I have forgotten? Though Gar attended the Baptist church, he was one of the finest basses in Ness County. Would he . . .?

Sure enough, Gar rose more ponderously than usual and joined the other three to sing one of Pop's favorites, "When the Roll is Called Up Yonder."

Three days later, the sons and daughters of Sam Kanaga gathered in Judge Lorin Peters' chambers for the reading of Pop's last will and testament. The only outsider was Elmer, who came uninvited to join me for the occasion. I expected Gar to object, but he only stared straight ahead, attentive to the judge's every word.

Out of the 1,700-acre estate, we three girls each got a quarter section—160 acres—plus $850 in bonds and an assortment of crockery, silverware, and antique pieces. The remaining 1,220 acres were to be divided between the two brothers. I couldn't believe it. Elmer nudged me, and I saw Ethel and Myrrl exchange glances. I almost cried during the reading of the rest of the document. My stomach churning, I determined to talk with Ethel afterward.

As we departed the courthouse, Elmer snapped, "Looks like the brothers count for more than the girls in the family."

"Elmer, I want to cry. Dad paid off Harold's debts and he helped the girls after they married. But he built a house for Gar, and Myrrl got the home place. I just don't know—"

Elmer's voice came like a growl. "I should have let him give me that infernal service station. Maybe you'd have gotten your share."

"I'm upset, but mostly, I'm hurt." Then I spotted Myrrl. "Myrrl! Could we talk?"

He stopped as if held by a rope. Ethel appeared beside us. We shuffled down the courthouse steps like monks in a procession.

These were my two favorite siblings, but I didn't know what to say. Then Elmer spoke up. "Claire feels like the girls got cut short in there—and I do, too, for whatever that's worth. Splitting 1,700 acres five ways comes to 340 acres and she and her sisters only get 160? I thought your dad made it a point to help all the kids—equally."

Myrrl took a deep breath. "I don't think we can second-guess Pop—"

"Myrrl!" I had expected a magical solution from my dependable brother. "You know Pop never favored one of us over the other. That's what hurts. I just can't believe Pop would do this to us on his own."

Ethel's eyebrows went up. "Are you suggesting Pop may have been influenced?"

"What else could it be? Let's ask Pearl if she knows something. Gar was forever pressuring Pop about things—plant Sudan grass instead of cane on the east quarter, replace the Holsteins he had all his life with Guernseys, then those oil investments. Getting himself put in charge of handling Dad's affairs would have been his next step."

Myrrl frowned. "Oh, I don't know. That's a very serious thing to suggest, Claire. You could never prove something like that. Gar would have a fit if you even mentioned such a thing."

"Well, I just might do it!" I felt my temples pounding. "It's so unjust, that his own daughters are less than his sons. That wasn't like Pop."

"But how can we know?" He swept his hands over his eyes and stared at his shoes.

Ethel slid between us and grabbed each of us by the elbow. "Well, why don't we talk to Pearl about this? If she's agreeable, the four of us can talk with Gar and see how he responds. Wouldn't hurt to try."

Elmer had listened to the discussion with interest. "Gar's a cold fish, and I doubt you're going to get anywhere with him. But even that would tell you something, wouldn't it?" He looked first at Myrrl and then at Ethel, before offering a humorless grin.

I took a deep breath. "I want to find out. Ethel, you'll let me know what you find out from Pearl?"

She nodded. "I'll try."

"But even if we do," Myrrl murmured, "how can anything be changed?"

9 John and Sons

Claire

Still disbelieving, I stared out the kitchen window of the house where Pop had lived alone for sixteen years. I was awaiting Ethel's call, where she'd tell me if my woeful disappointment was justified. So shameful, Pop just buried and me already questioning his will. More than awkward, disgraceful, what I was doing. But I plodded on, desperate to be sure of Pop's love, that he hadn't betrayed us girls.

Giving words to that thought made me want to throw up.

I couldn't let the accusation take residence in my mind. Pop had loved me, always called me "Babe." In that moment, I could see him, speaking to me, reaching out to grasp my hand.

The telephone. I stood, my eyes misty, and groped for the earpiece. It was Ethel. She'd talked with Pearl, who said having Myrrl read the obituary was enough. What about the division of the property—did she think it was fair? Pearl accepted it. Any thoughts why Pop wrote it that way? She said maybe Pop had gotten the idea that male heirs should receive more than daughters because they had families to support. Said she regretted how Pop wrote the will, that she couldn't understand it, either. Pearl didn't see how anyone could question Pop's intent at such a time as this, and his body hardly cold in the grave.

I heard Elmer come up the front porch steps. I'd had plenty of issues with his family. Now it would be his turn.

He didn't keep me waiting. "So, what did your sisters have to say about the will? They going to challenge—"

"No! It's not fair, but Pearl doesn't want any further confrontation with Gar."

Elmer frowned. "You three sisters going to let your brothers get twice as much land as you do? Why's that? I never thought your father would make the sons more worthy than his daughters."

I grasped the cameo necklace that had belonged to Mama. "He . . . he didn't. Pop always treated us the same . . . Pearl thought maybe it was an Old Testament practice, the sons getting more because they had families to support."

Elmer fairly snorted at that. "Old Testament? Bringing religion in is just a way for people like Gar to use it as a club to take advantage, run other people's lives. Another reason why I don't need church in my life, for crying out loud."

"Elmer, I don't want to discuss it anymore. Let's drop it. I tried my best. I never said my family was perfect."

"You can say that again. Let's go home."

I hadn't considered what kind of inheritance I might get from Pop. Rather foolish, as if I expected him to live forever. Most of the drive home, I debated betwixt thankfulness over what I did get and what I should've gotten if Pop had split his estate equally among us five siblings. Might as well forget the what-if, and accept the what-is. If word of our objections to Pop's will got out in the community, people would see we were no better than Elmer's brothers.

I turned toward the boys in the back seat. All three asleep in a jumble of limbs and quiet breathing. "Elmer," I said, "It'll never do for your brothers to learn what kind of an inheritance I got. They'll expect—"

"I'm not going to discuss it with them, or the folks. Why should I?" He raised his hand to scratch the back of his neck. "But they're not dummies. They'll know we got something."

I gave him a sharp look. "I got something. Not we."

"So, you. All right. You've got it, but we've got a joint account, the last time I checked."

"You know what I mean, Elmer. I don't need to remind you that you've always been the one deciding how we spend our money. With this inheritance from Pop, I'm determined to have final say. Not one dime will go to support the needs of your . . . your do-nothing brothers."

Elmer's lower lip puckered. "I don't intend to support them. They aren't the only ones in the family. Their kids, the folks . . . You can't leave someone in a bind if they're not in a position to get out." He paused and gave me a look. "Isn't that the Christian thing to do?"

I gasped. "That's unfair, Elmer. The Christian thing is to care for our own family, first and foremost. Others can help John besides us. I haven't had many nice things for myself in years. I'm not giving up on this."

༺∽༻

Maggie had taken in John's youngest seven years ago, after his
wife Moselle died in childbirth. We couldn't help back then; I was
expecting our first child in a matter of weeks. Those who knew
John declared he likened fatherhood to a bad case of the hives—
something to be avoided.

As if a windstorm had torn through his house, John's children
were carried away. The three oldest girls married to avoid
permanent servitude within the family. The eldest son, Bill, joined
a threshing crew that started cutting early wheat in Texas and was
bound to finish late summer in Saskatchewan.

John got Moselle's relatives in Adams to take the two
youngest girls. That left the two middle boys, Kenny and Tommy. I
didn't want to have anything to do with that pair. Of the nine John
had fathered, it seemed only fitting that he assume responsibility
for the rebels. He finally took those two with him to Colby in
northeastern Kansas. He bragged he could land a job up there with
his connections. I rolled my eyes.

It would've been no concern to us, but I knew from
experience, trouble on one branch of Elmer's family tree
eventually bore rotten fruit elsewhere.

From the living room window, I stared across the road where
Sammy and Dickie watched Elmer tinker with the carburetor on
our newly acquired Ford tractor. Pop would've looked at them and
said, "That's God at work."

Another reason why I miss Pop—he'd see God in places I'd
never think to look. Maybe I should read my Bible. I pulled it off
the top of the buffet and onto the table. Without purpose or
direction, I began reading.

The words hazed over, like our frosted windows, and I flipped
the pages . . . from Ecclesiastes to Nahum to Malachi. No wonder
people found it difficult. I almost closed the heavy book; I had
ironing to do. Then Malachi became Matthew, and I began to read:
No man can serve two masters . . . Ye cannot serve God and
mammon . . . But seek ye first the kingdom of God, and his
righteousness; and all these things shall be added . . . Therefore
whosoever heareth these sayings of mine, and doeth them, I will
liken him unto a wise man, which built his house upon a rock:
and the rain and . . . floods . . . and winds. . . beat upon that

57

house; and it fell not: for it was founded upon a rock.

The words swirled before my eyes, like flotsam caught in an eddy. For the first time, they spoke for my benefit, to me alone. ". . . on a rock. A rock. On a rock . . ." Satisfying. But to my life, at that very moment?

My reading became a late evening practice, after I put the boys to bed. Elmer seemed not to notice my disciplined study, but once he said, "We need to get together with Ray and Edith for a few games of pitch, instead of sitting around here by ourselves."

ৎৡ

Elmer's brother Earl went up to Colby and got an earful from the law. He stopped in at our place as we were finishing evening chores. We gathered on the front steps to hear his report. He looked grim. Clearly defeated, he said, "Main reason I volunteered to go up to John's was to get that jack and chain he borrowed from me . . . He wasn't even home!"

Elmer shook his head. "For a mechanic, I figured you'd know better than to loan your tools—especially to John."

"That ain't all," Earl took out the makings to hand-roll a cigarette. "Them two boys was running wild! John's been gone since Tuesday, and the sheriff's fit to be tied. He musta been watching John's place 'cause he showed up like stink on a skunk. Told me in no uncertain terms we'd better find John, and get him there—quick. Said them kids are tearin' up the town, to hear the neighbors tell it." Frowning, Earl threw down his half-made cigarette. "Got me so worked up, I can't even roll a smoke . . . Anyways, that sheriff says he's gonna lock John up if he doesn't look after his kids . . ."

For once, Earl's prophecy was on target. John returned to Colby, but not to assume responsibility for his sons. The sheriff promptly put him in jail for non-support.

Earl and his woman, Gertie, flew in like crows bearing bad news. Gertie cawed, "Elmer, if you don't get John out of jail, they'll put them two boys in the orphanage up in Leavenworth."

"How did you hear about all this?" I'd heard Gertie's exaggerations before.

She shot me a scornful look. "Why, we was at Mom and Dad's, and John's brother-in-law Weldon, he came over from Adams and told us, of course."

What a know-it-all. I wanted to tell her off but knew that

wouldn't help. "Well, if Mr. Weldon was so concerned about John, why didn't he go up to Colby and bail him out?"

Earl cleared his throat. "Said they'd done enough, taking them two girls." He seemed to anticipate my next question, and quickly added, "Broce is expecting me to be on the road two outta every three weeks, so I can't hardly help out, neither. In fact, I don't get my first paycheck for a week and half, and John needs to get back to his boys right away, or like—"

"Or like he says," Gertie interrupted, "those boys are going straight to that orphanage!"

"Besides," Earl resumed, "I'll hafta stay down at Elk City for three weeks straight, so ain't nothin' I can do."

Elmer scooted his chair back and stood. "Never mind, I'll go up and see what's going on. If John's in a jam, I'll see about getting him out. Colby's the county seat, so the proper authorities will be available."

I didn't say anything. There was no way the whole affair could turn out good for us.

৵৵

Elmer returned from Colby, worn out from the 400-mile round trip. He'd bailed John out of the lockup, but as the story spilled out, the circus hadn't folded its tents. Elmer grumbled about John's double-talk—he'd had to go out of town to look for work . . . the sheriff was running for re-election and wanted to slap somebody down . . . the boys were misidentified, and so on.

Ten days later, Henry Ausmus came over with a phone message. The Thomas County sheriff had telephoned for Elmer to get up there or else. When Elmer brought a load of cane feed in from the field, I relayed Henry's message and asked what it meant.

He said, "It means somebody has to go get those kids, or the county folks will take them to Leavenworth. Yeah, like Gertie said. The sheriff has no choice. Those boys can't be left unsupervised. He's not going to cut John any slack now—if and when he turns up."

I caught Elmer's sleeve. "Well, get Earl to take those kids. Don't you do it."

He shrugged his shoulders and heaved a big sigh.

My argument was already lost. I wanted to chew nails. "Elmer, we've got three children of our own—all under the age of five!"

"I know how old our kids are. But nobody knows where John

is, and even if they found him, it'd be the same thing over again. No telling where those boys would be farmed out to."

"They are not our responsibility. They're John's. Elmer, why won't you make him do what's right? I wanted to reach over and grab Elmer by the front of his shirt and make him listen. "How old are those boys? You shouldn't have to look after them."

"Kenneth is fifteen, and Tommy's maybe twelve. I can't leave them on the street, Claire."

"They are John's responsibility. He's the one who bred that mess of kids."

"He won't do it. I hate to say it, but I know he won't, and we might as well drop that subject. We'll keep them here until one of Mosie's relatives takes them in."

"That won't happen, Elmer. Hassie said they're going to send the two younger girls packing to your folks. They'd be fools to take in any more of John's kids after this."

"Don't be so pessimistic. You don't know what they'd do."

"Hassie said she and Weldon will not take those boys. In fact, none of his kin made a move to help get John out of jail. We don't know where the rest of that tribe lives."

"Saint Joe, Earl said. Mosie had an uncle in Fort Smith. I have no idea how to find her relatives. What it comes down to is those kids don't have a home. I can't turn my back on them."

My hands flew to my neck. That's exactly what Maggie said— Elmer still obligated to be the caretaker of the whole bunch. What about us? Is his family always going to have priority over ours? When choices involve his folks, Elmer always gives them the benefit of the doubt. I wanted to scream. "I don't like it. Guess I'll have to make the best of it. I'll need your help. It sounds like those kids are a pair of hellions."

"Okay, Claire. You'll get help. I won't leave it all up to you."

After a tense first week, Kenneth and Tommy began to show their colors. I'd never seen such insolence. It was all I could do to keep from flying off the handle. The boys defied me the minute Elmer stepped outside. Things came to a head at the end of the week. They'd lain in bed until well after Elmer went out to feed the livestock.

I began sweeping the kitchen floor and stopped for Kenny to move his feet so I could sweep around his chair. He made no effort to get out of the way. Such disrespect. I tried to keep the anger out of my voice. "Can't you see I'm trying to sweep? Lift your feet."

Slowly, he turned away. I ignored his insolence and finished sweeping. Putting up the broom, I heard a snicker.

Kenny held a cigarette in his hand, waving it in a figure eight. He exhaled a cloud of smoke in my direction.

"Give me that! We told you boys there would be no smoking," I said.

"Nobody tells me what to do," he snarled.

"Well, I do. Put out the cigarette and give me that pack," I felt my forehead throb.

He extended his arm as if to surrender the smokes. Then he tapped his ashes onto the floor I'd just swept, a smirk crossing his face.

Elmer's footsteps sounded on the front porch. Kenny quickly crushed the cigarette on the sole of his shoe and flicked it toward the trashcan. Like two feral pups, the boys sprang to their feet, backs to the wall as Elmer came in.

"Elmer! This kid has cigarettes. You've got to do something with them! They're spiteful and unruly—no respect." I was close to tears but steeled myself not to show it.

"You boys go to your room!" Elmer barked.

They slouched toward the back bedroom, Kenneth's face twisted in scorn.

Elmer said, "What's going on?"

"Elmer, I've been trying to tell you. They want to take over! When you're outside, I get nothing but disrespect. Kenneth just now pulled out a cigarette. Where he got it, I don't know. When I told him to hand them over, he scattered ashes on the floor, just to spite me! He smirks instead of obeying! I shouldn't have to put up with that." I felt my body trembling as I spoke.

Elmer listened, his face like flint. He turned and called toward the bedroom, "You kids! Come in here!"

They shuffled into the kitchen, defiance written across Kenneth's face and Tommy's eyes darting between Elmer and his brother.

"We wasn't doin' nothin'!" Kenneth insisted. "She's just tryin' to push us around."

"I'll do the talking," Elmer said. "Sit down. Now, what was the agreement when I brought you down here?"

"We ain't done nothin', I told you. She's just makin' it up,"

Kenneth said.

"Elmer, he's lying." They've never been disciplined. I can see that. "They're either going to do what you and I tell them to do or they go back to John."

Elmer's voice came out like rolling thunder. "I asked you what the agreement was—now are you going to abide by it or not?"

Kenneth curled his lip. "Nobody tells me what to do."

"Is that right?" Elmer stepped over to face him, inches from his nose. "Well, you'd better decide if you're going to stay here, because you're not running this house."

He ducked his head. "Nobody's tellin' me what to do. I'm leavin'. Tommy, come on."

"He's staying here," Elmer rumbled. "If you want to leave, I'll take you to Liberal and pay your bus fare to Colby. It's up to you. But if you leave, you're not coming back."

Kenneth hissed an obscenity I couldn't quite hear.

It was enough for Elmer. He roared, "Get your clothes together—now!"

Elmer and Kenneth had gone. Tommy, his face streaked with tears, had burst outside. Probably ran to the barn. I discovered the quiet carnage the boys had created in the short minutes Elmer was outside—dumped garbage in the room, chairs and a table overturned, pencil marks on walls and two of my doilies ripped to shreds.

We wouldn't have had this problem if Elmer had stood his ground with John. Never should've taken those boys in.

Forced to accept the irresponsibility of Elmer's family or the sweep-it-under-the-rug shenanigans from my side of the fence, I wanted neither. It looked like we were saddled with both. Maybe my family was no better than Elmer's; we were just more sophisticated in getting our way.

10 Maggie Married

Claire

If I'd known I would have to put up with the likes of Elmer's family, I might've thought long and hard before marrying him. Showing up at all hours of day or night and expecting a meal or a place to sleep, his brothers were not only lazy but inconsiderate. They smoked their filthy cigarettes in front of our boys, but Elmer had his pipe—what could I say?

We'd been married thirteen years. A few months after our third son, Jerry Elmer, was born, Elmer showed signs of actually considering my opinions. Not all at once—he wasn't that kind of man. Frankly, I wasn't the kind of woman to make it easy for him, either. Both of us were more prideful and argumentative than he or I would ever admit.

One stormy argument on a stormy day started in the house and then spilled outside—so the kids wouldn't hear—until we both got so cold, we had to damper it or go back inside to get our coats. I think that's when Elmer and I realized we needed to concentrate more on listening to one another rather than insisting on our own way.

I stopped trying to change my husband and began praying for him. Maggie was behind that. Not only did she encourage me, she helped me understand that tribe. And Elmer began to set down some rules for his family.

Maggie helped me see my husband wasn't the blind apologist for Will and Mary Grace and his mostly no-account brothers. After all, Elmer had grown up in that family, a family led by easygoing Will, who did just enough to get by, and often not that much. As the eldest, Elmer had inherited the mantle of family leader, and sometimes provider. That probably drove him to go on the road in traveling sales, where he developed legerdemain with people—as he called it—which brought him a success unknown to any of his kin. He joked that if I hadn't distracted him, he'd have probably run for governor. That all came, of course, well after my first marriage broke up.

I don't dwell on that anymore. After I met Maggie, I once asked her why God put me through the heartbreak of marriage to Harold. Survivor of eight years wed to a drunk, Maggie said she couldn't blame God. The nettles and bogs wrought by her precious self-importance simply led her from one adversity to another calamity. Just like her brothers. "Until they get right with God, they've just got themselves to go on." She'd hugged me and continued, "Jesus doesn't purpose to harm us but he wants to be part of our lives. He couldn't do that while I ran everything my way."

I had asked how that applied to my moral husband, whose blatant sins were smoking a pipe and cussing now and then. Her big smile, then, "Next time, sis. Next time we'll talk."

It had been two weeks since Elmer sent Kenny back to Colby, and we were getting ready to go see Maggie in Liberal. I was in the back bedroom getting the boys dressed when a car backfired outside the house.

A black Model A Ford sat in the yard. Elmer was peering out the kitchen window. "That is a smart aleck! Driving like he's at a racetrack. Claire, keep the boys—"

"We're getting ready. They're not going anywhere. Who is it?"

"Haven't seen him in three years, but it looks like John's oldest boy, Bill. He took off with a custom threshing crew, Texas to Canada . . ." Elmer struggled to get his mackinaw over the bunched-up sleeves of his shirt. I guided his arm through one sleeve and he eased outside.

I shooed the boys back into the rear bedroom and watched as Elmer approached the Ford. A broad-shouldered man in his mid-twenties stepped out of the mud-spattered coupe, holding a cigarette in his right hand like it was about to go off. He wore a green Trilby hat, patterned ascot, and brown leather jacket. Must be good money on those threshing crews. Wished I could hear what they were saying. Elmer probably snorted to himself; he'd once said that only a gangster would wear a Trilby. He made no move to initiate a handshake, which surprised me. Instead, he stood with his arms folded as John's son Bill talked . . . and talked, one arm resting on the car door. Finally, all the air seemed to go out of the young man.

Elmer planted one foot on the bumper of the Ford and leaned

forward. I couldn't see his eyes but by the set of his jaw and the way he stabbed the air between them, I had an idea of the tenor of what he was saying. He made a wide sweep of his arm toward the pasture and pushed the bumper with his foot in a sudden dismissive movement. The car rocked as if in surprise as Elmer dropped his foot to the ground.

The door tremored and the visitor jerked his arm down, eyes wide. Mouth twisted into a snarl, he flung something to the ground—his cigarette, which I'd pick up later. I realized I'd been holding my breath. He slid back into the Model A, started it, and backed away. He must've been mad as a hornet, because he killed the engine. Finally started, the car sent a spray of sand behind as he roared away toward the Kansas state line.

Elmer came in, shaking his head. I started to ask about the visitor, but he held his hand up. "I'll tell you on the way into town. Are the kids and Tommy ready?"

"They've all eaten. There's food on the table. I'll nurse Jerry on the way." Tommy and our two oldest sidled past me. "Hold it, boys. You're not going outdoors—not with those clean clothes."

Elmer helped himself to macaroni and baked beans as I herded our crew outside and into the car. Three were enough; having John's son added more work but I knew we had to do it.

Elmer motioned for me to lean toward him, then lowered his voice as he recounted his set-to with John's son Bill. "I hadn't even seen Bill since he was a kid, so him coming out to the farm was quite a surprise. Figured he might be trouble, by the set of his chin . . ." He glanced in the rear-view mirror, careful that Tommy not overhear.

"What did he want? Why did he come to our house?" My throat felt constricted, the way I felt anytime Elmer's crowd came around wanting something. "We don't have . . . we can't take care of that bunch."

"Take it easy, honey. I got it under control." He sighed. "He's a young man full of himself. Sees himself as caretaker of John's family. Which I can understand, since his dad is nothing but talk. John's always been that way. Probably provoked Bill into that stupid approach, coming out to the place with no notice, no warning. Then he started telling me how we've denied them their rights, their fair share."

"That doesn't make any sense at all, Elmer. What do we owe them?"

"Nothing, absolutely nothing. He's a scissorbill, anyway."

"Scissorbill? Elmer, what are you talking about?"

"You never heard of a scissorbill? Sweeney was a scissorbill—on the sales crew."

"I never cared for Sweeney, but I still don't know what you're talking about."

"Entitlement, honey. Like a bum who thinks he could be president—if he decided he wanted to be. Anyway, young Bill is a scissorbill. That trait runs in John's family. You saw how Kenny acted. We might expect the same from the one in the back seat."

"Oh, no, Elmer." My forehead throbbed. "We've got to separate ourselves from your . . . people."

We rode in silence for several minutes. No, blotting it out wouldn't make it go away. I said, "So, what did he want?"

Elmer cast a glance sideways to me. "You won't believe this. He wants to be in charge of deciding where the folks live, who'll pay for it, who'll stay with them . . . A young man out of touch with reality."

"I've never heard the like. That's hard to believe. And, based on what?"

"Because he should be in charge. Because he's who he is." Elmer shook his head. "It's crazy. I'm afraid we haven't seen the last of that kid."

After a stop at the creamery, we went through the slushy streets of Liberal to Maggie's trim house a half block off Kansas Avenue. Coats on all the boys, we finally had our troop ready to visit their favorite aunt. A short swarthy man answered our knock, his face indistinct until he widened the slit of the partially opened door. His dark eyes glinted like onyx out of the gloomy interior. Who was this? He asked what we wanted. Elmer told him we'd come to see Maggie MacLaren.

"There's no Maggie MacLaren here—Maggie Strickler, yes, but what's your business with her?" He didn't invite us in, nor did he smile. I pulled on Elmer's coat sleeve, just to check if we were at the right house. All correct. What's going on?

Elmer frowned and backed off the stoop. Maggie appeared behind the stranger, a blush to her cheeks. "Lee, let them in! This is my brother—Elmer and Claire, his wife. I told you about them."

I tried to catch Elmer's eye as she took our coats. What was going on and why hadn't she said anything about this strange man? I thought Maggie trusted me. This seemed disloyal. Hadn't I bared my soul to her without hesitation? But I was more interested in this . . . this Lee. A scar lay across his left cheek—like a pirate, I decided. He was no Errol Flynn but maybe he could've been, with more polish. His compact frame was only a couple inches taller than Maggie. He looked Indian and was probably a mechanic—by his skinned knuckles and the grease under his fingernails. I caught the smell of alcohol on his breath and looked sharply at Maggie.

Maggie grabbed the man—two strange men, all in the space of five hours—by the left arm and pulled him to her. "This is Lee Strickler . . . and I am now"—she flashed a saucy smile—"Mrs. Lee Strickler—for all of three weeks!"

Elmer didn't hesitate. He kissed his sister. "Congratulations, Sis. Sneaked one in on us, did you?" Then he extended his hand. Lee took it, hesitantly, it seemed.

"Yes, I didn't want to make a big fuss, so we went down to Woodward and found us a JP. We spent the weekend at Boiling Springs. Left the kids with Jenny. She loves having them, but I'll pick them up this afternoon."

I glanced at Lee and sensed he was waiting for a nod of acceptance. I blurted, "I'm happy for you both. You've been alone long enough, Maggie." I felt like I was babbling but didn't want her to think we disapproved of her man. Although I already had doubts.

She beamed and pointed to four meringue pies on the table. "So, we all have something to celebrate. The triumph of truth and love over defeat and loneliness. Why not? Here—I was going to take all four out to the truck stop, but they won't miss one pie. Let's have the banana cream. Okay, everyone?" She set the table and in minutes we were having a party.

"Good pie, Maggie." Lee grabbed her hand as she went by. "This woman knows how to cook, and she's nothing like my ex, let me tell you."

"Oh, Lee, I think you would eat anything I fix." She hugged him to her. "He makes me feel special—even brought me some posies yesterday. Lee's a full-time mechanic at Doll Cadillac, so now I can stay more days with the kids and less time baking pies." She paused. "I'll still do some pies, of course—brings in some extra money."

I knew what the extra money meant—she couldn't allow

herself to depend on any man a hundred percent. "Yes, every little bit helps. We just sold our produce at Fairmont's but saved a gallon of milk and a dozen eggs for you."

"That's mighty nice. We can use that." Lee smiled for the first time since we'd arrived.

Maggie told how she and Lee met—introduced through a mutual friend at the VFW. "And that same night, Earl showed up with his new 'friend,' Gertrude. She's, uh, different. I wish he'd stayed with Mae. Gertrude dominates things—you can't get a word in edgewise."

Elmer interjected, "Earl brought her out to the place a couple months ago. She thinks she should run things—like someone else we ran onto today." He put his hand up. "Later, I'll explain. Anyway, it makes me wonder what Earl was thinking when he hooked up with her."

Maggie grimaced. "He got tired of Mae's nagging. Can't say that about Gertie. She just tells Earl what to do."

Time for us to go. I began collecting the coats and hats. "Uh, we wanted to talk with you sometime about finding a place for the folks, but that can wait . . ."

Maggie sprang to her feet. "You just got here. The party's not over. Sit, Claire." She whirled to snatch the coffee pot and took a quick swipe at Tommy's face with a hand towel. "So, let's talk. Elmer, we need to figure some things out for the folks, and I'll help organize it, okay? Let's just suppose . . . how much would a two- or three-bedroom house cost . . . say, an older home?"

He said, "Shouldn't be more than two–three thousand. Depends where and what it is. What's that got to do with a rental?"

"Why don't we look . . . uh, something more substantial, even permanent like?"

"Permanent?" Elmer frowned. "You're barking up the wrong tree, sis. We can't—"

"What are you kids sitting around here for?" Using my command voice, I stood while placing a hand on Elmer's shoulder. "Go play outside. We're talking." I shooed them out the back door and returned, "Elmer, you forgot about Tommy's nosiness."

She gave Elmer a coy smile. "Look, I'd be willing to chip in if we could get your brothers to help out. We need to do what should've been done a long time ago—buy Mom and Dad their own home, in some little town around here where Dad can putter around his garden, walk to the grocery store . . . where they can be out of our hair, for heaven's sake!"

He glanced at me before answering. "Well, you're assuming your brothers will jump at the chance to spend their money just to help us. Not very likely."

She said, "But it's helping them. Being responsible for their own folks, for a change."

He said, "I doubt they'd buy that, sis, but anything is worth a try . . . Earl is a good bet to put in. I'll talk to him. John? He hasn't given me a red cent for that nothing place down at Adams. Maybe he'd see the incentive, to keep the kids off his hands—"

Maggie interjected, "Well, that's behind everything he does."

"I can't get anywhere with John," Elmer said. "You'd be the best one to get money from him, sis. I'll see Jim over at Buffalo. Beatrice never has cared for the family, but she's always let me in the house. And Bud? We'll have to see if our little brother can—or will—come up with the money—we'll have to catch him first." He lifted a sigh. "It's worth a try . . ."

I said, "It sure is. Your folks should have been in their own place twenty years ago." I was afraid to believe we were talking seriously about a permanent solution to Will and Mary Grace's housing. I was sure something would come up to spoil the deal. Most likely, any one or all of the brothers. "Elmer, in the fifteen years we've been married, I think they've spent half of it in my front room. If they'll stay put, I'd go along with this."

"Sal, I can't promise anything, but Maggie's got a good idea. I should've thought of it before now."

Maggie arose to retrieve a handful of clippings from a kitchen drawer. "Take a look at this." She proffered a list. "Houses for sale. There are at least seven houses here in Liberal in that price range, also selling in Kismet, Hooker—anywhere you want."

I shook my head but didn't say what I was thinking. They'll be lucky to get fifty dollars from any of them besides Earl. But it's something we haven't tried before. Anything to keep them from settling in my house.

11 A House for the Folks

Elmer

Every time I tried to get a real home for the folks, something came up to knock it into a cocked hat. Dad never had any money to speak of, and he lost the one plot of land that came his way, so anything for the folks was mostly up to me. Even as a kid, I remember us living hand-to-mouth. By the time I was eleven or twelve, I was hiring out to local farmers for five, sometimes seven cents a day. Later, Jim and Earl brought in support. Every penny went to feed our family.

When I was about fifteen, it hit me that I was the primary wage earner for our family. Dad talked about doing; lately, he hadn't done. Likable but not industrious, he put in a garden every new place we moved to, and Mama had a knack for getting value out of pieces—covers, ties, lids, handles, holders, and such. She never came out on the short end of a trade. Somehow, we usually had enough.

At twenty-two, I left home to make my own way, beholden to no one. That eventually took me to Deluxe Art Studio, headquartered in Chicago. I convinced them I could represent the company, making personal calls to sell their products—picture enlargements and frames.

Over the past twenty years, I must've tried a dozen ways to set the folks up in a living arrangement they could manage—rent-to-own, or as caretakers of property. It ended whenever the money did, as Dad never put his shoulder into getting a job. I tried to interest him in tenant farming, but he didn't have the get-up-and-go. Frankly, he liked being taken care of. When Bud, the youngest, moved out, Dad figured it was us kids' turn to take care of him and Mama.

I remember when Earl called to tell me that's exactly what Dad decided. I was in Youngstown, Ohio, at the time, and Earl wanted me to come back and talk sense to Dad. I told him I couldn't drive 1,300 miles at the drop of a hat; they'd have to sort it out on their own.

Maggie would have told Dad nothing doing, but none of the brothers would back her up. The situation had corroded into a door rusted shut when I finally got back to western Oklahoma three months later.

I made good money in the twenties with Deluxe, so I had fairly deep pockets. Not to brag, but I knew I could take care of the folks, and I did. Earl or Maggie helped out when they could.

When Claire and I married in 1930, none of my kin attended the ceremony. I didn't even give Claire much advance notice that I had a brief window in which to get married. A year later, she met the folks. I had neglected to tell her part of our income was going to support them. In fact, I didn't tell her a lot about my family, although she asked me plenty of times. Not that I was ashamed of them. I wanted her to meet them first and then draw conclusions.

For someone who prided himself on his self-confidence, I asked myself why I avoided peeling back the layers of self-disclosure. Uncle Joe, Dad's younger brother, hit it on the nose: "You peel an onion, you get more onion. But the deeper you go, the stronger the smell." Yeah, Elmer, smell from what? That you might be pegged as being like your own father? Dad never aspired to much, never owned much, and lost all of what he held title to. You afraid Claire and her family might judge you as being cut from the same bolt of cloth as your dad?

Twitchy about my drinking? Nah. I can hold my liquor. I puzzled over the women I'd known before I met Claire. They were history, and they'd stay history. There was my first marriage, to Florence. That flame blew out within the first month because of her constant campaign to change me into Billy Sunday. After a year of her hammering, I'd had enough.

I had a son, Durward. I knew I couldn't take him with me when I left. Broke my heart.

Still in traveling sales a thousand miles away, I had little chance to see my boy. She made it harder, rabid to run my life. My profession, my "paganism," as she called it, my friends, the car I drove and style of clothes I wore—all fair game. The mere suspicion I'd been drinking meant there'd be hell to pay. My infrequent visits to see Durward became fewer still.

He was eight years old the last time I saw him. I didn't intend it that way, or that that time would be the last. When I finally saw Durward again, he was a strapping eighteen-year-old . . . and I didn't recognize him.

Shameful. I let my son down . . . I could hardly be called a dad.

All those years without laying eyes on him. Good intentions . . . but I didn't look him up. Didn't want to deal with Florence. Took the coward's way out. I failed to be the father my son needed me to be. Yeah, that's reason enough to hide.

I remember when Claire found out I was sending money every month to my folks. Lost some hide over that one, mostly because I hadn't been upfront with her about it. With the Depression putting everything in a squeeze, we left Deluxe to set up shop in Kansas City. Two weeks later, she met Dad and Mama and found out they were moving into our apartment—all in one evening. She had a conniption, again because I hadn't told her beforehand. Yeah, that and the fact they took over our only bedroom.

The folks only stayed with us a few months—hardly a bother, from my perspective. She didn't see it that way; said them living with us kept her and me from establishing our marriage— according to the Bible, she said. According to the Bible? We went back and forth on that. When I told her she was starting to sound like Florence, she shut it down right quick.

Maybe that's why she and Mama didn't get along. Mama clammed up when I asked, and Claire would just change the subject.

Earl showed up to take them down to Tulsa to stay with him and Mae. That lasted until his marriage started to unravel. Anyway, the folks stayed with either Earl or me over the next several years. Claire did not like having them "crowd in on us," as she put it. Not a bit.

The entire scenario of moving the folks in and out, here and there, had turned into a circus. Maggie and I knew we had to put an end to it, for decency's sake, if nothing else. Dad would be eighty in December and Mama wasn't far behind. But we needed extra money to pull it off. Only one source, get the brothers—Jim, Earl, John, and Bud—to contribute. That was about as likely as snow in July, but we had to try.

Maggie kept the issue front and center. Anytime she had a chance to talk to any of them, she'd hit them up. Usually, with something like "Don't you think it's a crying shame the six of us haven't gotten the folks into their own place before they wither up

72

and die?" They'd try to brush her off, but she told them it was a disgrace. And it was. Then she'd follow up with a letter—except to Bud, the family vagabond. No one knew where he was. Mama didn't even know which state he lived in.

I'd been trying to get commitment, starting with Jim and John. First thing they wanted to know—how much will it cost? They should've been thinking value—value to Mama and Dad, to them, all of us. That's why none of them has a pot to . . . to use.

They're always thinking short-term, just like Dad. Mama has gone along with his lifestyle—what choice did she have?

Anyway, I planned to put a deal together with a long lead time, "contingent on such and so." The old hay-shakers around there hadn't met the likes of me. I still had my sales experience with Deluxe—selling to bigshot executives, bankers, preachers, and politicians. Those I likened to my hogs, pushing their way up front, making noise, always demanding.

Hard for me to give Maggie support of any kind. I had to keep my farm going. As May turned to June, I still hadn't planted milo. Everybody from Dumas to Dodge was looking up at the sky, wishing for rain. When it came, I'd be ready to plant with the rest of them.

First though, I had to get Ansley off my back—the folks' landlord down at Adams. He whined about extra cars parked at Mama and Dad's rental house every night, some for up to five days. Probably true. Likely John and his kids and their sponger friends taking advantage of food that Claire and I had taken to the folks. Ansley wrote, said he was tired of being ignored. Said I had thirty days to fix the problem or the folks would have to move out.

I didn't say so but I was tired of being ignored, too. Forget Ansley and his cracker box apartment. I found a two-bedroom house on a double lot in Tyrone, a sleepy little burg on Highway 54 eleven miles southwest of Liberal. The seller must've pegged me for a rube, asking $3,200 for the place. After I ticked off things that needed fixing before I'd even talk about buying the property, he changed his tune.

We settled on a selling price of $1,350. Still, that was a wad. Maggie and I couldn't bridge that gap. If the house deal fell through and I couldn't get Ansley pacified, we'd have to move the folks in with us. I didn't even want to think how my dear wife would take that.

Then I slipped up and Claire picked up on it like a bulldog;

73

asked if I planned to kick Tommy out in the street. Holy cow, I'd forgotten about the extra kid . . .

๛

The war over, we began seeing several variations of farm tractors in the neighborhood. I talked with Stucks Potter; he keeps up on machinery. Said he liked the Ford tractor. I'd been farming with horses ever since we moved to the Panhandle, but I could see we'd always be limited to how much land we could handle. Maybe I'd have to give up my team of draft horses.

Using a general rule of thumb of an acre a day with my team, Stucks said the Ford 8N model tractor could do three times what my horses would do. Claire resisted going further in debt but Myrrl had already ordered a Ford tractor. Big brother Gar, of course, had to be different. He had an International-Harvester Farmall. That convinced her, so we got a Ford 8N. It had a four-speed transmission, power takeoff, drawbar, and three-point hitch.

Late June brought the rain Claire said God had sent. Tempted to argue her point, instead I began planting milo at first light on the eighty acres east of the house. Midmorning, I saw Ray's pickup coming from the south. He stopped at the end of my row and waited. I shut down my new tractor, ears ringing. Horses don't make the noise of an internal combustion engine. I motioned for him to follow, and we headed to the shade of the lone cottonwood thirty yards inside the field. He waved off the offer of a drink of water from my gallon jar while I slaked my thirst.

He'd left two bushel baskets of Edith's produce at our house, the first of four deliveries from their garden. In return, we'd give them ham hocks and spareribs after our fall slaughter. He said they were going over to Harper County for the weekend. Edith's clan was having a shindig for an ancient aunt's hundredth birthday.

I told him about us lobbying the brothers and asked if he and Edith would make a nice friendly visit with Jim and Beatrice, up the road from the aunt's homestead. "Jim's never once put up Dad and Mama. Earl and I have had them stay with us for weeks or months at a time.

"The folks haven't stayed at Jim's, mostly because Beatrice and Mama can't get along. Five seconds in the same room and they'll lock horns at the drop of a hat." I pulled out my pipe,

74

wanting to fire it up. "But she's partial to you and Edith. If she buys in, she'll get Jim on board. Give Beatrice my word we'll never ever ask anything from them again."

"I'll give it a shot, Elmer. You know that Beatrice ain't overly fond of your people, and it's not just your mother. Prackly everything with your family has gone sideways, mainly because of Jim. He's as impulsive as a car-chasing dog, but he won't take the initiative to pull up his pants if it's breezy outside. On the other hand, Beatrice treats Edith's house plants like they's spun gold." Ray gave a big sigh. "Tell me what needs to be said, how much they have to kick in—"

"Two hundred and twenty-five dollars, same as everyone else."

Ray shook his head and whistled. "That's a lotta dough from Jim. No chance of a bank loan, even if Beatrice would allow it. Probably doesn't even have a checking account. He'd need a spell to get that much coin together."

I shrugged. "I know, I know. But I can't finalize the deal if I don't know who's going to put in. We'll all benefit. It's a mystery why any of them would hold back—"

"Jim's got Beatrice. Boy howdy, we don't wanta rile her." He took off his hat and fanned away a cloud of gnats. "I'll stop by Monday and let you know how the cow chews the cabbage. Uh, no offense to Beatrice."

Claire

In western Oklahoma, a calm July day less than ninety degrees is a blessing in itself. A good day for drying early corn outside. Our resident mockingbird was still warbling at ten o'clock, so it looked to be a glorious morning. I had three screens set up on frames back of the house when Elmer called from the front, "Ray's here. Let that be, if you want to hear what he has to say."

Good-bye, glorious morning.

Ray had already joined Elmer at the table. After greeting him, I went to the pantry and returned with a jar of blackstrap molasses and spooned a dollop into his coffee.

A wide-eyed look up from Ray. "Well, thanks, Claire!" His teaspoon picked up the rhythmic tick of the mantel clock, clinking inside his cup. Finally, he dropped his Stetson on the floor and rubbed knuckles against his temples, as if to activate brain cells. I could almost hear the wheels turning. The cup in both hands, he slurped and sighed. "These small things are the lifters of life. You know that, don't you, Elmer?"

Ray gave a little cough to launch his unaccustomed effort at expressing a personal opinion. "Not the best timing for our visit, Elmer. Beatrice gave us a blow-by-blow account . . . Seems your brother John showed up there last week when she was at the neighbors', having her hair done. Didn't take much for John to cajole Jim into going 'someplace for excitement,' according to the kids. When Beatrice got home, they said, 'Daddy went to Englewood with Uncle John to see a friend' . . . Whoo-ee! Beatrice knew it wasn't no 'friend.' She was fit to be tied.

"You know Jim. He can resist anything but temptation. She'd already determined not to chase him down. I guess Jim snuck back home a day later, claiming John had rushed him to the Shattuck Hospital because he come down with food poisoning."

Ray leaned forward, tapping his finger on the table. "Beatrice knew that was hogwash. Jim never eats out; he's tighter than bark on a tree." Eyes wide, he continued, "She's not a woman to be trifled with. She cranked up and tore into him again—for maybe the tenth time, I'd guess. Jim kind of blended in with the wallpaper but finally got his nerve. Wanted to know why you're in such a toot to get a house and why in Tyrone? I tried to explain but the Watkins man showed up and they plumb forgot us. Edith left her plants on the table and we headed home."

Elmer's eyes sought those of his cousin, as if expecting more. Ray chugged the rest of his coffee and stood to leave. "We did have a fine time at Aunt Bessie's birthday party. She's as spry as a spring chicken. I bet she'll last another fifteen years."

12 The Fairest Rose

Claire

Two weeks later, Earl came out to the farm to plead mercy. Whether out of fear or respect, he made every effort to stay on Elmer's good side. No way would he disappoint his big brother. One of the brothers had apparently told Earl that Elmer held him up as an example of financial accountability. His soon-to-be ex-wife, Mae, exploited that to her advantage, and was demanding that he send her $145 to prevent garnishment of his wages.

Earl had brought along Gertrude, his "friend" with the outlandish floral dresses and overbearing manner. So oblivious. They stood in my kitchen that very moment, perhaps expecting I'd bless their flagrant adultery. No matter. It appeared Earl was hidebound on spending any extra cash on a divorce.

Too bad, Earl had been Elmer's best hope to join him and Maggie in raising the money to buy a house for the folks. That left only Elmer's two youngest brothers, John and Bud, which would be like depending on goose feathers to build a fence.

We left the older kids with Ray and Edith, who lived across the section. Then Elmer and I went to Liberal to talk with Maggie, whom we hadn't seen in weeks.

Lee opened the front door and, without a word, melted into the gloom of the living room. We stood there—me with the baby—but finally went in and sat on the divan.

I whispered, "Why's Lee here? Doesn't he have a job." Elmer just shrugged. Why had my sweet sister-in-law ever teamed up with a man as crude as Lee? I crossed and then uncrossed my legs. Something wasn't right. Maggie would've had the venetian blinds in the living room open. Lee was . . . unusual. We hardly knew him, but that didn't excuse treating visitors this way.

Finally, Maggie came out wearing a raggedy old house coat I'd never seen. She looked as if she'd been on a bender, her skin like bleached parchment and eyes dull as sandpaper. She sat, then turned to extend her hand to touch my fingertips. Static electricity arced between us and we both laughed. "I apologize. Everything's a wreck. Lee, honey, could you get them coffee?"

He'd stayed off to one side. Why doesn't he sit with us, or at least join the conversation? He reminded me of a lost bird coming in for a landing but hadn't found a perch among a strange flock. Maybe he thought a nursemaid had to hover until called upon.

Stirred to action, he began rattling about the kitchen. His mumbling and clattering said he didn't know where anything was. So inept, probably hadn't bothered to learn.

Like the rest of that family, Elmer seemed unsure how to respond to Maggie's distress, as if a kind word or question about her health was unseemly or unmasculine. Instead, he rambled about Jim and Earl, and asked Maggie if she'd seen Bud.

She gave a short, quick laugh. "Nobody's seen Bud. Amazing that I expect my brothers to keep their word." Her humor was back. Then she began coughing.

I quickly arose and went to the kitchen. Returning with a glass and towel, I let her sip and then wiped her face. It struck me that the two men apparently couldn't accept that the spirited woman they'd known was suddenly a stranger. I drew my arms around her. "My dear, dear, sister, has this mess of getting money out of your brothers got you down?"

Her breathing calmed, she kissed the back of my hand, saying, "John's . . . car threw a rod . . . took every last dime he'd saved." A pause and she continued, "He said he'd swear on a stack of bibles that it took all . . . two hundred dollars he'd put in Citizens Bank to get that car fixed."

"John only makes allowances for himself." Elmer snapped. He sighed, deeply, the air coming out in a slow hiss against his fist. Finally, "Guess I took on too much. Uncle Joe had a word for that. He'd say, 'Elmer, don't dig up more snakes than you can kill in an afternoon.'"

"Wait. You'd better hear the rest of what she has to say!" It was Lee, silent until then.

What? What was Maggie doing?

She slumped back in the chair, her body crumpled like a wet dishrag. Gracie, just home from work, came in and stood quietly beside her mother, caressing her back. Maggie clenched and unclenched her fist around a handkerchief, as if to massage it to life. She began to weep. Lee was beside her in two strides, his arm around her, whispering to her.

"So sorry . . ." Her voice almost falsetto, she said, "I'm going to have to drop out, too. You see . . . I'm sick." She regained control, her breath catching. "I got test results from Doctor Hilbig last Tuesday. He had me come in. Told me I have . . . I have . . . cancer. My uterus."

Her words trickled across the space between us, corrosive as acid, kindling a fear I hadn't known since Mama died. I felt unhinged, unmoored. Elmer put his hand over mine, and I drew myself to him, our baby between us.

Lee took Maggie to Halstead, north of Wichita, for radiation treatments. A few days later, Elmer dropped me and the boys off at her house while he went to get a distributor cap for the tractor. Maggie greeted me with a long hug. We had a cry together, and I asked about the doctor's prognosis. She said Doctor Hilbig had recommended surgery in Wichita, a wish they couldn't afford. Jenny Washburn had told her that treatments at the Halstead clinic would be cheaper than hospital surgery and besides, it had worked miracles for her aunt who lived in Topeka.

Maggie recited the medical lingo they'd told her about radiation's effect on the human body. I looked at the tragic face of this woman I loved, her features once as sharp as if carved in crystal. Now I saw only blurred despair. Her hands were trembling claws, which she tried to still in my presence.

Elmer returned, and after a hasty good-bye to Maggie, we went home. By the time we passed Skinny White's place, Tommy and our boys were all fast asleep in the back seat, so I told Elmer about Maggie's condition.

He listened, his knuckles taut to whiteness over the steering wheel. Finally, he spoke. "I ran into John at Humpy's News Stand. He tried to dodge me, but I saw him first. I asked him when he was going to have his share for the folks' house—"

"He doesn't have any money, does he?"

"No. He'll never have it. I just wanted to make him admit it."

"Your folks will have to stay in Adams."

He grunted. "Too late for that. John did have some information. Ansley, the landlord, has had a bellyful of their violations—and promises to fix them. Neighbors are stirring it up, adding complaints about noise and parties. They've got thirty days to find another place."

"We can move them," I said. "There's other rental houses—"

"No, Claire, it's too much. I want it over and done. We'll buy the house in Tyrone ourselves and move Mom and—"

"We'll do no such thing!" My hand flew to cover the white spots on my neck. "We don't have that kind of money! And we absolutely can't go in debt to put them in a house!"

He paused, just enough to signal he had other ideas. "We do have that kind of money. We've got that quarter section from your inheritance—"

"Elmer! That's for us—for our family!" A flash of heat coursed through my body. He was suggesting betrayal. The boys stirred in the back seat, and the baby burst out crying.

Elmer spoke without emotion. "We wouldn't have to use it—if there were other options."

My breath caught. That was his not-so-subtle reference to working again in traveling sales. "So! You're making it my fault because your good-for-nothing brothers fail to come up with their share. And you want my inheritance for your folks! That is . . . just selfish, Elmer!"

Ignoring our baby for the moment, I simply glared at my husband. Then I slowly leaned over the back of the seat to pick up our howling child, swiveling back to hug him to me. He cried the rest of the way home, which gave me a perverse pleasure, giving voice to my own anger.

Neither of us broached Elmer's unkind suggestion over the next few days. Callous, that's what it was. The frostiness between us stretched weeklong. We had forgotten how to deal with strong differences of opinion. I knew my outburst had given Elmer pause, but he would bring it up again. I needed outside counsel.

I telephoned Maggie from Blanche and Henry's. She sounded like the old Maggie—upbeat and full of vitality. While I wailed about Elmer's intention to use my inheritance for the folks' house, she listened and prayed with me. Hearing her ask God's will and direction calmed me. Before we signed off, she insisted I come up right after her next treatment.

Leaving the boys with Elmer, I went to see Maggie the following Friday. I took a cooked pot roast, mashed potatoes, and two pies. Lee and Gracie were both at work when I got there. I drew water for compresses and sat beside her bed. We talked, two sisters filling our well of need with love and the relationship we'd forged over the past seven years.

Despite the pain, her voice was strong. "Claire, it's like we've always known each other. You're the sister I never had. We've been so busy being wives and daughters and sisters of men, we haven't allowed time—stopped to discover who we are . . ."

Were those words meant for me, too? My blouse chafed my neck, and I sought to loosen it. Could I find my way without Maggie? Placing another cool washrag on her forehead, I stammered, "M-Maybe so . . . Pop, he actually insulted me, though I never confronted him . . . Took me out of school after only the ninth grade. Like I had no say in my own future!" I touched the cloth to Maggie's closed eyelids. "But Myrrl told me Dad stopped his schooling after ninth grade, too. So it wasn't just because I was a girl, but that Dad wanted us there to work on the farm." The thought was upsetting. "But it was my life, for me to find out who I was!"

Maggie bit her lower lip and moaned. I worked faster, repeatedly dipping the washrag into the cool water, wringing it out and pressing it to her forehead.

She finally spoke. "Our preacher told us about Jesus talking with a madman who lived in a cemetery. This wild man ran up to Jesus and stopped—like he realized for the first time that he stood before God's Son . . . The man needed to be healed. But that wasn't what Jesus did—not immediately. First, he asked the man, 'What is your name?' Imagine that. So this wild man—standing there without a stitch on—admitted all the bad he'd done. Pastor Fultz said that's what God wants from us—to admit who we are—then he can heal us. Isn't that something?"

"Yes," I stared at her, the cloth dripping cold water onto my dress. "That's something . . ."

Another tangent. "You were very close to your sister Ethel, weren't you?"

"Yes. She went to nursing school, so I felt like I could do better, too. That's why I went to cosmetology school . . . So many women doing things. Amelia Earhart inspired everybody, the women anyway. When her plane went down in the Pacific, I cried for a week."

"Oh, Claire, you've done things, marvelous things. You've seen Niagara Falls and Chesapeake Bay, had banquets with chefs serving lamb and lobster. You saw President Hoover. You were part of history, sis!"

81

"I think of that sometimes . . . But that was another life—before the Depression. Now, I'm just here, Elmer and me building a life for our boys on our little farm . . . I told you what Elmer wants to do. Use my inheritance to buy a place for your folks."

She didn't seem to hear me. I started to repeat myself, give her the whole story. . . .

"Oh, Claire, you shouldn't have them living with you again! Do what it takes to get Mom and Dad in their own house. She's been dragged from pillar to post. Dad never saved anything." Her body stiffened, color draining from her face, and she waved her pale arm, a flag of distress.

I dashed to the bathroom and grabbed the slop jar on the run. She vomited, her frame trembling and perspiration coursing down her face.

Wiping her mouth and face, I whispered "Jesus loves you" to her until the ragged breathing stabilized. As she slept, I put the roast in the oven to re-heat it, wondering—if radiation treatments are supposed to kill cancer, why do they make her feel so rotten? I wish I could do something about her pain . . .

Her words came to me like spidery scraps of anguish floating on motes of air . . . whatever it takes—I want Mom and Dad in their own house. If Maggie felt that strongly about the house . . . So unfair. Resentment rose in my throat. I nearly gagged but shook it off. Fairness could not be part of the equation if I was doing it for Maggie. By an act of will, I shut myself out.

Three days later, I returned. Jennie Washburn had come several times from next door to cook since I'd been there. Looking around at the heaped laundry in the bedroom, I doubted if Lee understood his wife's needs. If he did, he couldn't deliver.

Maggie asked me to sing the old hymns to her. Close beside her bed, I began to sing. "The Old Rugged Cross," "When the Roll is Called Up Yonder," and "Amazing Grace" were her favorites, and I sang them all.

I never again brought up the issue of a house for the folks. Maggie needed at least to have that wish granted. I gave her a pain pill and soon she was fast asleep. Cornbread in the oven to go with baked beans—it was all done when Lee came in from work.

Driving back to the farm, I retraced my conversation with Maggie. Elmer would bring up the Tyrone house. He did, the very next day, and I listened, determined to not overreact. Maggie told me to accept folks where they are, and not to expect them to be sensitive to my feelings. "You can't change other people, just yourself. Only God changes people."

My inherited land sold in two weeks. Elmer quickly closed the deal for the house in Tyrone and moved his folks in. I'd never had such a bitter pill to swallow. Not only did I lose part of my inheritance, but irresponsible John came out best. He had a home for his three youngest as well as a place he could camp anytime he wanted.

Maggie's condition spiraled downhill. I sang to her and did all I could to ease her pain. In shining moments, she talked with a desperation born of the knowledge that life would soon be over. Crowded days and memorable conversations melded together like a dreamer's collage, interrupted by radiation treatments that ended when Maggie said she could endure no more.

Death came like a dove of peace, finally bringing the serenity and honor that Maggie seldom found in her lifetime. I wept and prayed with Billy and Gracie, her living legacy.

Her brothers and parents seemed unable to process this first loss to the family. With no religious tradition, they left the funeral arrangements to me. When it was over, they resumed their lives with little discussion or understanding that they had lost the fairest rose among them all.

For me, I'd lost not only my dearest friend, but also a sister in spirit. Maggie had been my last backup, the one who pointed me to who I was.

For weeks afterward, I'd begin most mornings with a pen, my Bible, and the black bound volume before me. I'd ponder the question "What is your name?" Most days, I wrote nothing. As the words came, I began to see glimpses of promise, of self-discovery I'd never known.

13 Elmer Buys Cows

Claire

One thing Elmer and I both believed—land ownership gave us special status. I never liked that word—it sounded pretentious—but I liked what it meant. We could make our own way. Create our own destiny, if you want to make it sound important. Having land, owning it, would make us self-sufficient so we wouldn't have to kowtow to anybody. Getting the four-hundred-dollar down-payment to Federal Land Bank took everything we could muster, putting us in debt to the tune of three thousand dollars for our farm. It was the right thing to do.

The note stipulated twice-yearly payments. All we had to do was harvest decent crops or sell a few head of livestock each time. The very thought of debt terrified me.

Then the rains came. For the first time in years—a good rain, wonderful rain that came slowly, over several days. And no hail.

By mid-June, Elmer had the milo planted. Two weeks later, he told me to bring the boys out to look at the milo field. Row upon row of brave green shoots patterned the ground. I began to believe we could prevail. Before Maggie died, she said the rains would come, that we'd make it on the farm. We just had to be careful—no risky ventures or serious mistakes.

A month later, on a windy afternoon, I glanced out the kitchen window. Something in the corral—looked like whirling animals in a dust storm. Red cattle . . . rangy and wild . . . stampeding about the corral. Not ours—where'd they come from? Had they broken into the corral?

Then I spotted a two-wheel trailer within the fenced area. I'd never seen the trailer or the animals before. Then I remembered an idle comment Elmer had made a few weeks before. He'd gone with Ray, advisor on all matters livestock, to the cattle auction in Liberal. They brought back those crazed brutes—for Ray?—but why leave them in our corral? I'm no sissified farm girl, but those animals looked mean! Watch that kick, Elmer! What is going on? My temple pounded. My husband better have a good story for this freshly unloaded farce.

In a matter of minutes, Ray hitched the trailer to his pickup and left. Elmer took his time coming into the house while I fidgeted between the front door and the kitchen window. He seemed preoccupied as he cleaned his brogans across the boot-scraper and came up the steps. He nearly walked right past me but jumped when I spoke. "Are those Ray's cows?"

With a nonchalance that would have disarmed a deputy, he said, "No, they're ours now."

"Ours? We don't have any money! How could you pay for them?"

"I wrote a check."

"We've got exactly thirty-seven dollars in the bank." Writing a hot check? I never thought Elmer would pick up his brothers' habits. "I know those cows cost more than that."

"Not so much. They're mostly yearlings—from down near the border—so that brought the price down. Ray said it was too good a deal to pass up. Don't worry about it. I've got an appointment with Naylor at People's Bank—"

"The bank? Shouldn't I be party to any dealings with the bank? Surely, you're not talking about another loan. Are those wild-eyed brutes diseased? What if they've got hoof and mouth? Blackleg? They could contaminate—kill off our entire herd!" I was fired up. Out of the corner of my eye, I noticed Sammy and Dickie had stopped playing in the front room and were watching us, their eyes wide and mouths open.

"Settle down, Claire. There's no way Ken Varay would auction diseased stock. They wiped out hoof and mouth in this country before the Depression. And Ray said those animals would already be dead or they'd be lame if they had blackleg. They came by rail from west Texas. He'll be here first thing tomorrow with serum, and we'll have them all vaccinated by noon."

He pulled out a chair—rather arrogantly, I thought—and gestured toward the percolator. "Hand me a cup, will you? And sit—you'll feel better." I stayed where I was, my jaw set. A grimace flashed across his face. "Okay, stand. The bank won't—"

"The bank? The bank is not my concern." He acts like I'm speaking Greek. "And I'll sit when I want to! Yes, you'd like for your wife to get you a cup . . . while you go out and buy a herd of

85

cows." I sent a cup skittering across the checkerboard oilcloth. He lurched up and barely caught it. "But you don't discuss the more important matters with your wife? You're missing the whole point, Elmer. I'm part of this family—"

"No one said you weren't. And it's not a herd—it's six. Like I said, mostly yearlings, a couple cows. But don't get so het up about the bank. Naylor was impressed with how we're running the farm. Said so last time he came out—"

"I'm not het up, Elmer Hall! You're not listening. You just want to run things like you did before. We had this talk a long time ago—about listening and respecting, doing things together—but you seem to have forgotten." I grabbed a towel; my nose had started to run. The baby awakened and was setting up a good squall from the back bedroom.

"Claire, Claire. You're blowing this all out of proportion. Easy to increase the principal to cover the cattle." He raised his voice so as to be heard over Jerry's howls.

Sammy stepped in from the front room, waiting for a chance to state the obvious. "Mama, J-Jerry's crying."

"Thank you, honey." Bringing my volume up to a near shout, I bawled, "Your father will take care of him. He likes to do things on his own." My arms crossed, I gave Elmer a withering stare. When he blinked, I turned to Sammy. "You and Dickie go outside, right now."

Elmer flung a splash of coffee at his cup; half of it darkened the oilcloth and ran off the edge, dripping to the floor. "You don't have to talk that way, Sal. Why don't you let me handle the farming, and you take care of the house?"

"Really?" I was ready to fight. "I believe you were going to take care of your youngest son before you made any more decisions about what I should do."

Our baby boy had gotten used to being picked up within thirty seconds of his first yelp. He'd now reached the shriek level, which brought to mind the tortured saints Mama made me read about in *Foxe's Book of Christian Martyrs*. I turned my back so I wouldn't have to witness Elmer's graceless departure to attend to his son.

Elmer was gone a long time; it seemed like half an hour but probably less. I had plenty of time to think about the exchange. Easy to imagine how it really went . . .

It's as plain as the nose on my face . . . He's planned it all, probably for months . . . buy cows . . . get tractor . . . sell the team . . . borrow more money . . . get a new car . . . do this . . . do that. Claire's duty is to cook and take care of the kids. Don't need her uneducated opinions. Start with whichever opening breaks first. There's Ray—let's go to the sale ring . . .

Disrespect fueled his thinking. That and being as oblivious as a doorknob. Yes, add denial that I could add anything to the complex planning required to run our farm. My feelings are hurt, and he doesn't try to understand me. Too busy defending himself, even though he knows he's wrong. It's his selfish ego. A new word I'd learned from Maggie. If the husband thinks his wife isn't as smart as he is, he can just ignore her.

Our differences of opinion had ascended step by step, sparking old annoyances into smoldering divisions that would burst into flame, capable of scarring and scalding whatever relationship I thought we had. What I thought didn't matter.

My breath caught. I began sobbing. Pushed the towel to my face. Oh, God, where are you? Just when I need you—

From the back bedroom, Elmer, talking to his son—our son—who chirped back at him. Chirp—talk. Chirp—talk. Back and forth. It sounded like they really understood each other. How does he do that? Giggle and Elmer's snort. The naughty sound of him blowing a big kiss on Jerry's fat little tummy. Shrieking giggles. "Let's go see Mama. Go see Mama."

I stepped to the wash basin and splashed water onto my face. Leaned over to the oval mirror on the wall. Fluffed my hair. More water, dry my face. Quick, quick. Fluff my hair.

The baby shrieked and giggled as Elmer tossed him in the air. Don't drop him! I quickly sat, not sure what to do—stay on the prod so I could pour more thunder on my husband's head? Greet the laughing pair with a pretend happy face?

Elmer answered that one for me. "Claire, how do you diaper a kid without poking yourself with those infernal safety pins? Took me three times to wrap that thing around him so it would stay. Man, was he a mess! Uh, you'll have a few more towels and washcloths to wash. I had to clean myself up, too. But we had fun, didn't we, little cowboy?"

"Mama, Mama." Our boy had spotted me. Daddy was forgotten.

I held out my arms. Baby Jerry burrowed against my neck, cooing contentedly. Elmer followed as I took the baby into the front room. When I sat on the couch, Elmer joined me, letting his arm rest lightly over my shoulders. We remained like that for a time, the silence broken by the sighs of our child. The pall of conflict had lifted. Our souls began to commune. Yet we needed to distill and cleanse our vessel of relationship, as one might wipe dregs from a goblet before its reuse.

Elmer spoke first. "You do quite a bit there, taking care of our three little farmers. Yeah, you do a few other things around here, too. This one, um, kinda stretched me . . ."

I gave him a sideways glance. "Now that you're qualified, maybe you'd like to take over the house and let me handle the farming?"

He kissed me then. Whispered apologies before and after. He laughed when I told him about my pity party—how awful I thought he was.

We had been at this place before. Maybe not quite the same place, but near enough to know that telling the truth goes a long way.

The folks were finally in their own house. Probably built at the turn of the century, the single-story wood frame structure had high ceilings, plank floors, and plaster-and-lath interior walls. Elmer and I had repaired the broken, replaced the missing, painted everything that didn't move, and cleaned the place inside and out. It cost a major part of my inheritance from Pop, but for the first time in sixteen years of marriage, I felt like I could rule my kitchen without interference.

Thankful for that, I boxed up a dozen jars of canned goods for Elmer's weekly trip to Tyrone, population 350. "Tell your mother not to give it all away. That food is just for them and the kids living there— John's three youngest, isn't it? The canned vegetables and meat should last two or three weeks."

Word would get around. John and his boys, probably Bud too, would show up "to see Grandpa and Grandma." The thought of it gave me a headache.

When forty pounds of beef disappeared from the folks' larder in little over a month, I told Elmer he had to put a stop to his brothers and their crowd mooching off his parents—mooching off us, really. Either that, or butcher another steer.

Elmer gave me a tired look. "I suppose we could cut back.

Mom's chickens are big enough to fry. That'll help out with what we give them. She about had kittens when Dad turned the cacklers loose in the garden, but he just laughed. Told her that's how he got rid of grasshoppers."

Wonderful, that something worked. Most of their garden was sprouting or planted. Mary Grace said she was going to teach John's girls how to can vegetables. Yeah, good luck with that.

৵৵

From the front step, I held the baby on my lap and watched Elmer clean the carburetor on the Oakland. Sammy and Dickie Lee played nearby in a sand pile. If Elmer couldn't get the car running this time, we'd have to replace it—somehow. My mouth felt dry at the thought. I should've been pleased with the fine weather, highlighting little diamonds of light on the dew-drenched lilac bush, but grief was a hard taskmaster. With both Pop and Maggie gone, it left just me and God.

Maybe just me, if I couldn't penetrate access to the Almighty.

I turned back into the house, realizing I hadn't read my Bible in weeks. I pulled it off the top of the buffet and onto the table. Back to reading God's precious Word, how had I fallen out of that discipline?

Elmer seemed not to notice, but he saw everything. One evening as I began reading, he suggested stopping by to see friends in Liberal, Dave and Lorena Scott. They often hosted pitch parties which sometimes lasted all night.

Playing cards—always a lot of fun—but I wanted to tell him how my special reading time fed my soul. That would've been too much for my husband. As far as I could tell, he still saw God as an enemy. But I also knew the Heavenly Father wouldn't allow us to block him out of our lives—as long as people were praying.

And I would be praying.

14 Outdoor School

Sammy

When our twelve-year-old cousin Tommy came to live with us, Mama told me and Dickie to behave and get along. She told Tommy to behave, too. I knew he didn't have a mama anymore, but Uncle John, his daddy, came to see him sometimes. Mama said John came to get a free meal, but she was glad Tommy got to see his daddy, anyway. I was glad my daddy doesn't leave 'cause I want to see him every day.

My daddy told Tommy that if he'd work hard, he'd earn extra pribleges. Daddy started farming with our new tractor, so he didn't use the horses anymore.

Tommy said it wasn't a real new tractor, 'cause it was older than a new one. But it was new to us, and that's what counted.

When Daddy finished cultivating, sometimes Tommy got to drive the Ford tractor back from the field while Daddy brought the pickup home.

For Tommy's thirteenth birthday, Mama baked a chocolate cake. We all waited for Uncle John to come but he didn't. We ate cake, anyway.

Then Daddy said he had a different kind of gift for Tommy, but we all had to go outside so he could show us. He had Tommy get in our old Chevy pickup; then Daddy showed Tommy how to drive it. He said if Tommy was going to stay with us then he needed to help do things around the farm. So Mama didn't have to all the time.

Tommy said he already knew how to drive 'cause the Corzine boys had taught him how to use the clutch in their Model A and Mama said, "Oh, not them wild boys!"

Daddy looked at Tommy. "Well, let's see what you can do, Mister Know-It-All." Then he got in the other side so he could watch Tommy shift the gears and hopefully go down the road without killing someone or running the pickup in the bar ditch.

Tommy stepped on the starter, but the pickup jumped and died. Daddy told him he should've taken it out of gear, so Tommy tried again, and then again. It never did start.

Daddy got out and waved for Tommy to get out, too. "That's enough. It won't start now. You flooded it." He shook his head. "Those Corzine boys only showed you part of what you need to know. They don't know as much as they think they do. And I'll bet they been stealing from my watermelon field every summer."

"Oh, what makes you say that, Uncle Elmer?"

Daddy stared at Tommy. "I set time aside to give you a break. You couldn't curb your know-it-all attitude to be taught by me. As if I wouldn't know more than those rowdies. Those boys are trouble. We'll do this another time. Come on, we've got work to do."

Tommy didn't drive the pickup that time. He said bad things, but not so Daddy could hear. He wanted to use the pickup to take out Georgia Duvall. But not till Daddy let him.

Me and Dickie went into the house when Mama took Baby Jerry to change his pants.

We sat and had some more chocolate cake.

๛

After Tommy finished his chores, he took me and Dickie with him hunting out in the pasture. Hunting was mostly for us to find new things, and Tommy knew lots of stuff.

Dickie and me thought our dog Shep was the best dog. Mama said Shep was a good dog but the best ever was old Ring. She told us stories about Ring saving Daddy from the great storm, and how he would bring in the cows by himself. He was so quick, he could kill rattlesnakes without getting bit.

Daddy said Shep was too slow for rattlesnakes. But he got excited every time we went outside. He raced around the yard from me to Tommy to Dickie until we left to go someplace.

We went north of the barn where the little pond is. Right away, Shep scared up a noisy bird with skinny legs that ran across the ground instead of flying away.

Tommy said, "That's a killdeer. Watch what he does."

Dickie called it a silly bird. It fell to the ground, crying like a little baby.

Tommy said, "It pretends it's been hurt . . . Watch! See, Shep thinks he's going to catch it."

The killdeer flew up every time Shep jumped for it. He barely missed it, every time. "Look at him!" I said, "He . . . he almost c-c-

91

caught him! Get it, Shep. G-get it! Oh, no . . ."

Dickie pointed. "The silly bird is coming back . . . Shep! Wait, Shep!" He grabbed Shep around the neck, but Shep ran anyway, and Dickie skidded into the water. He let go when he shoulda held on. Mama had warned him not to get his clean pants dirty. He was in trouble.

The silly bird landed, dragging one wing on the ground while it kept on running and crying so pitiful, Kill-dee! Kill-dee! It sounded awful, like it really did have a hurt wing.

Shep ran after the pretender bird, but Tommy called us back. "See, over there on the ground? That's where its nest is." He pointed to a spot, but Dickie never could find it. I couldn't either, but I acted like I could.

Tommy said since it rained, we might find wildflowers out in the pasture. Dickie picked two bunches for Mama. Tommy laughed and said they were weeds, but Dickie didn't care. Then Tommy hollered for us to come and look. "See these plants with purple flowers?"

We ran over to look, and Dickie picked one of the flowers for Mama's bouquet.

"Wait a minute," Tommy pulled out his jackknife. "I call this Injun bread. It's good to eat . . . No, Dickie, wait! Not the leaves, just the root." He dug into the ground and pulled up the root. It looked like a white carrot. He scraped off the dirt with his knife. "You boys want some?"

"You g-go first," I said.

"Sure," Tommy cut a piece and started chewing it. Then we all ate some. Shep stuck his nose in because he's always hungry.

The sun was about to go down, so we started back to the house. We had lots of new things to tell Mama and Daddy. Dickie was proud of the bouquet of flowers he gave Mama. She said how beautiful it was and went on how much she liked getting flowers. I guess she didn't know they were mostly weeds, 'cause she gave him a kiss while she wiped his nose. Mama never did say anything about Dickie's wet pants, either. She just pulled them off him "like peeling an onion," she said. Then she dusted his bottom with powder.

Daddy said, "I don't want you boys messing with that wild turnip—that 'Injun bread,' as Tommy calls it. Not until you're a lot older, and you know what you're doing." He looked over at Tommy, who dropped his eyes.

Daddy didn't smile the whole time. "That wild turnip, or parsnip—whatever it is—is a dead ringer to another plant out in the pasture. A plant that's poison. You boys listening?"

Both of us said, "Yes, Daddy, we won't." We didn't want to disappoint Daddy.

"That's good," he said. "You boys are too young to tell the difference. Tommy calls it 'Injun bread' but it looks a lot like locoweed. Locoweed is poison. It'll make a horse go crazy. Don't fool with it." He looked at Tommy again. "Tommy and I have already had a talk. He won't be careless about such things again."

☙✍

Tommy waved at us to follow him toward the big pear tree. "Come over here to see the kingbirds. Come around here . . . no, over here." He pointed up in the tree. We crowded around him. "Hey, don't get too close. Look . . . right up there. They're almost like meadow larks—yellow breast—except they're not as big and they make a lot more noise—"

"I can't see," Dickie pushed in front and stepped on my foot.

"Get off me, Dickie!" I pushed him. He never looks where he's going.

Tommy said, "Aww, you're not looking the right direction to see them. Their nest is up high where the leaves are thick. But—are you listening? Those kingbirds will dive-bomb any cat that gets too close . . . You boys watch the birds. I gotta finish my chores."

Dickie and I stood looking up in the tree. He said, "We need a cat."

The next morning, after we all ate Mama's pancakes for breakfast, Tommy ran out to catch the bus. We told Daddy about the dive-bomber birds. Then Dickie and I went out and sat on the front step, watching. We waited a long time.

I said, "We've got fourteen c-c-cats, so we—"

"Look, Sammy! There's the sneaky gray cat. I bet he heard the kingbirds. S-h-h-h-h."

We held our breath while the cat with the crooked tail ran across the road toward us. He went past the old tamarack tree and dug a hole in the sand.

Dickie whispered, "He's just going to the toilet."

Daddy came out and sat beside us, sipping from his coffee cup. We watched that cat go right toward the pear tree.

Before he knew it, the kingbirds came like dive-bombers!

Zoom! Zoom! We all laughed when the scaredy-cat ran away. The kingbirds made a lot of noise afterward.

Daddy said they were scolding the cat, telling him not to come back. He didn't.

Daddy went back into the house. Dickie looked around and said, "Gonna find that kingbird's nest." Off he went.

Zoom! Zoom! Those birds were so fast Dickie didn't see them coming. They hit the top of his head and he started yelling and crying, 'cause he's only four years old. He ran right past me—into the house.

I laughed, but Dickie didn't.

Mama came out just then. She said, "Your little brother was mad at you for laughing at him."

I shook my head. What can a six-year-old big brother tell his little brother if he doesn't want to listen?

But Dickie didn't go near the big pear tree for a while. I didn't, either.

Mama said for sure I'd go to first grade in the fall. So every time after Tommy came home on the school bus, I'd ask him about his teachers and what he did at Greenough School. Dickie and I already knew most of it because we all went there to watch basketball games and for box suppers and meetings of the old people. I stayed with Mama or Daddy just 'cause. I didn't tell anyone, but I didn't want to get lost in the big gym with all those people around.

Dickie didn't care if he got lost. So Mama always had to leave Baby Jerry with Daddy while she went looking for him when it was time to go home.

The last time we went, she found Dickie sitting on the basketball bleachers, right in the middle of a bunch of high school girls, the ones Tommy talked about all the time. They wore red lipstick that made their lips look like big apples. And they wore dangly earrings and chewed gum and laughed at everything he said. Or what anyone said.

Afterward, Mama told Daddy all about it. She said Dickie was talking a blue streak and those girls were lapping it up like Old Tom drinking milk out of a saucer. They were having such a good time, she didn't want to interrupt. Then she got worried about what he was saying, so she slipped over where she could hear.

Dickie was telling about when Daddy cussed the preacher tinhorn that came to our house.

Roberta Monroe asked what Daddy said and Dickie told them. At least some of it, because they shrieked and laughed before Mama grabbed him by the arm.

Katharine Weybright stopped Mama from leaving. She said how handsome Dickie was with his long eyelashes and dark eyes and not a hair out of place. I bet if she had a gallon of Wave-Set put on her head she would have all her hair slicked down, too.

When Daddy drove us home, Mama told him we'd lost all of our family secrets. She said he needed to stop cussing around the boys. Especially when "the preacher tinhorns" came around. I asked if Reverend Holder was a preacher tinhorn. Mama started laughing. She told me not to call anybody that, but she was still laughing. Daddy never did laugh, and when he asked Mama if she'd ever told us boys about Harold, then she stopped laughing, too.

I asked Mama who Harold was, and if I could have a stick of gum, too.

She turned around in the front seat of the car and stuck out her hand to Dickie: "Give me that. Open your mouth. Now!"

She made him lean back and open his mouth. Then she made him twist around every direction so she could see down his gullet. Probably like a mother kingbird feeding its little ones. She should have had him open his hands.

That night, he put enough Juicy Fruit on the bed post to last a year. It smelled good but I didn't want any of it.

Mama never told me where they lost the family secrets.

15 Hog-Killing Season

Sammy

A kick to my leg, and then another. Still dark but I didn't have to see to know where it came from—right beside me, Dickie, pretending to be asleep. I got my left arm mostly out from the sheet . . . Y-i-i-i! Thumb caught.

I sat up, but he didn't move. Maybe he really was asleep and dreaming again. So he kicks me? Little brothers. If I clobbered him, I'd be in trouble. Maybe Mama's fixing early breakfast. Time to get up, just in case.

Went into the kitchen. A rifle . . . was on the table. Daddy's .22 rifle. Just laying there.

Moving closer, I stared at dark blue steel and wooden stock. Wondered what it would feel like to pick it up and hold it. My right hand kinda floated out—

"Get away from there, Sammy Earl! Don't touch that!"

I jumped and caught my breath. Should've known not to fool with a gun.

It was Mama, screeching almost like Grandma. "Elmer, get this thing off the table!"

For once, Daddy moved quick when Mama spoke. "Okay, okay . . . Sammy, get away from that! Don't ever touch a gun if one of us isn't around! Told you plenty-a times."

He bent down so his nose was almost touching mine. He didn't say anything at first. "Okay, son. No harm done. I just went back in the closet, looking for—"

Tears ran past my nose and onto my upper lip. "S-s-sorry, Daddy. I didn't p-pick it up. I j-just wanted to . . . to . . . ."

Mama's arms came around me. Hanky in hand, she reached up and wiped my face. "Don't want anything to happen to my boys. Daddy wanted to clean the rifle while you were still asleep." She looked across the room at Daddy. "He'll be more careful next time."

"Where's breakfast, Mama?" Dickie ran in from the bedroom. Then Tommy came in. We were all ready to eat.

Mama put out a platter of hot pancakes. So good. Daddy said, "Listen up, boys. We got that hard frost I've been waiting for. Good butchering weather. Monday we'll start with a barren sow—actually a gilt, as she's never farrowed. She's in the pen this side of the mean one that ate half her litter."

"Oh, Daddy," I remembered. "Th-th-that's the one you told us to stay away from."

He poked me and grinned. "So, you do remember what you're told, don't you?"

We all nodded our heads, and Tommy said, "So that's why you had the .22 rifle out this morning—you're gonna shoot her. I'm a good shot, Uncle Elmer. Can I do that, uh, for you?"

Daddy glanced at Tommy. "I'm not going to have a thirteen-year-old kid waving a gun around and getting somebody hurt. There's a lot more to handling a gun than hitting a target. I already asked Earl to come out. He's an experienced shooter, which is what we need."

Daddy said Uncle Earl used to be a policeman for Rock Island, and some things I didn't understand. Uncle Earl coulda been in the movies, with all the stuff he did.

For a change, Dickie didn't ask a buncha questions. We listened while Mama and Daddy named who they expected to show up on butchering day. Ray would help Daddy anytime with animals, 'cause he was his cousin and they were friends besides; and Edith and their daughters Ruby and Violet would help Mama in the kitchen.

At least Mama hoped they were coming so she could introduce Ruby to Wayne Buffalow, Lew's youngest. She said he was a real sheik, but never did tell me what a sheik was.

They didn't count on Blanche Ausmus coming to help. A cow had stepped on Henry's foot, and he'd probably stay home. Mama asked if John was coming but Daddy shook his head. He didn't come to Tommy's birthday party when Mama baked a cake.

Mama got up to take the hot water off the cook stove. She told Daddy to tell Lew, since he's still sad over Kate dying and he would have fun with us.

Tommy left. Mama said he was pouting. He wanted to shoot the gun. She whispered something to Daddy and then she went back to the bedroom to get baby Jerry. We could hear him chirping like a cricket.

One of these days, Daddy will teach me how to shoot. He

called for Tommy to come back to the table. Then Daddy told us he had to go to Liberal to see some people and he would drop us off at the picture show.

Mama had us wash up and get our nice clothes on first. We were all ready to go by the time Dickie found his shoes.

઒ન૭

Daddy gave Tommy the money for the Saturday matinee at the Plaza Theater. There was extra for Milk Duds and maybe popcorn if we shared. Tommy stood in line and me and Dickie watched other kids come in. Noisy, acting like big shots. Pushing one another. They stared at us, whispering and pointing, like they knew we weren't from there. Didn't have any manners, but what do you expect? They were Liberal kids. Our cousin Gracie said that's the way the Liberal rowdies acted. Better for us to stay away from them because they bullied little kids.

I wished Tommy would hurry or them rowdies would come and push us around. If I had a gun like Randolph Scott or Tom Mix, they'd keep back, but all I had was a slingshot and it was home. I told Dickie, "N-next time, I'll bring my slingshot."

Tommy came with our candy. "Take this. They ain't got Milk Duds—just licorice."

Dickie pushed in, stepping on my foot, like he always does. "Where's mine, huh?"

"Dickie, g-get offa my foot." I gave him a shove. If I hadn't, he woulda stood on my foot all afternoon, and Mama said I had to take care of my new shoes 'cause they had to last till next year. Dickie was wearing my hand-me-down shoes, so he didn't care if they got scuffed up.

Tommy gave Dickie his licorice. When he gave me mine, he asked, "Did you say slingshot? You can't bring a slingshot in here."

I didn't want to talk about it. "If I had a gun like Tom Mix, I could keep them back."

He looked at me funny, but I said, "Hurry, the n-newsreel is already st-starting." That was my favorite part because it showed our soldiers and sailors blasting the Germans with tanks and machine guns. American planes dropped bombs on ammo dumps and airfields. Airplanes zoomed over Tokyo, in Japan. I loved the music and the big guns.

Tommy brought a bag of popcorn, and after he ate some, he passed it to Dickie Lee, who was sitting between us. He dropped it

98

before I could get any. Good thing I was quick 'cause some of it dumped out in the foo-foo hair of the fat girl in the row in front of us. She turned around real quick, but I acted innocent. Dickie started giggling and everybody told him to shut up. We told him he'd better quiet down or the rowdies would come.

The cartoon started—Bugs Bunny and Daffy Duck—so everyone forgot about spilled popcorn and the rowdies. The big show was Randolph Scott, my favorite. He was the good guy in Abilene Town. Halfway through, I remembered popcorn, but couldn't find it. No wonder, Dickie was laying on it!

I tried to get it loose, but he wouldn't let go. Good grief. He was sleeping on it. I pulled the bag out from under him, but it ripped and he still didn't wake up.

Only six pieces left for me—but Randolph Scott got the bad guys. He whipped them because he was brave, and he had a Winchester.

If I had a gun, I wouldn't shoot anyone, but I'd let those rowdies know who was boss.

Elmer

Me with my rifle in the crook of my left arm and my butchering crew beside and behind me—we must've been a sight as we crossed the road to start the whole shebang. Earl and Ray would help with the heavy work. Lew and Henry had enough experience to improvise if we needed changes to get the job done. Our kids brought up the rear. A windless chilly day, so we wouldn't have to contend with blowing sand.

Ray suggested we look at the scalding vat and butchering area beside the barn. He'd seen it but, savvy as he was, wanted the rest to have a look. He tugged on the block and tackle and peered up at the cross timber I'd anchored between the two black locust trees. He grunted okay, so we trooped south around the corral.

I held up everyone near the loading chute. As Henry and Lew caught up, I signaled the others to quiet down so we wouldn't spook the hogs. The hog sheds extended west as a narrow wood frame structure with adjacent pens opening to the south. Our quarry was in the fourth enclosure.

I had updated everyone after Henry and Blanche arrived. Didn't mince words with the kids; told Tommy and the boys they were to stay out of the way and be quiet. Distractions made me nervous as a cat. Shooting and killing, anything could happen.

Lew showed up first, but without his boys. Glad to see me but he looked rough. He'd be good for advice; Lew could talk the pants off a policeman, and always ready to talk politics with anyone who'd listen. Nobody did, which suited me fine. We could talk later.

Henry made quite an impression when he and Blanche arrived. Swaddled in wrappings, he looked like he'd come from a war zone rather than being stepped on by a cow. The bandages and swollen jaw muffled his speech. He said the cow wasn't supposed to be in the barn. She spooked and came out full tilt about the time he started to go in through the same narrow door.

Henry said he came just to maintain family harmony and save his sanity. It seems that Blanche had driven the old International one time. Remembering that day still made Henry's head hurt. Afterward, he had to rebuild fifty feet of Reuel Rushton's precious fence that Blanche ran over. Sore foot and all, it was simpler to drive Blanche over to help Claire.

After giving the rifle and cartridges to Earl, I waved my workers toward the fourth pen. Our approach brought the pig out of the shed, grunting eagerly. "She's the one we want. Probably close to 250 pounds, bigger than most slaughter pigs. She thinks we've come to feed her." I nodded to the boys and they surged up, next to the pen. "Keep your hands and toes on this side of the fence. It's okay to look now, but just for a minute. And stay away from that one." I pointed toward the adjacent pen.

Eyes big as saucers, the boys stumbled back like their pants were on fire.

Good. Fear could be a good thing. Any common farm animal that would eat its young was a danger to anyone and anything. I watched Sammy and Dickie as they stared at the huge sow snuffling for tidbits around her trough.

Sleepy-looking, even docile, that sow could be cat-quick. I hadn't told Claire, but I carried a club anytime I ventured inside her pen. Several weeks previous, I'd had to renail a loose board on the inside of her pen. Figured it would only take a minute, so I didn't do the smart thing. Should've lashed a couple fence panels together to separate my workspace from her. I'd barely started when I glanced up to see her a-coming. I vaulted my fifty-eight-year-old carcass over that fence like a gazelle.

When I returned from retrieving my hammer, she tried it again. I caught her in the snoot with my newly made billy. Boy, did she scream. When I go in that pen now, I advertise my enforcer and she backs up, raging in frustration. Ray said I better sell her.

"Okay boys, listen up." I waited. "When Earl comes over with the rifle, clear out. You can watch but stay back. Understand?" I waited for assent from each one, including Tommy, then nodded behind us. "There's my sled, already hitched to the tractor. That's to get her to the scalding vat. Things have to move quick, once she's down."

"The boys will be here with me, Elmer." That was Ray, one hand on Sammy's shoulder and the other on Dickie's. He nudged them to one side where they could see.

Lew had waited for Henry, and together they approached at Henry's gimp-pace, sharing stories of other butchering days. They quieted as they saw Earl, braced against the outside corner post of the pen, rifle pointed to the sky. Both followed his gaze into the empty pen.

From my position at the near corner, I nodded and swept an arm upward, toward the shed. They understood, settling in back and to the left of me. The audience was ready for the star of the show to come out into full sunlight.

Glancing behind him again to make sure the area was clear, Earl slid a round into the chamber. No talk. A rooster crowed from back of the house; another answered.

Our subject, white with pinkish highlights, appeared ghost-like within the darkened rectangle opening. She ambled out a few steps and stopped about thirty feet from Earl.

He brought the rifle barrel down in a steady arc. The stock against his cheek, his chest and shoulders rose and relaxed. An alien noise, little more than a pop, broke the morning quiet.

A small dark spot appeared an inch or so above an imaginary line between the pig's eyes. She shook her head, as if annoyed at the reddish-black seepage starting to flow down her jowls. Then she turned and ambled back into the darkness of the shed.

Earl let out an oath and glanced at me, eyebrows raised.

My fingers clawed for my double-bladed pocketknife, sharp as a whistle. I flicked the big blade open and thrust it, handle-first, at him. My middle brother bounded over that board fence and, knife in hand, crept to and through that dark opening. Stunned by the fact the pig didn't go down when hit, I wondered if Earl was going to face an enraged animal in the shed.

Ray came up beside me. "He should be able to get her outta

there right quick." Apparently seeing the alarm on my face, he added, "Don't worry. He's doing it right. Need to get her out here in . . ."

The gilt appeared in the opening, prodded along by Earl on its right side. The instant she was completely outside, he flashed his right hand under her jaw and drew it back toward him. Its throat cut, the animal hit the ground into an instantaneous pool of blood. He shook his hands as if to dry them and brought my knife over. I stuffed it in my pocket and headed to the tractor.

Ray unwired the front fence panel and he and Lew unhooked the sled and dragged it into the pen. Henry nudged the boys back out of the way. Tommy joined Ray and Earl to muscle the carcass onto the sled as I backed the tractor in for hookup.

I gave Sammy and Dickie a choice of riding with me on the tractor or running to tell Mama about all the excitement. I knew what they'd do.

It was a little crowded on the tractor but me and my two farmers rode like conquering heroes over to the scalding vat where they could oversee the activities of my work crew.

Claire

I had six buckets ready to go when Sammy rushed in to tell me Elmer was ready to scald the carcass. Edith and her girls helped me carry buckets of hot water across the road to the rectangular wooden vat next to the barn. Tommy was sitting on the fence, watching, so I signaled Elmer. A word from him, and Tommy joined our bucket brigade. Earl winched the carcass into the trough. As soon as water covered the carcass, he and Elmer began scraping off the hair.

I'd already set out pans, a meat grinder, bone saw, and a brace of knives. Edith and her girls joined me in working on the large pork sections brought into our kitchen work area. Hams, chops, and bacon went into a scrubbed wheelbarrow, which Tommy pushed to the milk house for curing. I made sure to supervise his work, aware of his carelessness. Extra fat went back to the kitchen to reheat on the stove. When it went jelly-soft, we poured off the lard and set it aside.

Fat went into large pans on the propane range. It sizzled and stung our arms and face, but I loved the savory smell. I set the girls up grinding sausage, forming patties, and putting them in Mason jars. We topped off the sausage with lard and then sealed each jar.

That all done, we heated another pot of grease and began a donut-making operation, a family tradition since I was a girl. Word of that brought the boys into the house. One donut apiece, then I sent them with a boxful out to the butchering crew. They delivered in a hurry, returning for more donuts.

The workday ended after dark, everyone worn out, but satisfied and well-fed. We sent our volunteer helpers home with a tidy package of meat for their own tables, knowing we'd soon be called on to help with their butchering day.

16 Crime and Punishment

Elmer

Six in the car, heading back to Forgan, but it might as well have been me alone. Gave me time to think about the day. Claire kept me company for a couple miles out of Tyrone. She couldn't get over Mom's proclamation, "I'm thankful none of my boys is in jail."

I about ripped a stitch. Finally told Claire that's an achievement back in Kentucky where my mother grew up. My dear wife didn't appreciate my amusement and soon joined the kids in dreamland. Being around Mom too long wears on anybody. Claire would do well to let her bark-bark go in one ear and out the other, like I do. She won't—can't—because she's still trying to please her own mother, dead almost sixteen years. I'd never tell Claire, but her mother was a lot like my ex, Florence. Glad I'm done with that trolley ride. Hard to believe Claire and I both had controlling women trying to save us from ourselves.

Claire was unhappy about missing her church meeting, but it was time to see the folks. They won't be around forever. I was all for her taking the boys and Tommy to church, but I didn't need to listen to her sky pilot tell me I'm going to hell.

A chirp from the back seat. What a sight, our little men sprawled against one another like jackstraws. Sammy, way too serious for his age, but he'll be ready for school this fall . . . Dickie Lee always has ants in his pants; got his mama's good looks and not afraid of anything . . . And my littlest Indian, Jerry Elmer, that everyone says favors me. Fifty-six years since I was two. I can't imagine it and fear for them—a world out there, full of traps and tarnation. Wish I could walk them through it. I'll have to be teaching them how to be young men. My partners.

Oops, take a deep breath. Needed to wipe my face with a bandanna before my good woman caught me bawling like a baby.

Any time we visited the folks, Claire and I both tried to be alert for how our boys hit it off with John's kids. Joyce and Phyllis—usually no problem, as they wanted to impress older brother Tommy with how grown-up they were. Him staying with us, they got to see him more than if he lived with his dad.

Corky was another story. Any trouble, Corky was usually behind it. Only a month older than Sammy, but Mom said he defies her. Maggie said Corky was drawn to trouble like filings to a magnet. Early on, the kid pegged his grandfather as an easy touch. Had to put a stop to that real quick, so earlier—that very afternoon—I had Claire send the other kids outside. Corky knew something was up and tried to slip away with the rest of them. I grabbed him by the suspenders as he ran toward the back door.

Only six years old, but what a mouth! We'd heard his vulgarities before, so Claire was ready. She handed me a washcloth lathered with Lava soap. A quick mouth scrub wised that kid up real quick. I felt like a bully but didn't let on. After I laid down the law, Corky took it like a good little soldier. He wasn't fooling me; I knew he and I would butt heads again. I needed to plot strategy with Dad.

Tommy and his sisters were talking with the Grice kids from across the street. Claire shepherded our two older boys and Corky to play in the vacant lot north of the house, so I asked Dad to show me his garden. Early June, the season that his plants should be flourishing. I followed him and closed the gate of his chicken wire enclosure behind us. "Dad, do you ever get any help in the garden from John's kids?"

"Not if I have anything to say about it." His voice turned to a low growl. "See that?" He pointed to a heap of crushed and uprooted plants behind the manure pile. "I turn my back for five minutes to tend to your mother and left the girls in charge of watering. Corky and two of his buddies slipped through the gate and I get this."

"That's outright vandalism, Dad. That young tough wanted to hurt you. Did you take a belt to him? '"

"I'm not sacrificing my garden to teach those kids responsibility. Mother and I depend on what I raise and what she puts up, and of course, what you and Claire bring over. If I get little or nothing out of this patch of dirt, I—"

"Dad, didn't you hear what I said?" I moved closer and faced him directly. I peered into his eyes—no confusion, just determination.

"Yes, I hear you. I said it's not my job to teach those kids responsibility. Corky is—"

"Dad, what I want to know, did you confront the kids and Corky specifically, about what they—" At that moment, a chill crossed my forehead. A quick turn of my head to locate our boys, to see Corky or the older kids. I held my breath. No sound but the occasional car on Highway 54. Where was the last place I'd seen them? I called and waited. Nothing . . .

I strode toward the gate and practically ripped my fingernails off getting it unlatched. Dad's voice sounded behind me, but I didn't answer. The idea of that unrestrained child menace had taken root in my mind, forming fear that our boys were in danger. Suddenly I needed to know my boys were safe. I tore into the house, slowing when I barged into Claire and Mom sitting in the kitchen, waiting on something to cook. Without explanation, I asked if they'd seen the boys.

Claire stood. "Is something wrong?"

"No. No, just want to make sure they're not into any mischief."

"They should be out in the north vacant lot. I told them to stay there."

I went out the door without answering. No surprise, the vacant lot was vacant.

A sun-bleached pickup came around the corner up ahead. Might be Grice, the neighbor. He angled across the street as if to intercept me. What now? I waited, trying to recall his first name, as he glided to a stop, his arm hanging out the window.

I eyed him from the anonymity of my wide-brimmed fedora. Ruddy complexion, red hair, hawkish features, and an unblinking stare gave the impression of a street fighter.

His voice came out flat, but there was no mistaking the testiness behind it. "You looking for three young boys, one with a smart mouth lives across the street with the older couple?"

I ignored his insolence. "Could be. You seen them?"

"You'll find them where the street's littered with green gourds. They're having a party, chucking those baseball-size gourds out at traffic. That's flat-out dangerous—startles drivers, gourds flying through the air, banging the side of their car. If those kids was mine, I'd tan their hides." He shifted into gear, revved his pickup, and chugged away.

I turned and glared after Grice—Ross Grice, I recalled—but

106

got ahold of myself. If I was in his shoes, I'd be hot under the collar, too.

I soon spotted the scamps and my relief was replaced by anger. Focused on their mischief, they didn't hear me coming. I slipped in behind them and let out a yell that would've woke the dead. It took all my self-control to keep from rolling on the ground and howling with laughter at their reaction. Comical. They must've filled their britches.

Knowing they were going to get a licking on the spot, Sammy and Dickie started crying. Instead of paddling them, I read them the riot act, and then I had them pick up every one of the gourds—including the flattened ones—from the pavement while I kept watch for cars.

I didn't include Corky in the last part of my punishment; he wasn't my responsibility, but I hoped Dad—or better yet, John—would deal with him. I marched the three of them back to Mom and Dad's house. I took my boys aside and ordered them to go to Mr. Grice and personally apologize for their offenses.

I couldn't have ordered a more demanding task. They cried all the way over to the Grices and all the way back. I made it easier for them by arranging for Grice to receive their confessions in private, while I hovered in the background.

My boys had learned a valuable lesson. Ross Grice learned something about me, too. From that day on, he never failed to tip his hat or give a salute anytime we crossed paths.

We must've made the twenty-nine-mile drive to Tyrone from the farm a hundred times. Claire gets worked up, knowing John takes advantage of the food we supply the folks. Bud, too—when he remembers he has family. I don't care about that. Mom gets to see her youngest son.

I caught Claire in the kitchen early that Sunday morning, fixing a banquet to take with us. I put my arms around her. "Mom already knows how to cook. You don't have to fix anything."

"I can't go over there empty-handed. That's not good manners."

"How long you been up?"

"Long enough." She elbowed me in the ribs. "You're in my way. I need in the oven . . . Oh! That tickles. Elmer! Stop it or you'll wake the kids."

107

"You're the one making noise." I waved at the pressure cooker. "What's in there?"

"Chicken and noodles."

"Dad's favorite."

"That's why I'm fixing it, Lover Boy."

My signal. I grabbed my gal Sal and gave her a kiss to remember the rest of the day. I still remembered it, twelve hours later. Over the next hill, and we'd be able to see our house.

After all we'd been through that day, it would be good to be home.

Sammy

Monday morning at breakfast, Tommy started teasing me and Dickie about getting in trouble for throwing gourds. I told him Corky started the whole thing, and he should've gotten in trouble, same as us.

Afterward, Mama told Daddy that Corky was the ringleader of that escapade. Daddy took Tommy outside and talked with him. It sounded like he was in trouble. Tommy never said another word about the gourds.

Tommy was real nice to me and Dickie the next day. He showed us three sparrows' nests in the locust trees by the barn. We learned that sparrow eggs take two weeks to hatch.

"Did you ever find the m-mockingbird nest?" I said. "He sings every morning before we get up. And where do m-meadowlarks build their nests? There's no trees out in the pasture."

Tommy shook his head. "You guys ask too many questions. When Short-Pants here gets bigger, I'll show you a badger den amongst the sagebrush."

"He means you, Dickie Lee," I said.

Dickie had more questions but after a while, I went into the house and told Mama what Tommy was showing us.

She was ironing shirts and sheets but stopped to look around. "Where's Dickie? Didn't he come with you?" She went to the north kitchen window and looked out.

"Oh, my stars!" She started yelling and crying and before she ran out the front door, she told me to watch Jerry, to make sure he didn't get into anything.

I got a lard can to stand on so I could see out the window. Mama was running across the road to the barn and waving her arms. I looked closer. Dickie had climbed up on the east side of the barn and was leaning out from the roof. He was trying to see in the sparrow nests!

Mama got to the barn in a hurry, and she started waving her arms again and holding her head and pointing at Dickie and down at the ground. He climbed off that roof real quick and Mama waited for him the whole time. As soon as his feet touched the ground, Mama grabbed his ear and pointed to the house. She followed right behind him, talking and shaking her arms.

I jumped off the lard can and pushed it back in the pantry, just like it was. I hurried to check on Jerry.

Too late. Jerry had gotten into the big flour tin. He looked like a snow man, having lots of fun. But I knew I was in big trouble.

We came back from Bethel Church and saw Uncle John's car parked by our house. Tommy didn't go to church with us, because he had a stomachache. I came back just in time to ask Mama if he'd feel like seeing his daddy and she said she'd seen some miraculous healings on Daddy's side of the family when food was put on the table.

Daddy was outside with Uncle John, telling him the price of pigs was going up. He wanted to sell some pigs, but his mean old sow made a bunch of problems.

Uncle John said it wasn't a good time for him and that Daddy might have to get someone else to help. I didn't know what Daddy needed, but I would sure like to work with Daddy.

Mama fixed a real good dinner, like always. Noodles and chicken, mashed potatoes and green beans. The chocolate cream pie was best.

Then she tended to Dickie. He had a stomachache, too. Afterward, she and the men sat around the table for a while and drank coffee. I was only six years old, but I liked to listen to the grownups talk. Sometimes they didn't want me to listen, but that time nobody said not to.

Daddy told Uncle John he could use help getting his young pigs ready to sell, but Uncle John said that it all depends. He said that a lot.

They didn't talk for a while, so I went outside.

Nobody else around to play with or talk to. I moseyed across the road to the pigpens. I decided I might take another look at the mean old sow again.

As I got closer, I got kind of scared, afraid she would see me. Didn't want her to look at me. Sand had drifted up outside a corner of the long shed. That made it easy to climb on top of it. I stood up there, so high with the wind blowing in my face, and looked all around. I began walking on the roof, pretending I was a sea captain on a sailing ship. Like I could spy down on everything.

Daddy had put bundles of cane on top of the shed last year, so the sheds would stay warmer. I pretended they were the deck of my ship and the bundles were ocean waves below me. There were some rotten ones that had fallen apart—just different kinds of waves. I hadn't decided yet.

Wham!

The sky went sideways and the roof of the shed came up to clonk me. My shin felt a sharp pain and I felt like a claw had raked across it. I didn't know what had happened, but I couldn't move much. I was hanging partway through the roof, almost upside down. It was dark all around me, except where my left leg stuck out the top. I tried to get my breath, but the air smelled like pigs. Ugly and close. I was awful scared.

I couldn't reach anything to grab to pull myself up. I slipped a little . . . lower inside the shed. Tried not to . . . Couldn't hang on much longer.

Under me, behind me, another light—the opening to the outside of the shed. I saw the feeding trough, and right beside it—a hog. I stared. The mean old sow. She was huge!

She grunted, trying to see what the noise was. Then she saw me, her bright piggy eyes shining. She started moving toward the shed, toward me!

Daddy called me "his big boy" but I felt so weak. Tried not to slip . . .

That old sow looked like a giant. Her body completely blocked off the daylight from the opening. I couldn't breathe . . .

Everything seemed darker . . . There was a hole of emptiness with smudged edges . . . nothing I would ever remember . . .

. . . I seemed to be twitched up into pink and blue clouds . . . higher than the top of a sea captain's ship.

Something was pulling on me. I tried to pull my leg up, but nothing worked. Pulling around my waist—how could she do that? I couldn't see but it kept pulling.

Her teeth were going to bite my leg—it would hurt so much. Tommy said pigs had very sharp teeth. I could feel the pain already . . . No. Not pain. Something had me . . . from behind. I couldn't see—tears. I knew I'd been crying, like forever.

I didn't want to cry but I was so scared. My body was being pulled up, up and out of that hole! Somebody's arms pulled me up and didn't let go. Then I was on the ground. Safe.

I was crying, but I could see. I turned around and it was Uncle John! He had pulled me out of that hole.

Uncle John had saved me from the mean old sow. Uncle John saved my life.

17 Perils of First Grade

Fall 1946

Sammy

The first day of school came before I was ready. Still too many questions without answers. Yet there I was, across the road from our house, waiting for the bus. Just thinking about everything made me feel like a little kid, which I sure was. I couldn't let Mom wait with me, much as I wanted her to. If she did, big kids on the bus would say I was a baby. That's what Tommy said. So, I pretended to be brave.

I wouldn't know anybody at school, except Tommy. Mom told him to watch out for me, but I knew he wouldn't. He acted like he didn't hear when I tried to ask him about things that popped into my head. Daddy told Mom he'd bet a dollar to a donut that Tommy was trying to act big because he was scared of starting high school.

The porch screen door smacked, and there was Tommy, sitting on the top step and just then tying his shoes. He didn't even look at me, like he didn't want to bother with me.

The week before, he told me the bus driver, Laverne Johnson, was big as a bear, but he said Laverne was always nice to him. A nice bear. Tommy bragged he was going to play on the Greenough High School basketball team, where Laverne played center. I knew guys with big muscles didn't have to be good to little kids like me.

I looked up the road north. Nothing in sight. Then my sack lunch fell plop on the ground. I stuffed three new yellow pencils in my blue overalls and reached down to pick up my lunch. My hands were so sweaty, I dropped my Big Chief writing tablet. Daddy said Mom packed enough food in my sack for a threshing crew.

Everything picked up, then I had to pee. I started toward the outhouse, which was back of our house. Mom hollered from behind Tommy. I looked where she pointed—a cloud of dust rose from the north. I turned around. The dust haze soon turned into a yellow bus that backfired as it slowed, and Tommy came over to the west side of the road, but not beside me.

The bus brakes squealed like Daddy's little pigs. I backed away, and the bus windows slid to a stop in front of me. Older kids at every window, staring at me.

The door flipped open. Inside sounded like our chicken house when we let the chickens out every morning. Cackling, crowing, and clucking with everyone talking at once. The first step into the bus was high, but I stretched and got in.

Laverne was big! He took a look at me and then glanced up into his mirror over the windshield. He hollered, "Roberta, help this little guy find a seat."

I didn't wait for her to help me. I plopped into the first seat I came to before I dropped my things again. A boy my size was in the next seat, but he didn't speak. Tommy went to the back of the bus where everyone was talking and laughing. I forgot about having to go to the bathroom.

The bus must've made twenty stops before we got to school. Mom had taken me there to meet my teacher, but I couldn't remember where my room was. Everyone piled off the bus, and I was swept up like a tadpole in a waterfall. Once outside, I made sure I had everything, and turned smack dab into a big pair of bib overalls. They belonged to a giant who bent down in front of me.

He had shaggy hair and sideburns down to his jaw. Wore a plaid shirt with sleeves rolled up just like Li'l Abner in the Sunday comics. He said, "Hi pardner, my name is Howard. What's yours?"

Pardner—that's what Daddy called me. "M-m-my name is S-Sammy Hall."

"Well, Sammy, I'm pleased to meetcha." He stuck out a hand as big as a skillet and shook mine with his thumb and pointer finger. "You must be Tommy's cousin, so you live about three miles southwest of us."

Howard was the first person to speak to me. I didn't know what to say.

He stood up. "Looks like Tommy took off to the high school building." He jerked his thumb toward the big brick building east of the playground.

"Yes," I said. "Th-th-that's where they play basketball."

"Oh, sure," Howard said. "You been here before, I'll bet. Well, don't you worry. I'll take you to the primary room. It's where it's always been, here in the old school building."

Howard reminded me of Ray and Edith's friendly old dog that

wagged his tail at everything, even rabbits. Boy howdy, I was glad to have someone look out for me. I stayed right behind Howard as he put his giant hands out in front of him to plow through the kids that had just spilled off the west side bus.

We went up the outside steps and through the double doors—from bright sunlight into the long dark hallway with high ceiling and squeaky wooden floor. It came back to me then—from our visit with my teacher. Chasing after Howard, I caught my breath as he stopped at the last door on the right.

"That there is the gym." He waved toward the end of the hall. "But you go here."

He motioned me into a classroom that smelled of cleaners, paste, and floor wax. Several boys in the back were talking like they'd been at school for days. They all seemed to be friends with everyone else. I didn't know anyone.

Mrs. Bish—I finally remembered her name—was dressed like she was going to church, with high heels, and hair pulled back like Aunt Maggie except she had dark hair instead of gray. She said, "Thank you, Howard. You brought . . . yes, I know you. You're Sammy Hall."

Before Mrs. Bish could say anything else, a skinny girl with stringy blonde hair and glasses ran up. "Teacher, where's the toilet? I gotta go . . . right now!"

Mrs. Bish pointed outside. "The girls' outhouse is in back, east of the bus barn."

Two boys stampeded in from the hallway. They bumped me out of the way and headed for the empty wooden desks.

I almost dropped my things again but decided I better get a desk, too. By then, a pretty girl came up and said the pencil sharpener wasn't working. She had long eyelashes and rosy lips. The whole room quieted down as everyone looked at her. Then a bell rang somewhere.

I slid into the only empty desk—right up front, under pictures of men that Daddy had told me were the greatest ever—George Washington and Abraham Lincoln. A blackboard went all across the wall behind Mrs. Bish's desk. Above was the alphabet, in capitals and little letters, and below that was the fancy alphabet, like Mom used when she wrote letters. At the very top, near the ceiling, was the American flag with all forty-eight stars and thirteen stripes.

Mrs. Bish went to the front of the room and read off

everybody's name, starting with first graders. Before she started the second and third graders, she went back where two boys were talking. They stopped.

She came back up front and pointed to what she had written on the blackboard. "This is the pledge to our American flag. We will stand facing the flag, with our right hand over our hearts and say it first thing every morning.

"All right, everyone stand on the left side of your desk." As she turned to face the flag, over her shoulder she said, "Together, with me—I pledge allegiance to the flag . . . of the United States of America, and to the republic for which it stands . . . one nation, indivisible, with liberty and justice for all."

We didn't say it very well, but as we sat down, she said we did good for the first time, and she knew we'd get better.

Mrs. Bish went through a list of rules: no one could speak or leave the room without her permission; no running in the classroom or hallway; no gum chewing in the classroom; keep your desk clean; don't interrupt when someone else is talking; respect what belongs to others; and raise your hand any time you wish to speak. We were to line up in the hallway every time we came in or went out of the classroom, like at recess and noon hour. The girl with the stringy hair—her name was Ruby— asked more questions.

Some were good questions, but the same boys at the back of the room snickered and made fun of her. Mrs. Bish didn't like that a bit and stood in front of their desks. They shut up.

When she went back to her desk, she said, "If you are chewing gum, you have permission to get up right now and throw it in here." She pointed to the wastebasket.

Everyone looked around, but no one did anything.

Mrs. Bish looked at everyone in the room, up one row and down the next. "I told you there's to be no gum chewing in the classroom. If you spit it out now, there'll be no punishment."

Still, no one moved. The bell rang.

She said, "That's the bell for morning recess. Line up in the hallway, first graders, then second, then third. Everyone is dismissed except for these six." She read off six names and told them they would have to stay in for recess since they didn't spit out their chewing gum. We knew Mrs. Bish meant business.

Every day after school, Mom asked how it went. It was usually good except for not having friends. Except I didn't tell her that. She went over my papers every week and told Daddy that almost every paper had gold stars.

The first time he saw my papers, he held them up. "Look at those gold stars. Do the other kids get stars on their papers?"

I said, "I don't know. I don't keep track. There's some who brag like they know everything. But they don't even get silver stars."

Daddy said, "I'd be careful, son. You don't want to be a braggart."

"I don't like braggers either, but those kids have lots of friends. I don't have any real true friends. Except for Howard."

Mom looked surprised. I wished I hadn't said that. She said, "Well, that's not true. Some of your cousins are real friends, like Uncle Myrrl's kids and Aunt Pearl's grandkids. They're always glad to see you boys."

"Yeah, but they live up in Kansas and we don't get to play with them very much."

"You have more friends than you know about." Then she said, "Who's Howard?"

"H-Howard is . . . Howard," I said. "He's—"

"That's Phil Harris's boy—really a grown man." Daddy said. "He's not much for book learning, but he stays out of trouble and looks after the little guys, something we could use more of in this country."

"Well, the braggers have friends," I said, "and they're not nice to the kids that don't have friends." I didn't want to tell him that sometimes they made fun of me, too.

Mom said, "Do they try to run over you?"

"Well, they make f-fun of Ruby. She's kinda cross-eyed, so she asks lots of questions."

Then Mom said, "Oh, I forgot those cookies." She hurried over to the stove.

I said, "There's another girl, in Mrs. Houston's room. She's really big—almost as tall as Daddy—and she walks funny, like she has to lean back to keep from tipping over. Her name is Patricia Cox, and she's always by herself. The smart aleck boys call her D-Drusilla, but she just ignores them."

116

Mom set a plate of cookies on the table. We could talk about braggers another time.

≫≪

Pretty soon I knew the names of all the first graders—Phyllis, Ruby, Larry, the twins Keith and Kent, Jimmy, Cletus, Tina Joy, Edna, Bobby, Pauline, and Larry and Kenneth, the Mennonite boys. But I still didn't have a friend.

I liked school, anyway, because Mrs. Bish taught us to learn all sorts of things. I got a gold star for being first to count to a hundred and another one for finishing the Dick and Jane reader. It was easy because Mom had already started me reading. Some of the kids couldn't read a word, but I didn't call them dummies. No one likes to be made fun of.

We played games at recess, like hide-and-seek. I was good at Red Rover and tag because I could run fast. I tried to talk to other boys, but no one wanted to be my friend. It helped if you were related. Larry was cousin to the Taylor twins, and they were cousins to Cletus. Several lived close to one another so they already had friends. Everyone seemed to know everyone else.

One of the twins was talking about a party the week before. He said everybody wanted to sit by Edna, the pretty girl. Some of them went into another room, and he said they'd been kissing! That made me jealous. I didn't want to kiss Edna, but I didn't like anyone else kissing her. Maybe holding hands at recess behind the school building, but getting close enough to a girl to press my lips against hers was scary.

I told Tommy about the party, and he acted like he knew all about such things. He said, "When I take out Georgia Duvall, I'm going to smooch her right on the lips! You know if you have a girlfriend, you have to kiss her on the mouth."

"On the m-m-mouth? I d-don't want to."

Tommy laughed. "Oh, you're afraid to kiss girls, aren't you? Maybe you need some lessons."

"No. I don't want any l-l-lessons, either," I yelled.

"Well, Uncle Elmer said I could have the pickup this weekend, and I'm going to take Georgia out on a date. I'll kiss her. Then I'll tell you about it."

I didn't want to talk any more about mushy stuff. I was just in first grade.

Afterward, Tommy told me all about his date with Georgia.

But he was in high school and they were so grown up. High school girls wore lipstick, pleated skirts, and dangly earrings. They were more dressed up than Mom when she went to town. And the boys weren't boys at all. They were men. Bill and Gilbert Corzine wore sideburns an inch below their ears, and Gilbert's Adam's-apple stuck out like a wedge of cheese. Laverne was just all muscle. They all joked around with the girls, especially Roberta Monroe and Kathryn Weybright.

I kind of made some friends at school but having one of Mom's sugar cookies was the best way to end any day. On the way home just before Thanksgiving, I was thinking about those cookies as the bus chugged over the last hill. Our house was just ahead.

Roberta went past me to the front of the bus. She whispered to Laverne, and then went back to her seat. The bus clanked to the stop at our house, so I made sure I had all the pictures I'd drawn that week, plus my Big Chief notebook. I was thinking of the weekend ahead when I caught a sweet smell, like a bouquet of flowers. Then an arm came around my left shoulder, nudging my face to the right.

I wondered why Laverne was looking back at me in the big mirror, a silly grin on his face. Then another face and red lips blocked my view. Roberta Monroe pushed her lips on my face, kissing me, all over my face!

I was under attack. Could barely breathe; couldn't see and thought I was going to die. All I could hear was the other kids laughing. They were laughing at me. I was so mad. And embarrassed.

I remembered the bus had stopped at our driveway. Blinded by tears, I stormed off that bus and ran for the house. I had to escape that awful girl and the laughter from the open windows of the bus. They were still hooting as the bus pulled away.

Mom met me at the door, asking what was on my face. Dickie wanted to know everything. I told him to just shut up and leave. I told Mom about that awful Monroe girl. She shushed Tommy, who came in with a smirk on his face. Then she gave me a glass of cold milk and warm sugar cookies.

Before anything else, I had her scrub off the lipstick that had ruined me before the whole world. After three cookies, I felt a lot better. The sooner I forgot that attack, the quicker I could start my life over.

Mom asked if Tommy had said anything about kissing, and I

told her. She said she and Daddy were going to have a talk with Tommy, that he probably had a hand in the whole business.

৩৵৶

The high school, across from the playground, was a lot nicer than our old grade school building. The classrooms had big windows and indoor toilets. We had outhouses at the north side of the school grounds, one for the boys and one for the girls. Mrs. Bish warned us that the boys better not play near the girls' outhouse or we'd be in trouble. Of course, the girls would never go over to the northwest corner where our outhouse was.

Being a kid means you have to do what your parents tell you. Most of the time, that's all right; but when they make you do things that might cause you to be teased, that's not all right.

Mom said she didn't want us boys to get sick, so Dickie and I had to wear long-handled underwear, even when it wasn't cold. Even in September. I was sure none of the other kids wore long underwear. At least the ones who rode their bikes to school, because they rolled their pantlegs up. I knew I would get teased if they saw my underwear.

It was safest not to go to the toilet when other people were around. I'd never use it if I had to pull my pants down.

One morning, everything was late, and I didn't have enough time to go to the toilet before the bus came. Then our driver was late getting us to school. At recess, I ran to get to the outhouse first. But the fifth and sixth graders were already there, so I had to wait till noon.

The morning dragged on. Noon time and we lined up in the hallway to go outside. It seemed to take forever, but finally I could go. I ran.

Nobody else in the toilet and I shut the door. I was too late.

Cleaned up the best I could. No one else around. Everyone else playing all around the school yard. I didn't want to get close to anyone, or they would know.

I sat on the west steps of the gym where no one was playing outside. Kept my head down and after a while, I heard footsteps. They stopped next to me.

"Sammy, why are you crying?" It was Patricia Cox, the big girl everyone made fun of. How did she know my name?

She picked me up like I was a feather. "Why, Sammy, you dirtied your pants."

119

I really started crying then, but she didn't make fun of me. She sat me down beside her and said I would be all right. I knew that was true because she stayed with me the rest of the noon hour, even though I smelled bad. No one would bother her. She would have pounded them.

The rest of that day was like a fog. What I remembered was that Patricia Cox cared for me. She was wonderful.

I don't remember anything else about her.

Wherever you are, Patricia Cox, I love you.

18 Hope and Reason

Claire

Elmer must have walked out into our wheat field twenty times the spring of '46 to gauge the harvest yield. Reliable as sunrise, he'd pull heads of wheat from scattered locations and then roll them between his palms and count the grains from each head. "Sixty grains in that one, but I got eighty-five from two others."

All we needed was what Elmer called "a decent crop," sufficient for seed to plant the following year and enough to support the family till next harvest. The Great Depression, compounded by the Dust Bowl of the thirties, made such hope pathetic, even embarrassing, for anyone stranded on the Great Plains.

We'd been farming in the Oklahoma Panhandle ten years, yet not one solitary year had given us "a decent crop." Most years, it seemed we survived by the skin of our teeth. Greenbugs, drought, plagues of grasshoppers, hail, or an early freeze could ruin a wheat crop any given year. Mostly, it had been the drought, worsened by the wind. By January, Elmer was cautiously optimistic it would be the breakthrough year and bought an old Case tractor to pull the Baldwin combine. Optimum weather in the fall and no pests . . . if we got a good snow and a few soaker rains, we'd only have to face the specter of hail. I told him I was praying about that. He nodded his head and muttered that "We need all the help we can get."

Inspired by his optimism, I blurted, "Oh, that's like something I was reading just last night, exactly what you're doing . . ."

He looked up, his index finger still pushing the grains around in his opposite palm. Finally, "Yeah. Well, tell me."

Permission, he said it's okay. Deep breath. Not meeting his eyes, I bubbled the words out in a hasty froth. "It's a short story—a parable by Jesus, actually—where he told about a farmer scattering seed . . ." I ventured a glance Elmer's direction. A doubtful look. Keep going. "He threw seed out by the handful, but some of the seed fell among rocks, like it was going in one ear and out the other, as if it was all Greek to them. So, the devil comes

121

and takes it away and . . ." Is he listening just to humor me? Well, he said to go ahead. Throat's dry. Jesus, help me. "When troubles came, it died. That seed died. Other seed fell on the footpath and the birds ate it—just like the worries of the world. He kept flinging seed . . . some of it fell in with the sandburs and devil's claw. Briars—those are the cares of the world. Of course, that choked the life out of it."

I lifted my hand, which seemed barely attached to my arm. Can't believe he hasn't interrupted. "But other seed fell on good ground, fertile soil. Just like what you were telling me . . . Some of it bore thirty-fold, and some sixty-fold, and others, a hundred-fold!" He's still listening. At least, I think so.

"It's like the dry years in our part of the world, isn't it?" He's taking in everything I said.

"Well, Bert McCarter just showed up to ride the combine. I gotta go," he said. "We have to get this. In case they're . . ." He went over to talk to McCarter. When he was done, Bert nodded and scrambled up the vertical steel ladder to the catbird seat on the Baldwin combine. Elmer cranked up the tractor, checked to be sure McCarter was ready, and away they went.

I watched from north of the house as Elmer started cutting on the eighty-acre field next to the house. It was hard to believe our wheat harvest was underway. I felt like cheering. A quarter of the way around the field, the tractor and combine stopped. An exchange between Elmer and Bert, then they began waving back at me. Something was wrong.

Tommy wanted to drive the pickup to Elmer. Not a time to practice driving. I shook my head, dismissing him with a frown. I climbed into the pickup and revved north on the road, then downshifted to head east into the field to follow the swathe cut by the combine. Elmer listened to my whole telling . . . Lord, help us fix whatever problem caused him to stop.

I pulled up behind the combine, expecting to help repair something. No. Elmer waved me alongside the machine. He pointed to the grain bin. Already full. Can't be. But it was. Elmer simply needed me to offload the full grain bin.

As soon as I stopped the pickup under the bin, McCarter levered the slide gates open and a waterfall of golden grain poured onto the pickup bed.

Elmer, pulling straw from one of the elevators, got it cleared and beckoned to me. "Claire, this looks like forty-five— maybe fifty-bushel yield this year. For this eighty-acre field, that could be . . ." He squinted, then said, "Four thousand bushels. At two dollars a bushel, that's eight—"

"Elmer! We've waited so long, so long, for things to go right." I dropped my head and breathed a prayer of thanks.

He raked his hand over the pile of grain in the pickup. "Back out a third for expenses and breakdowns, we'll still net four or five grand . . ." He looked up at the sky and did a three-sixty. "No clouds, but we better get in gear just in case." Suddenly he pulled me to him and backed out of sight next to the combine. I got a passionate kiss right then.

Finally breaking free, I murmured, "You better get back to cutting wheat before we forget ourselves."

Wheat harvest done, Elmer sat at the kitchen table, tallying grain receipts from Security Elevator. I heard him talking to himself while I put the finishing touches on a shirt I was making for Sammy. "Claire, I think we can do it. Remember the promise I made—about the house?"

I looked up from my sewing machine. "Elmer, you're joking. Don't tease . . ." He looked as solemn as a judge. "You said when we could afford it, we'd add a room . . . Can we?" I arose and went over to him, pulling his face to mine. His chin rasped against the softness of my arm, sending a delicious tingle over my back.

He held me, a lingering embrace that took my breath. I wriggled free and whispered, "You'd better behave or you'll wake the boys . . . Now, when am I going to get my house fixed up?"

"Whenever we can get Rodkey out from Liberal. We tell him what we want. He tells us what it's gonna cost. You said you want indoor plumbing, but that doesn't come cheap. Don't forget I get a garage out of the deal—and a machine shed."

". . .and a wind-charger so we can have electricity—" I said.

". . . better figure on a good used car—" He echoed.

Before anything else, we paid off the $640 owed People's National Bank. By the time Clark Rodkey added a third bedroom, an enclosed porch and new kitchen, there was only enough left for a used Chrysler sedan, a wood frame garage/machine shed and a single-basin cold water sink piped from the well house. No matter.

I felt like God had rediscovered us again.

At the end of summer, we took the boys and Tommy on a first-ever family vacation to Colorado. The highlight of the trip was the cog rail steam train to the top of Pike's Peak from Manitou Springs.

A sharp wind knifed across the 14,115-foot summit, taking breath and body heat as we stumbled out the train door. A snow flurry drove everyone toward the nearly invisible terminal house. Everyone but me. I had told Elmer to take the kids; I wanted to look across the plains stretching to Kansas. Calling "Don't get lost," he pulled the boys like a chain of paper cutouts behind him.

I bit my lip and pulled the coat collar up over my ears. Wind whistled around the squat structure, whipping snow sideways. It reminded me of two stormy trips from home to Epworth Hospital. The first was when Sammy was born six and a half years before. The last journey was one of many to care for Maggie before she died. One life gained, one life lost.

It made me feel like I was close to heaven . . . near Mama and Pop and Kate and Maggie. I tried to fix their faces in my mind, but each visage faded, colorless and indistinct. How could that be? Maggie's only been gone three, four months . . . How would I have managed without Maggie? She always told me to look for the best. Sometimes, you'll get what you want, and it'll be just the way God planned it. Tears flowed down my cheeks. The indifferent wind iced the moisture on my face and in that moment, I decided to memorialize Maggie, somehow.

Our adventure ending, the cog train took us back down through the spruce and pine forests to Manitou Springs. After telling Elmer I wanted to get something to commemorate Maggie, I found a household furnishings store and bought a table lamp with a plastic base designed to look like marble. Elmer looked at me with a question in his eyes when I returned but kept still. Back at our lodging, I told him Maggie said we'd someday have electricity at the farm. When it happened I wanted to be ready. He gave me a tolerant smile and told me there'd always be pretties to collect.

I sighed. That little lamp was a hope signet to take back home, wrapped in newspaper and deep longing. Of those before me, Maggie and Pop always pointed me toward hope.

The next year, Rural Electrification Administration crews extended power lines to the Ausmus house—and stopped, a mile-

and-a-half away. Afterward, each time I opened the storm door on the west porch I'd look past our elms and wonder when those power lines would connect us to the grid. My little table lamp would have to wait in the bedroom closet until Maggie's promise came true.

Myrrl and Grace came down from Ness City, bringing Gary, their youngest, the same age as Sammy. I was pleased to have family visitors—especially my favorite brother. Myrrl's plainspoken manner enlivened conversations but it put Elmer on edge anytime the topic turned to religion.

Elmer liked the folksy pair, too, but he became irritable when trapped with any of my relatives longer than thirty minutes. None of them smoked, drank spirits, or uttered epithets stronger than "whillikers" or "fiddlesticks." Elmer didn't rail against my family's taboos out of spite; he simply felt it would be hypocritical for him to pretend to be something he was not. Once, he told me he wondered if my people truly believed in the rules they appeared to practice, or were they simply expressing a lifestyle that had been handed down to them?

I didn't try to answer but attributed his question to the bugaboo of religiosity from our clan, real or imagined. The other men in the family seemed intimidated by Elmer. He told me their steady politeness felt as phony as a three-dollar bill.

We gave our guests a tour of our recent additions. Elmer joked about the boys having to sleep on the floor. Most visits, the men would spend half a day looking over the cattle herd or sitting in the shade of the big pear tree, talking politics, farm prices, and the weather. That particular day, a sharp wind came up, piling tumbleweeds against fences. Too bad for us but the boys would not be contained all day indoors. They went outside to entertain themselves.

Penned inside, we rediscovered adult conversation. My tendency to worry drew me to the kitchen window about every twenty minutes. Grace caught my frown. "Let those kids worry about themselves. If one falls in the stock tank or gets chased by a wild cow, Gary is big enough to rescue them."

Myrrl set the pitcher of tea on the table. "And if he doesn't get there in time, that's just one less kid to worry about."

I tried to laugh with the rest. "Well, Tommy's old enough to take care of any emergency but sometimes I catch him teasing Sammy and Dickie Lee."

"If he gets out of hand, we'll hear about it," Elmer said. "Then I'll have a talk with him."

That provoked a discussion about bullying, indifferent parents, and bad behavior. My brother freely invoked scripture to support his views. He talked at length about communism spreading in America, and the end of the world if things kept getting worse. I caught my breath each time, expecting a reaction from Elmer.

Before long, the electricity in Elmer's demeanor manifested itself. He raised a hand. "Myrrl, you really don't believe all that stuff, do you? 'New world order'? 'Gog and Magog'? That's weird, if not crazy. I didn't even hear that stuff when Florence was trying to get me to join her holy rollers."

Myrrl ignored the jibe and took off on another topic. "Such a long dry spell—at times I was tempted to doubt, but God showed his faithfulness this year. It looked like the wheat wouldn't make enough to get back the seed, but we were blessed with a bumper crop."

Elmer eyed him with a sound like "Mmpf."

I caught Grace's eyes and quietly brought kitchen cleanup to a close. We eased over to the kitchen table and sat with the men.

Myrrl said, "The Lord has a timing in all he does. We have so much to be thankful for."

I was groping for a diversionary topic when Elmer blurted, "What do you mean, 'given us a wonderful crop'? Maybe he gives you everything, but I work hard for what I get."

Myrrl looked up, his eyes wide. "Oh, I know you work hard, Elmer, but God is really the source and giver of all that's good." He paused a beat for acknowledgement and when none came, plunged ahead. "I guess I just wanted to say that I really feel loved by the Lord—"

"You know. . ." Elmer paused as he scraped ash from the bole of his pipe into a heavy glass ashtray. "What bothers me is that when something goes good, it's because God did it. But what about the hard times? Bad people, like Hitler, gassing all those Jews? Whose fault when it took almost four years after Pearl Harbor before MacArthur won in the Pacific? Nobody is praising God for that."

"Elmer, you're just looking at all the bad things," I said. "What about good things, like my sis? You saw the pictures on Ethel and Ed's piano—all four of her sons came home. And you didn't have to go at all, because you got an agriculture deferment from military service."

Myrrl spoke up. "The Bible says all things work together for good, to those—"

"That's what my first wife used to preach at me." Elmer's voice came out like a spaniel's bark. "Fine words but just not true. When dishonesty pays because crooks have connections; when the bank takes a man's horses and plow and he's got nothing left to work off his debts . . . Big shots getting rich off another man's hard luck—I don't see any of that working for good."

"Well, Elmer," Myrrl said, "we sometimes need to see things from God's perspective."

"How's that going to help—especially when we could just as easily have had another drought year?" Elmer asked. "Just believe, and things will get better. Religion expects you to like it or lump it. That's asinine."

"Are you saying you don't believe God is good?" Grace asked, a smile on her lips.

Elmer squinted and puckered his lips as if searching for an answer. "I didn't say that. I just don't believe religion—all the rules and 'thou shalt nots'—really works for day-to-day life, when grasshoppers eat your crop or a rusty nail causes lockjaw or machinery breaks down in the middle of harvest or . . . you see my point?"

"Yes, I understand, Elmer," Myrrl said, "but have you ever given your cares over to God when bad things happen?"

Elmer stared at him, incredulously. "What's that supposed to do? The grasshoppers have destroyed the crop and Kate Buffalow's dying of lockjaw. No way is reading the Bible or listening to a preacher going to fix that!"

"Well, of course not—" Myrrl's turn to search for the right word.

"If I may join the discussion. . ." It was Grace, her smile disarming and friendly. "I don't think you're looking for God to be a fix-it helper, are you? Jesus, God's son, didn't come to this earth to shield us from all the hurts that are part of this life. He himself was whipped and beaten. They spat on him, out of pure hatred. He was nailed to a cross—for your sins and mine. He knows what it's like to suffer."

127

"So, why would he let a good woman like Maggie put up with all she did? She went through hell, and for what? She was already a mighty fine woman, and I don't see why a caring God—if he does care—should require her to go through all that."

My heart pounded like a drum. Maggie's death. Elmer can't get past that hurt. In a small voice, I said, "Elmer, I don't know why Jesus took Maggie to heaven so soon. I believe God will help us understand what we need to know. He loves us. Maggie understood that, Elmer. She knew Jesus like she knew you and me, and she believed that Jesus came to show us how to live. But don't think for a minute that Jesus doesn't understand or care what we go through."

Elmer pursed his lips and gave me an agitated look. "You can't tell me Maggie had to have her insides eaten up with cancer! She'd never have chosen that, if she'd had a choice!"

"We don't always get a choice, Elmer," I spoke so softly I could hardly hear my own voice.

"So we just take what's dished out to us?" he snapped.

"It's not 'just us' taking it, honey." In the stillness of the room, my words pounded like a blacksmith's hammer. "The hard times come—sometimes. Grace is saying that the difference is that . . . Jesus is with us. He shows us how to live . . . He gives us power to go through it all."

Elmer cleared his throat, his Adam's apple bobbing. I expected him to stomp out of the room. Then he said, "Is there any more of that pecan pie? Myrrl, you want some coffee?"

19 The Consolidation Faction

Fall 1948

Claire

Elmer heard the rumors first. Ray Clapp, a rancher with three boys in Greenough School, pulled him aside at the blacksmith shop. Ray said he and Lila had been approached by people in the community complaining about our school.

He didn't give any names but said if Elmer knew the membership of the bridge club, he'd have an idea of the people involved. Ray shook his head at the things being said about Greenough. Everything was bad—teachers, classes, unruly students, kids smoking on school grounds, even complaints about the basketball uniforms. They insisted something had to be done and wanted Ray and Lila to throw in with them to consolidate Greenough with Forgan and Turpin town schools.

Ray told Elmer there was no way they'd join any effort to disband our school. Consolidation would destroy the community.

Knowing rebellion often dies a natural death, we waited and listened. Something was going on. Then we heard an outspoken member of the school board resigned, no reason given.

I wanted to learn if there was substance to the rumors. The best place to find out would be at our Home Demonstration Club meeting, always the highlight of my month. Aside from homemaking skills I learned from the Ag Extension agent, I got to know other women in the community. I hadn't realized how starved I was for women friends outside of family. Elmer chided me about it being an old hens' gathering, but he always asked afterwards about what we discussed and who was there.

The first Tuesday in October, Elmer dropped me off at Blanche and Henry's house. "If you don't get the goods on the consolidation crowd at your old hen meeting, it means they've given up."

The smell of fresh-baked cookies wafted out the door as I entered. Dort Emrie saw me first. "Claire, you're just in time.

Everyone's atwitter with all the talk about that petition going around the neighborhood."

A chorus of greetings swept over me. Besides Blanche and her daughter-in-law, Avis, six other neighborhood friends sat around the room. While Blanche's platter of sugar cookies circled the room, I joined her in the kitchen to help serve coffee and mix Kool-Aid. "My word, I should've come early. Sounds like the gals are pretty het up about this. Elmer and I are too."

"Well, my stars, Claire, it is serious business. I think we ought to talk about it. Come on."

Marie Glover and her daughter, Norma Jean Huling, entered to another cascade of greetings. Avis brought in two more chairs from the dining room.

Blanche held up her hand for quiet, and said in her creaky voice, "Hazel, our County Home Demonstration lady, called to say she couldn't come today. But I swan to goodness, it sounds like we oughter be dealing with this school consolidation commotion anyways. We can talk about flour for bread-making next time."

Goldie Beard said, "We'll be here all morning if we just talk about what we're afraid of. Gladys, you and Jewell have been teachers. Why don't you tell us what those people are trying to do to us?"

Crisp as always, Gladys Eagan adjusted her glasses and looked around the room to make sure she had everyone's attention. "Pure and simple, the Consolidation Committee—that's what they call themselves—they want to close down the Greenough elementary and high schools so our children will be sent to Turpin and Forgan. They emphasize Greenough is a country school, as if that automatically makes it bad. They say Greenough has failed their kids, using a limited curriculum, poorly taught. No art or music to speak of, no foreign languages, and math and social sciences are inadequate—"

"Even if that's true," Marie's huge thumb punctuated each point. "Which I don't think it is—who's to say Turpin or Forgan would be any better?" She paused. "They just want our kids to play on their ball teams . . . and they want our tax money to buy new band uniforms and put new roofs on their ramshackle buildings."

Jewell Rushton interrupted the chorus of agreement. "Money talks. They claim cost efficiencies and the ability to attract experienced teachers. They ignore questions about parental participation, the danger of larger school environments, and lower

130

graduation rates."

Dort piped up, "Our kids will have to ride their busses all over creation—over muddy roads, snowstorms. Weather in the Panhandle can change in half an hour. Greenough kids will have the farthest to travel, too. Who's behind all this, anyway?"

A good question. Few in the Floris-Greenough communities had ever traveled beyond the Panhandle. Fewer still were those who had ventured more than a day outside the seventy-seven counties of Oklahoma. Busing kids out of the neighborhood would be an aggravation.

Velma Wakefield and Lila Clapp began ticking off names of those who'd asked them to join the consolidation movement. It was the bridge club bunch.

"What gives them the right to judge our school?" It was Norma Jean. "That sounds biased to me."

"How can we protect our kids?" Dort wailed. "It's a known fact that gypsies have head lice. Every fall, Johnny Long imports a crew to pull broomcorn."

"Don't be silly," Gladys said. "Those are Indians, not gypsies. He brings them up from the Cheyenne-Arapaho Reservation, down near Canton."

Goldie turned from admiring Blanche's new floor lamp with the tasseled shade. "Cleanliness and personal hygiene have nothing to do with causing head lice, anyway. Most children get them from—"

"Forgan had one—if not two—shotgun weddings after last year's senior trip," Marie said. "That's of greater concern to me and Bert than a case of head lice."

"There's more at stake here." I heard my own voice and was surprised at how childlike I sounded. Get over it, Claire. Pop always told me to speak up if I wanted to get my two cents in. "Elmer and I moved here thirteen years ago—first, to the Jennie Washburn place, until we got a chance to buy the Eagan place—named after your in-laws, Gladys, as you know. We belong here. It's been hard but . . ." I was getting emotional but didn't really care.

"Keep going, Claire. We hear you." Marie patted my hand, bless her heart.

Blanche chimed in. "For them that don't know, Claire's seen a lot of grief, and me and Henry have followed her most of the ways, haven't we, dear?" She leaned over and hugged me.

131

I took a deep breath. "Greenough community is . . . community, our very lives. Belonging, shared sacrifice and shared grief. Kate and Lew Buffalow were our first visitors when we moved here . . . came with a platter of fried chicken and an angel food cake. Didn't know us from Adam, but they reached out to us. Remember how everyone came around in support when Kate got lockjaw and died?"

A murmur around the room. For me, another deep breath. "Our neighbors, the people we run into at Virgil Adams' Grocery or Forgan Lumber Yard, those who nod in recognition at the clinic or Doyle Davis's drugstore, none of them really know much about us. Most don't ask where we came from or what we did before. But we were accepted into this community, just the way we were. Now, our school isn't perfect, but it's built on the same kind of sacrifice and caring. That's what community is, and that's what's at stake here."

Blanche rose to her feet. "Clair-ie, I couldn't have said it better. Don't you ladies agree?" She began pouring another round of coffee without waiting for an answer.

Clair-ie?

Goldie and Marie told about the girls' basketball team beating both Forgan and Turpin the same year. Everyone had a favorite memory of community suppers, school carnivals, caroling and Christmas programs with treats for every kid, the Halloween costumes, Easter egg hunts, even voting at the school.

The meeting closed with agreement that the best way to defeat the consolidation effort was information—remind people about the strengths of our school and plans to overcome the shortcomings. We were convinced that splitting the school would break up the community.

The sound of the dog barking interrupted my ironing. I glanced outside—not a car I recognized, and it was parked awkwardly, like they'd never been here before. A tall, distinguished looking man emerged—our preacher, Reverend Holder. And Mrs. Holder too, the boys' primary room teacher the previous year. How nice, but what a surprise. I set the iron aside and wiped the table.

The couple always appeared a bit upper-class, hair slightly graying, dressed in the well-ordered way that implied higher purposes in life, as if they were perpetually going to or coming from an important meeting.

When Elmer met Reverend and Mrs. Holder at school functions, he'd muttered the pastor's hands were so soft that he "doubted the man had ever done a lick of work . . . unless reading books and telling people they're going to hell was real work." Typical for my husband. He rarely had anything good to say about "the church crowd," even though that included me and the boys. We'd never had the Holders over for a meal or a visit, as Elmer was suspicious of church people and their agendas, which he suspected were designed to change everything in his life.

My mind racing, I tried to recall if I'd ever admitted why my husband never darkened the door of Bethel Church. Because he was a "misguided heathen," as Brother Heitschmidt might have called him. Had the preacher come to try to convert my irreligious husband? Elmer would be fit to be tied. I exhaled when I remembered he was repairing the pigpens across the road, the three boys with him. His hammer pounded in the morning quiet, each blow like a gunshot.

I pasted on a smile and opened the porch screen door. "Brother Holder, what a surprise to see you in our neighborhood. Come on in. I've got a fresh pot of coffee going."

They both looked up at the sound of my voice. I could have sworn they flinched. Then I noticed Reverend Holder carried, not a Bible, but a white folder. The wind rattled the leaves on the big cottonwood just as he started to speak. He put his foot on the first step and kicked up his volume. "No. No, we only have a minute. Wanted to talk with you and . . ." He hesitated, as if unsure whether to include Elmer in whatever he was advocating.

In that instant, I knew. The preacher came to our house because they wanted something from us. He had not come to minister to my family or to witness to my husband. For the first time ever, I mistrusted my pastor, the leader of the congregation where I gave alms, where I prayed and sang and fellowshipped with other neighbors of the Greenough neighborhood.

Leona Holder started to fill the gap her husband had left. "We're going around the neighborhood to—"

A dust devil choked off her words, whisking both with blowing sand and ground debris. I genuinely liked Leona but could scarcely suppress a giggle as they covered their faces and spat to expel the grit that fouled their mouths and maybe their dispositions.

"Hurry, come in," I called. "That breeze just came out of

nowhere." By then, the limbs of every tree and bush scissored back and forth in response to the impertinent wind.

Eyes watering, the visitors lurched up the front steps and onto our screened-in porch. I invited them to sit at the kitchen table and quickly brought out a newly purchased box of tissues, straight from Duckwalls Dime Store. By the time they'd swabbed their teary eyes and faces, I'd served steaming cups of coffee. Trustworthy or not, I was determined to treat them as special guests. After all, I'd been taking the boys to Bethel Church nearly every Sunday over the previous thirteen months, ever since Sammy began second grade and Dickie first grade.

Reverend Holder leaned back, apparently warmed by the coffee. He picked up his folder and hurriedly replaced it—face-down—on the table. Leona stared at him, her eyes narrowed.

I pretended not to notice either the mysterious folder, or their obvious frustration. By ignoring their ruse, I kept them in the role of guests, thereby forcing them to act accordingly. They knew nothing about my work with Deluxe, working under the tutelage of my savvy husband in our earlier life. I felt giddy, even empowered, as I gauged the ease with which I took control of the situation—graciously serving refreshments to visitors who unexpectedly showed up, presuming their agenda would trump whatever I was doing. Refusing my libations after I'd rescued them would be unthinkable.

"Leona," I said, "I've wanted to tell you that you were Sammy and Dickie Lee's favorite teacher. Sammy did so well in spell—"

"Yes, because he's a fine reader. Phonics makes reading easy." She steepled her fingertips and broke into a broad smile.

"Dickie is much more confident expressing himself. You should take credit for that."

"Oh, I do. Thank you." By then, she was beaming.

The pastor cleared his throat and almost touched the folder, which lay before us like a hand grenade waiting for its pin to be pulled. "Claire, I—we've come to ask if you'd be kind enough to support an effort to . . . to strengthen the education of our children." He thumbed the folder open and spun it so the text faced me. "We're circulating this petition to propose a consolidation of Gree—"

"Really? Elmer and I were talking the other day how Greenough School has done so much to—"

The front door banged open, and our three boys rushed in,

followed by Elmer. Reverend Holder's arm uncoiled like a spring-loaded trap, smacking Leona's coffee cup and sending a brown wash across the oilcloth. His hand quivering, he half-stood, and then sat.

Elmer glanced at the visitors, then ordered the boys to take their coats off and go to their bedroom. He struggled out of his jacket. "I was wondering whose car that was. Holder, isn't it?" He stuck out his hand, and the pastor started to rise once more. "No, keep your seat."

Reverend Holder said, "Yes, pleased to see you again." He eased back into his chair.

Elmer moved behind the vacant chair but remained standing. "So, what brings you to this neck of the woods?"

I flourished a coffee-soaked dishtowel. "They're here about the consolidation. They want us to sign a petition." I waited for Elmer to meet my eyes, then sat.

Elmer's expression eclipsed, as if a window blind had been drawn. He did not sit. No one spoke. Time seemed stuck. Silence lay upon those of us around the table like an iron shawl, not easily shrugged off.

Sounds of the boys in the back bedroom rose and fell, reminding me of the intrusive gnawing of a rodent that had awakened me from sound sleep twice that week. Outside, a piece of roof flashing argued against the wind that had loosened it.

Finally, Elmer broke the peace, which was not peace. "This paper . . ." He leaned over to glance at the document. "You want us to sign this? Have you no respect—for us, for our school, for the community?"

I had seen other men wilt before Elmer's withering gaze and felt genuine compassion for Reverend Holder. He and Leona had high hopes for their two sons, both in high school. Marie Glover told me they were upset Greenough didn't offer a single foreign language, and the annual grade school operetta could hardly count as a real music program. But nobody had to read tea leaves to know that a school split was no place for a preacher to take sides. I guessed the Holders had been pressured by others of the consolidation faction to participate.

Quietly, Leona arose, her hand on the arm of her husband. "James, we should go—now."

I wanted to stop them; begin the whole morning over. Give this man who exhorted others to repent his own chance at redemption in the eyes of the community, in the eyes of my husband, who would see only hypocrisy.

As the Holder's Plymouth backed up to return in the direction from which it had come, I knew I could never again take the boys to Bethel Church. Not only would Reverend Holder be a hypocrite in Elmer's eyes, how could I sit under the teaching of a pawn of people committed to destroying our community?

20 Battle Lines All Around

Claire

Start all over again. That's what we'd have to do, being that our community was being torn apart by people we'd thought were with us. I'd held Pastor Holder and his wife in such high esteem. I guessed they didn't care, or didn't realize, that Greenough School was the glue that held our community together. Bethel was one of half a dozen churches that drew people from our school district. Within each church, most congregations had divided school allegiances. It was suddenly so complicated.

I wanted to cry.

I told Elmer I was going over to talk with Blanche. He said I was wasting my time, that Blanche could tell you the piddly details of everyone's personal lives, but she couldn't see the big picture.

I went anyway.

Her daughter-in-law, Avis, was there when I arrived. I'd gotten to know her in the year since she and Charlie moved back to Beaver County. She was fairly tall, had jet-black hair, and wasn't afraid to speak her mind. I wondered where she got her gumption. Charlie was just the opposite—laid-back, like his dad. One would think she was a big-city girl. Not so, she grew up in Guymon, the biggest town in the Panhandle, but hardly a metropolis with only 4,700 people.

Blanche served us coffee and special cookies. "Girls, them's 'date bars.' Different than what your mama made. Help yourselves—got them from Ragsdale's, last time we went to Liberal.

"All the grocery stores is pushing store-bought bread, and they make oodles of money on it, but for the life of me, it just doesn't compare to homemade bread. I know it's easier for a young mother like Avis here to pop open a sack of that store-bought stuff, throw some butter and a wedge of cheese or Spam on it, then expect your child to—"

"Mother, didn't you say Claire came over to discuss how we're going to stop the school consolidators?" Avis rolled her eyes.

Blanche acted like she hadn't heard her. "Clair-ie, were you as confused as I was during the Home Demonstration Club meeting? Everybody talking at once—we never did get assigned our secret pals."

"We'll do that next time." I snapped. Blanche and her new pronunciation of my name was getting on my nerves. "All the ladies were upset about the consolidation mess. I wanted to stop that bunch. The truth is, we don't really know the score—what's at stake . . ."

Avis leaned forward. "It could be the life of Greenough School. Maybe more than that, once this all sorts out. People are in the dark. Which means we're pigeons about to be plucked."

Blanche frowned. "Oh, Avis, how you go on. We're not like those big-city Texans you been golfing with."

"Wait and see, Mother. I think you're in for a big surprise."

"Can't you see it, Blanche?" I took another date bar. "They've been working behind our backs. I was floored that my own preacher would take sides. Outright deception is what it is."

Avis nodded. "I suspect it all began with a small clique, meeting behind closed doors, biding their time until they could take charge. Who would believe a well-oiled conspiracy—plotting against country folks? We have no idea how long they've been scheming to pull this off. At least a year, maybe two. And no one saw it coming." She paused. "Maybe they've got a case. Our music program is nothing to shout about. No foreign languages. I'd like to know what it is."

"You surely don't think so, do you? And even if they do, why not bring it up in an open meeting? Are they afraid of the truth?" I gave Avis a look, but she didn't meet my eyes.

Avis and Charlie had recently moved from Dallas or Wichita, I didn't recall which. She held a dose of the cynicism I picked up in traveling sales. "Elmer thinks money is at the bottom of the whole thing. This bunch is organized—got their petitions printed up and teams out canvassing the neighborhoods. They want what they want. He said if they get the district boundaries changed, they can send their kids to Forgan or Turpin without paying tuition."

Blanche looked at each of us in turn. "You say clique? Why that's awful. Really, a clique. Plotting against their own neighbors."

Clique, yes. I imagined late night meetings, riddled with conspiracy and secret plans.

"Charlie said they probably figured they'd never get what they wanted if they didn't plan an end run, as he put it. Our little country school is really not very sophisticated in lots of ways—too confining and parochial."

"Parochial—you mean Catholic?" Blanche's eyes widened.

I said, "They could've brought their complaints before the school board, like when Laverne Johnson was called on the carpet for racing his east-side bus to school to beat the west-side bus coming in. Menno Wedel should've faced the music too, but no one turned him in."

"No, Mother—not Catholic." Avis waved her hand dismissively. She turned to me. "Racing buses? I didn't hear about that one. That's the sort of item they'll push front and center—makes Greenough look bad. It's not quite the same as two girls getting pregnant on the Forgan senior trip. They kept that under wraps. Somebody should've been fired."

"My stars, I never heard . . . such goings-on," Blanche murmured.

"Charlie and I were up half the night talking about this. Likely, they've already contacted the State Board of Education. I'd be surprised if they don't already have it sewed up. Barring a miracle, they'll close our high school within a year, maybe two. I hate to be so blunt about it, but like Charlie says, face facts."

We didn't lose our high school, not right away, anyhow. Since no one knew exactly where everyone stood on consolidation, a current of suspicion poisoned the well of easy familiarity. Invitations to neighborhood card games dried up; friendly smiles at Adams Grocery or Coldwater Hardware were sometimes forced or divided into "us and them." Family victories, worries, and crises that used to be shared became hush-hush—even among neighbors. Trusting, giving, and receiving had become risky within larger circles, lest motives be questioned. The neighborliness we'd prized so highly had turned rank. Like a pork roast left out of the icebox too long, it had become suspect, and was possibly spoiled.

I gathered sox and shirts that needed mending. A mindless task, but I wanted to let my mind drift. I recalled what it was like when we first came to the Panhandle, fourteen years previous. Didn't know anyone, but neighbors like Lew and Kate, Jenny Washburn, McCarter, Otis Minton—they proved we weren't alone.

139

Checking in on us after a storm, bringing back a stray calf, sharing tomatoes or cucumbers their garden, and receiving from what we had. Everyone liked Elmer's watermelons.

Extending their hands and hearts to us, they told us we belonged—that other people felt we mattered. Kate was so good about that. I'd always miss her. Why had God let her die that way? I could never let Elmer know I had such questions.

Would we have to verify our friendships? That seemed childish, the sort of thing my brother Gar would do. We never doubted close friends, the ones we could talk to without being on our guard all the time. I wondered if I was letting my imagination run wild.

Elmer came in, leaving the boys outside. He seemed distracted. He always had a lot on his mind, looking after his folks and trying to keep his brothers in line. Not to mention attending to me and our three active little boys.

I told him I believed Blanche was truly sorry about what my preacher had done.

Elmer shook his head. "You can believe her if you want, but I don't think Blanche knows what's going on half the time." He asked for some ice.

I chipped a piece off the block I'd taken out of the icebox. "Well, Reverend Holder and Leona should've never taken sides in this whole consolidation fracas. He surely knew how some of us feel about the school."

Elmer hefted the gallon jar of tea onto the kitchen table and dumped a generous scoop of sugar into it. I put in ice while he wrapped the jar with layers of burlap.

I said, "Did you ever hear why Raymond Watson stepped down from the school board?"

"I'd guess he favors closing our school. He wants out, with no conflict, no blame, and . . ." Elmer sighed. ". . . no responsibility."

"I wouldn't want to be connected with that consolidation bunch. I'll bet half of them work on Sunday."

"Claire, you can't bring religion into everything. Most people, me included, couldn't care less with what others do on their own time."

"Well, I care. I think it's an indicator of character, whether one chooses to honor God or worship at the altar of materialism."

"'Altar of materialism'?" His eyes narrowed. "Woman, what are you talking about?"

"I'm talking about people who try to live their lives without faith . . . in God." I flinched. Shouldn't have put it that way.

I continued in a rush so Elmer wouldn't take that as an arrow directed at him. "I'm . . . what I'm trying to say is the Holders' disloyalty seems more hurtful. Our school is the heart of this community. If Reverend Holder cared a whit, he and Leona would've never carried that petition through the neighborhood. They tried to deceive us. I'm not about to go to Bethel Church again."

Elmer finished stoking his pipe, and then sent a puff of smoke curling to the ceiling. "I bet you'll find hypocrites and crooks of every style and size in any church you wanta point to. I don't know why you bother with them."

I stared at him. "Wait a minute. That's not how it is. Church isn't for perfect people. I'm leaving that church because they broke faith with me, with the people at Greenough who depend on him to be our . . . our spiritual leader."

"We're using different words, but we're saying the same thing. You just won't admit that every preacher is focused on only one thing—power. They want to change everything about a person's life, so they tell people what to do. Setting themselves up as judge and jury. That's not how I want to live, or my boys either." He puffed another cloud of smoke to the ceiling.

"I can't believe you're saying that, Elmer. Those boys are as much mine as yours. They're our boys. Would you rather they grow up never attending church or hearing God's Word, like a bunch of street urchins answerable to no one?" I stood there, arms akimbo. I must have had fire in my eye, 'cause Elmer said not a word.

My boldness surprised me. I almost said *like some of your family* but he knew that score. No way could he defend his no-account brothers.

"Have it your way," he said. "You want to take them to church, go ahead, but I hope you don't plan on driving all over creation. Gas costs money."

"Why, of course," I shot back. "Don't you think I've given this some thought?" Actually, I hadn't. I knew I'd better think fast. Elmer could spot a phony argument in five seconds.

"Blanche!" I blurted. "Blanche and I have been talking . . . Her . . . She said they . . . her church has an excellent Sunday school teacher. Forgan's only eleven miles, about the same as—"

141

"It's four miles farther," he said. "Each way. Times fifty-two Sundays, and with gas at sixteen cents a gallon, you're talking an extra twelve dollars every year. Double or triple that for all the extra meetings these churches dream up, plus the extra wear and tear on the car, and we're talking serious money." My husband's mind was like a machine.

"Well, sometimes you have to make sacrifices for what's right. I didn't say we were going to join that church, but one of these Sundays, we'll go to Forgan, listen to their preacher, see what they have for the boys, and then decide."

Such a conundrum; I guess that's the word. I wanted Elmer to respect my views and try to understand who I was. Much as I loved him, he could be difficult. He always trotted out his beliefs like they came down from Mount Sinai.

Elmer was sure he had God all figured out. I was tempted to set him up to debate the next traveling evangelist coming through Beaver County.

⅌⅌

Blanche barged through our front door, her mouth a-going about something she found. What was she wound up about? I had set aside my morning to give her a perm.

My emotions still aflame over the school consolidation fiasco, I foolishly expected she'd have something pertinent, like a list of the consolidation conspirators.

"Henry took me down to Beaver—"

"You talked to Lee Hulse?" I grinned, bouncing from foot to foot.

"Me talk to the County Superintendent? I got no business with schools. No, I went to the Extension Office." She pulled a scented hankie from her brassiere and began wiping her glasses. "Our Home Demonstration Agent, Helen Delaney—you being new to the club, probably didn't meet her—she made a special point of having me stop in so she could give me the mimeographed sheets on how to use a pressure cooker. But that ain't all I found, Clair-ie—"

"It's Claire, just Claire," I mumbled. I had told Elmer that if she didn't quit making my name into two syllables, I was going to set her straight—friend or no friend. I took a deep breath and primed myself for the next time. Expelling air, I said, "So, tell me what you've got."

"The list of our secret pals!" She proffered a wrinkled envelope. "Helen gave it to me so's we'd get started with our secret pals next time we meet, which is . . . November twelfth, I believe. She can't come to our meeting. Has to travel over to Gate, being's they got new officers . . ."

I shook my head. Should have listened to Elmer. Foolish of me to expect anything different. Sighing, I motioned Blanche to a straight-back chair and draped a pair of dish towels over her shoulders. I commenced combing out the knots in her graying hair before trimming and setting her hair in curlers. She droned on about how she'd been so cautious to keep the secret pals list secret.

"Clair-ie, I—"

"Blanche!" I banged the hairbrush on the table.

"Eh?"

"Blanche, how long have we known each other?"

"My stars, what does that have to do with secret pals?"

I pivoted around to face her, trying my best to smile. "We've known each other for a good ten years, and you . . . you . . ." The skin across my face felt like it was stretched tight enough to make my eyeballs pop. I leaned toward that dear impossible lady, forming words of rebuke. She peered back over her granny glasses, her questioning eyes wide.

I couldn't do it.

"Is something the matter?"

"Blanche, tell me about . . . your church."

Her eyes lit up. "We built us a brand spanking new sanctuary, right on Main—"

"Oh, I didn't mean the building. Everybody in the county could see it go up, right from when you poured the foundation." I hadn't meant to ask about the Baptist church just yet; I'd barely decided to leave Bethel Church. "What I meant was, the people, your pastor, the—"

"Elzay Caywood is one fine preacher. Him and his wife are real good to come out and visit folks." She paused as if considering what to say. "Say, why don't you and the boys come this Sunday? Elmer, too, in case he's seen the light."

"It would just be me and the boys . . . that is, uh, if we decide to go."

"What's there to decide? You change your mind about Reverend Holder?"

"What time do you start?" I said.

143

"Sunday school at 9:45, church at 11:00, and we got Elzay trained so his preaching and the invitation are all done by 11:55."

"That seems like an odd time. Why so specific?"

"Sunday dinner is special, and they serve a good meal up at the Sunset Café. We need to get in there before the church crowd—that is, the other church people. I don't care to wait in line behind a bunch of prattling Methodists."

So it was that I told Elmer I'd be taking the boys into Forgan to the Baptist church on Sunday.

21 The Blizzard of '49

March 1949

Sammy

Big wet flakes flying sideways out of the northwest smacked my face. Some stuck to my eyelashes and eyebrows. Dickie and Tommy followed me to the bus as it slowed to a stop. We all had our mackinaws buttoned to the chin, mittens on, and caps with earflaps—except Tommy. He said Georgia Duvall didn't want a hat to muss his hair, so he covered his ears with a blue plaid scarf his sister Bonnie had given him.

Daddy said the wind came all the way from Canada, since there was less than five trees to stop it. It bent the battered tamarack beside the road almost flat, and the elms in front of our house whipped back and forth like they were fixing to fly to Texas.

We barely got on before Mr. Leukengay, the school janitor and bus driver, took off like a house afire. He seemed to forget the roads were slick until the bus skidded when he turned into Eagan's driveway, a mile and a half south. Good thing for him that Eugene and Edna hadn't gotten on the bus yet. They would've told their dad, who was on the school board. After that, he slowed down.

By the time Ruby and Lila Clapp got on and we headed west toward the schoolhouse, my feet were numb. No room up front by the heater. Dickie and I sat together, him huddled practically on top of me. For once, I was glad for long-handled underwear, but the plastic-covered seat still felt like a plate of ice.

Snow plastered over the right-side windows of the bus. Old Leukengay had the wipers going full speed, but the way he was hunched over, I bet he could hardly see the road.

At school, he stopped the bus with the door facing right into the wind. It almost blew us back into the bus. So cold. Two weeks before the first day of spring, but it felt like we were at the North Pole. A hat flew off. They might get it back—if they knew someone in Amarillo.

Mrs. Cates, our teacher for the first three grades, stood

145

outside the entry doors with a worried look on her face. I was glad our room was warm. The radiator banging away reminded me of Ed Jones bent over his anvil.

All morning, the wind howled like it was coming in to get us. Several times, Mrs. Cates went over to the high windows along the east side of the classroom to look outside. I liked her. She always had an encouraging word for everyone, even the kids who still couldn't read.

Nobody left the building for recess. Two groups of girls played jacks in opposite corners of the room. I followed some of the boys into the grade school gym, which was right at the end of the long hallway. For a while, we watched them try to play basketball. They didn't play long. It was an icebox in there, so I went back to the classroom.

Karen Cates saw me come in and smiled real big. Dickie said she was the prettiest girl in second grade, but I acted like I didn't hear him. She smiled at me a lot, which was okay until she got too close. If I didn't watch her, she'd squeeze my shoulder or arm, or grab my hand. That made me nervous. I didn't want to be teased. Other kids would say I was trying to be teacher's pet because Mrs. Cates was her mother.

Karen came right over and crowded close to me. "Sammy, I'm glad you came back. I told you I'm your friend. You'll be my boyfriend, won't you?"

I gulped. Tommy bragged that if a girl liked him, she would want him to kiss her. That was too much. My face felt hot. I didn't know how to kiss a girl. Tommy said it was a lot different than kissing your mother.

I tried to move away from Karen, but I was backed against the corner storage closet.

She stepped closer, giving me her big smile. I'd just come from that cold gym, but I had already started to sweat. I could tell she used fancy soap, not the Lava soap Mama made us use to scrub our hands. Karen asked me again if I wanted to be her boyfriend.

Just then, Mrs. Cates came back into the classroom and the bell rang.

⁓⦿⁓

Mrs. Cates stood behind her desk and rapped it with her ruler, which she'd never done before. "Children, stop what you're doing.

146

I want your full attention." Everyone turned around and looked at her. She stared back at us and said, "It's noon, time to go over to the high school building for lunch, like we do every day. But this isn't like every day. There is a very bad storm outside, so we're being extra careful today.

"It's still the same distance between our building and the high school, but it will seem twice as far because of the wind and blowing snow. Now, we might be going home instead of coming back here. So, get your homework, everything you need to take home."

She went straight to the first and second graders who were always losing their things. She told us third graders that once we were ready, maybe we could help the little kids who might've not got their coats buttoned or put their overshoes on correctly. It was always the same ones.

We lined up in the hallway like usual. Then she said, "All right, first graders, the sixth graders from Mrs. Wakefield's room will take each of you by the hand as we go to the high school building.

"Second and third graders, stay in line as you follow the first-grade children all the way across to the lunchroom. That wind is fierce, so stay close to the pupil ahead of you. Mrs. Wakefield and I will be at front and back of the line."

We bigger kids watched them leave. Dickie whispered, "I'm glad I'm in the second grade. I don't need no sixth graders to hold my hand."

We followed the first graders with their helpers through the long hallway, past the fourth and fifth graders, and out the front door. Lucky the door faced south, but as soon as we passed the corner of our building, the wind hit us. It took my breath away. Everything white, I couldn't tell the ground from the sky.

Dickie was still in front of me, and I had my hand on his shoulder. He turned around. "Sammy, gimme your hand."

I grabbed his hand. For once, he didn't try to do everything his way.

Just as we got to the swings, several high school kids came out of the flying snow and hovered beside us like mother hens. Roberta Monroe was me and Dickie's mother hen. I was glad to see her and pretended to forget she kissed me when I was in first grade.

When we finally staggered into the high school building,

everyone was gasping for breath. We stamped the snow off our overshoes and put them in a room Mrs. Cates told us to. On our way to the lunchroom, I saw Mrs. Cates and three other teachers gathered around Mr. Cates, the superintendent. She was talking really fast and pointing her trigger finger at him. They were saying school should already be dismissed . . . and I didn't hear the rest.

We had to wait in line longer than normal for lunch. Mrs. Leukengay, the cook, was grouchier than usual but I didn't care. I was hungry, and we'd soon be going home, like Mrs. Cates said.

I waited for Dickie to finish his beans and cornbread. He was so slow; I wanted to hurry up and go home. We got our things and walked along the side of the gym, where some boys were playing basketball. Tommy was there too, showing off for the girls. Guess he didn't want to go home. We did, so we went to the west windows of the high school gym to see if the buses had parked at their usual place. We looked out but no buses. Nobody else was waiting for the buses.

"C-c-come on, Dickie," I said. "Let's go out f-f-front. That's where they parked the buses."

We ran to the front, but nothing was out there. No buses, nobody waiting. Things were going wrong, and it made me afraid. Just a little.

The big Reznor heaters roaring at opposite corners of the gym made the basketball players shout louder, and kids running up in the balcony had two teachers yelling at them to get down or they'd be in big trouble. It seemed like the other kids were playing games or just having a good time. No one was trying to get the buses over to pick us up and take us home. I didn't want to miss the bus when it left, so I kept my coat on.

Then I saw Mrs. Cates come out of a classroom. She was still frowning but I said, "When is our b-b-bus going to take us home?"

"Oh." Her mouth dropped open, and then she got angry again. I wondered if it was something I'd done. "No one has told you? Well . . . we called all the parents who had telephones. But apparently . . . do your folks have a telephone?"

"N-n-no. We don't." I was kind of embarrassed about that.

"I'm sorry, Sammy. We can't reach them to tell them." She took a deep breath. "We will stay here . . . tonight. The storm's turned into a blizzard. It's already thirteen below zero and bound to get colder. No one should be out on those roads. We'll be safe here." She leaned down and touched my arm.

Her perfume smelled like Mama's. I missed Mama and felt sick to my stomach. Mrs. Cates was so nice. I wished she would put her arm around me, like Mama would do, but she couldn't do that. She was Mrs. Cates, my teacher.

She said, "You and Dickie will be warm and dry, and the superintendent will announce where everyone will sleep. You and your brother will be all right. Do you understand?"

I said, "C-c-can my daddy come and get us?"

"No, Sammy, it's too stormy. We'll be safe and warm, here tonight."

I couldn't think of anything to say. She smiled before she left, and I felt very sad. I went to tell Dickie.

He still had his coat on, like me, as we watched Tommy show off for Georgia Duvall.

"Dickie, we're not gonna g-get to go home."

"Yes, we are," he said. "Mrs. Cates said so."

I explained what she'd said.

He looked around, and then said, "I ain't never been away from home without Mama and Daddy—not for all night."

"Don't say ain't, and I haven't either."

"Is Tommy going home?"

"He's pl-playing basketball and making goo-goo eyes at Georgia Duvall." I didn't say more because my stomach started doing flip-flops, and I felt weak.

"I need to go to the bathroom." Dickie took off.

"Oh, Sammy, there you are." It was Karen. I was trapped.

"You're still my boyfriend, aren't you?" She put her arm on my shoulder and then slid it around my neck. "Can I have a kiss?" She giggled and moved right with me when I pulled back.

"I think I'm g-g-getting sick . . ."

"Oh, come over here, Sammy." She pulled me to a chair beside the ball court. "Here, let me help you." She sat beside me and tried to pull my head onto her lap.

My face felt like it was on fire—everyone looking at us. I jerked away and said, "I'm really sick . . . Gonna throw up." I stumbled to the restroom as Dickie was coming out.

I stayed there until the Corzine boys came in. When I came out, Karen was gone. I still felt awful, but I didn't want Karen to baby me or I'd feel worse. I walked over by the lunchroom.

Two other teachers had been watching me. One of them, Mrs. Wakefield, called me over and asked my name and a bunch of questions about how I was feeling.

"I . . . I'm s-sick."

She didn't say anything for a minute. Then she put the back of her hand on my forehead. "No fever. Sammy, you wish you could be home, don't you?"

She had kind eyes, but I just nodded.

"Sammy, you're homesick. Now don't you feel badly about it. Sometimes, being away from home can make anyone sick." She studied me awhile longer, her hand on my shoulder. "But you'll be okay. You come see me if you need to, will you?"

"Okay, I will."

Mrs. Wakefield was a nice lady, but I wanted to be home. I walked around the gym for a while and then decided what I would do. I got my overshoes and put them on, buttoned up my mackinaw all the way to the neck, and put my earflaps down. Then I put on my gloves and picked up my tablet and homework papers.

The main entry doors on the south side still showed lots of light. I went over there and stood outside the doors. For a while, I watched the swirling snow and listened to the wind howl around both sides of the high school building. Two high brick pillars rose like sentinels out next to the turn-in off Greenough Road.

Now that I was going home, I began to feel better. I hadn't gotten very far away from the school building when I felt the wind flog my back. I walked toward the pillars, and then past them, so I could look east along Greenough Road, the way home.

I stopped and looked straight east down the road. By holding my left hand up beside my face and squinting, I could almost see through the flying snow. Tried to see the ditches, where the edges of the road were. Took a deep breath; couldn't see them.

I shifted my gaze just a little. Henry and Blanche Ausmus's place was right beside Greenough Road, about a mile away. I squinted as hard as I could but didn't see any of their trees or their house or their barn. That was strange. Our house was three-quarters of a mile farther east and over a mile north.

I stared down the road for a long time. Everything looked so empty, except for the white. Everywhere. My legs began to shiver.

I worried what to do . . .

I started to go but something held me where I was. I thought for a long time what to do.

Maybe it would be better to wait a little bit. After the storm let up, I could go then. For a long while, I waited for the wind to stop blowing the snow so I could see. My toes felt cold.

I turned around and faced the school building. That wind seemed like it had gotten stronger, and my forehead hurt. I ducked my head and walked past the two brick pillars, keeping my head down all the way. It was hard to breathe. As I got close to the school building, the bite of the wind eased up.

I looked up, and there was Dickie. He said he'd followed me out the door.

We both went inside, not knowing exactly where we'd sleep that night. Somehow I knew, I'd turned away from danger . . . a danger that would've kept Dickie and me from ever going home.

Elmer

Eleven o'clock and still no sign of our boys. Claire was beside herself. I was mad. Mad at myself for even letting the boys and Tommy get on that bus. Radio reception had been awful, but by nine, every station was warning about blizzard conditions. What was that superintendent thinking? They should've sent everybody home already.

I'd spent all morning getting livestock into shelter, opening up both side aisles of the barn for the cattle and getting the horses into the working pen south of the granary. Had to keep them blamed horses—Ted, especially—separate from the cows. Diamond and Mabel and the rest never chased or kicked the other farm animals. Ted bullied smaller animals, just out of meanness. I made up my mind right then to sell him to Ray Amen, first chance I got.

Three sows were due to farrow within the week but other than that, I didn't worry about the hogs in a storm. I'd had three sows survive two days buried in a snowdrift. Pigs were smarter than most farm animals, anyway . . . Stop it, Elmer, you're just ignoring what you're afraid of—that our boys are marooned who-knows-where in that yellow icebox, covered by drifting snow this very minute . . .

After busting the ice in the stock tanks for the third time that morning, I parked the sledgehammer inside the barn and headed to the house. Moving my legs against the lash of the wind in two pair of ice-sheeted pants was like wearing armor while stumbling through a vat of tar. Shep kept his muzzle at my knee, his instinct guiding me through the swirling snow to the house.

Halfway across the road, I stopped to stare north. I wished . . . I wished my wishes were as good as Claire's calls to the Almighty.

All I had was the flame of my yearning. Surely, that ought to manifest a yellow bus out of that roaring storm. Within seconds, my forehead ached from the cold. I hoped to God my boys weren't stranded somewhere. As bitter as that wind was blowing, it would shock the life out of anything it could reach. Best not to think of such things.

I turned back toward the house. Had to keep my bearings or I'd stray off course. Everything white, I'd miss the entire house if I wasn't careful.

The porch door opened by Claire's hand. "Oh, let Shep in too! He's covered in ice. And you, oh, Elmer, Elmer."

I shed my clothes right there in the kitchen. Claire, always thinking ahead, had a pan of hot—almost too hot—water for me to soak my frozen feet. Then she pulled a blanket out of the oven and threw it over my shoulders and legs. Within minutes, I was a new man.

I could tell she'd been crying. What should I do? "Claire, I'll get into dry clothes . . . Saddle up Diamond. She's tough. We'll head over to Greenough. Get there and make sure our boys are not stuck in a snowdrift somewhere."

"Elmer, what if you can't make it? You'll be—"

"I'll be all right. Put some hot coffee in a hot water bottle. I'll carry it under my shirt, next to my belly." I stopped to figure the best route. "I'll go south to the corner, then head west along that cow path trail. It opens up on top of the ridge. Then the rest of the way to the section line east of Hinz's. A mile straight south to Greenough Road, then the half-mile jaunt west to the school. We got a good four hours of daylight left, maybe five."

With that, I toweled off and strode into the bedroom. Found my warmest wool pants and doubled up on everything.

I must've looked like a mummy; Claire put her hand to her mouth, and then said, "Elmer, I love you. Please be careful. We want to know if our precious boys are safe, but I don't want to lose you out there."

Bundled up and with my rubber bottle of hot coffee, I hustled across the road, leaving Claire with a hug and kiss and Shep for company. I knew she'd be praying. That wasn't in my bailiwick, but I felt better, knowing she'd be calling down angels or whatever she asked for.

A black mare in her prime, Diamond was part quarter horse and all heart. The wind at our backs, we swept past the double track at the section line before I knew it. Not because we were going fast but because I didn't see the fence corner posts on either side of the section line. My heart pounding, I reined her back. Her tracks were already erased, like we hadn't been that way only minutes before. Then, in the uncertain light, I made out a change in the pattern of drifted snow. Tumbleweeds bunched against my fence on the north side created a sizable snowdrift, and I headed her into the drift toward what I thought was straight west.

Head cocked against the wind, Diamond forged ahead through snow nearly up to her girth. Laboring and blowing, she finally burst through the mass, then moved smartly through a series of smaller drifts for the next quarter mile. But I could only guess the distance. Aware of a vague silhouette rising before us, I breathed easier.

I knew that hill. It rose a modest twenty feet above the surrounding fields, but the road gouged a severe cut—at least six feet—below the crest. Enough to swallow horse and rider if it drifted full.

Which it had. I cursed, unwilling to accept what I should've known. Through the shrieking barrage of wind and snow, I could see the top edge of the white wall rising before me.

I turned Diamond back the way we'd come; hope draining out of me like water out of a busted bucket. I hoped I'd be able to comfort my dear Claire.

And that our boys were someplace safe.

Claire

The storm roared all night, turning wearisome hours into heaps of anxiety and outright fear. In those moments of desperation, I called out to God from my fear, not caring if Elmer heard my prayers. I remembered that Pop had said—not once, but many times—fear was a necessary element of our survival, and even of our worship, for it prompts us to look beyond ourselves to a power, a Person, higher than our feeble hands.

The day after the storm began with a hopeful brightness lying in a thin band across the eastern horizon. Before I ventured outside, its gray threat began to turn to silver promise. In an act of faith, I plunged through drifts of snow across to the barn to do the milking, and Elmer went to the big garage, where the Ford tractor awaited. The bitter cold sky—still down to minus fifteen—turned a brilliant blue.

I heard the tractor start. Another prayer of thanks, as Elmer prepared the seven-foot sled he'd built months before. Together, we lashed blankets and extra articles of clothing to the sled. Elmer headed straight south on that windless morning, where he'd turn west on Greenough Road. I watched him as he broke through each drift angled across the road, finally returning to the house when the chill became unbearable.

My fifth trip that afternoon to slog from the house to the road and look south. That time, I was rewarded with the sight of a moving object, coming down the hill, toward us. Another prayer of thanks, and I went inside to prepare a celebration dinner for my beloved ones.

22 Tommy Decides

Elmer

As I waited, the morning sun glinting off the water in the stock tank took me back forty-five years to my parents' farm in Nebraska. For the life of me, I couldn't recall sassing my mother when I was a snot-nosed kid. Certainly not like Tommy had taken to doing lately. I'd probably done it, but it was contrary to my upbringing.

Mom had elevated despair to an art form—her way of dealing with Dad's say-much and do-little leadership of the family. Unlike Tommy, I hadn't allowed myself the freedom of indulging adolescent fantasies toward personal independence. Not while Mom and Dad, me and Jim and Maggie were struggling just to raise enough crook-neck milo, corn, and chickens to survive. John, Earl, and Bud had it easy, them coming later.

Tommy still hadn't showed. Guess he needed to be showed. I started up the Ford tractor and pulled the low two-wheeled trailer into the crowding pen tucked behind the shop building. A winter's worth of manure and trampled feed stalks had formed a foot-deep muck, sodden with spring rains. Couldn't delay removing the mess much longer; summer heat would make it hard as concrete. I dismounted and secured a shovel and pitchfork from the shop.

Shep's ears went up. He trotted around the corner of the shop to greet, who else? Tommy, rubbing his eyes, hair uncombed.

All innocence and blather, that kid had his mouth going the second he stepped into sight. He used a frequent ploy to divert attention from his shortcomings—bring up a totally unrelated issue, one usually tied to something he wanted badly. "Uncle Elmer, is there enough gas in the pickup to go to Liberal Saturday night?"

I ignored that and pulled out my pocket watch. "Twenty minutes after seven. Is this your idea of being on time for chores?"

He didn't have the guts to meet my eyes, but turned on his

155

whiny voice. "My bootlace broke. Aunt Claire didn't have extras."

"Don't give me that. There's work to do, but you delay coming out to do your chores over a broken bootlace."

"Work, always work." He punched the words, pointing to the ground, as if to smack them into the muck. "If we're not feeding these cows, we're castrating, dehorning, or cleaning up after them. In between, we're fixing fence or broke-down machinery, stringing barbwire around miles of wheat pasture, planting or getting ready to plant, repairing—"

"You got a home here, you know. A bed to sleep in and plenty to eat. That doesn't just appear without some sacrifice. You think you shouldn't have to work?" I squished my way out of the pen to face him.

His lip curled, he spat, "Well, it's not my farm . . ."

"You saying you shouldn't have to help because you don't own the place? What if I decided not to provide a place for you at my table under my roof because you're not my kid? Is that what you want?" I let my eyes bore in on him. Ungrateful pup, who does he think he is?

Toneless and barely audible, he mumbled, "That ain't what I'm saying."

"Well, you're not showing much gratitude for what we've been giving you. You're just complaining because I expect you to work to earn your keep.

"Don't you think you could tie a knot in your bootlace so you could get your hind end out here—on time—to help? Who do you think pays for your boots, your Levis and denim jacket? You think the food on the table and a place for you to sleep appears like magic? Yet, the first thing you got to say is 'Do we have enough gas in the pickup' so you can do your running around.

"You seem to think just by existing, you deserve what you want, when you want it." I stopped; better put a lid on the rest. He was incapable of hearing more from me or receiving instruction from anyone. A determined unwillingness to learn—just like his dad.

"Tommy, that shovel and pitchfork in the trailer are your tools for today. Load up that trailer from the pen. Then we'll talk about gas for the pickup. We'll be going to Liberal shortly. You could've come with us, if you'd been out here to help with chores. You weren't. That's gotten to be a habit. This will give you some time to think it over." I waited for him to respond.

156

Nothing. No apology, no appreciation for all we'd done for him. He had to be boiling inside, eyes squinted tight and jaw set, like he wanted to yell at me. The kid didn't have the capacity to admit his mistakes, to stand tall and take correction like a man. John had been the same; still was.

I realized Tommy needed space, so I cut it off. "Dinner will be in the icebox."

૭৶

The minute we got back from Liberal, I had the feeling something wasn't quite right. Anytime Tommy didn't go to town with us, I always made a point of bringing him an RC Cola, which he sometimes thanked me for. Probably still pouting, I supposed.

The dog was acting up, occasionally growling and looking down the road. He'd stop and give a woof, as if to declare a sense of trespass. I carried the groceries into the house while Claire started supper. "Say, you notice anything odd about the place?"

"Oh. I don't know. Why do you ask?" Her voice took on a sharp cadence. She caught her breath. Eyes wide, she said, "Elmer, where's Tommy?"

"Be right back." I launched myself out the door, skimming the steps and across the road to the crowding pen. A quick glance to be sure the pickup hadn't been moved.

The tractor and trailer—half-filled with black muck—sat in heavy silence as I came around the back side of the shop building. No Tommy, which I'd begun to suspicion would be the case.

I trudged back to the house, surprised at the wave of emotion that rumbled in my gut. Anger and frustration at Tommy's lack of appreciation, or even understanding, of what we'd sacrificed to make a place for him. Disappointed the kid couldn't see our taking him in offered a real chance to start his life on solid footing. He'd never gotten that support from his dad. John showed little interest in any of his brood; treated them like they were a nuisance.

I was bothered that it didn't need to be that way. If Tommy had set his self-righteous anger aside, he would've been able to see the value of working for a distant reward. But no, whatever he wanted, he wanted right now. He hadn't learned discipline, pure and simple.

Hardest to take was my sense that I'd failed. I had taken raw farm boys hired on at Deluxe and taught them how to sell, some with startling results. But teaching a smart-mouth kid discipline

157

and the value of hard work seemed beyond my ken. Tommy wouldn't amount to anything unless he learned who he was and what he could be. Maybe because no one ever told him. Chicken and egg—you either believe you're worth more than a tinker's-dam, or you prove it by doing something worthwhile first.

My own words stopped me. Tommy couldn't see value in himself, and his dad never gave him an example to follow. Any chance of teaching the kid value and worth would've had to come from us. But he never shut his yap long enough to hear it.

Claire met me at the door, wide-eyed and hands on her hips. "It's all gone, Elmer. Every stitch of clothes Tommy ever wore—cleaned out. He's gone, isn't he?"

I pulled her to me, guided her to the divan. We sat, side by side, neither one speaking. "Yes," I finally said. "The boy has gone. He thinks he's a man, but he's still a boy. Thinks he's got everything figured out, but he doesn't know squat."

"I'm glad he left." Her words came out as a hiss, spilling acid. "Never respected all we've done for him . . . Five years, he's had a home here. If not for us, he would've been on the street. Always held himself apart, like he was just waiting to break loose . . ."

I winced at her tone. She was usually more forgiving than me. I wondered if she'd had to put up with the kid's insolence because I hadn't paid attention. "Yeah, honey, he was kind of like a feral pup. But I'm not glad he left, at least not the way he did. That boy is going to find what it's like to be all alone. He'll be lucky to find a place to sleep for more than a day or two. Not one to save money, he'll miss some meals. Maybe someone will hire him on, take him in." I caught her teary cheeks. "He didn't leave a note, did he?"

She shook her head. "Elmer, such a smart aleck, he only thought of himself. Never considered others." Frowning, she said, "But how did he leave? Who would—"

"Probably walked over to Corzines. Got those boys, wild as they are, to carry him into town." I gave her shoulder a squeeze. "We did what we could. He's so full of pride and spite, he'd never come back here. But life goes on. You want to tell the boys?"

Try hard as I could, I couldn't get over the feeling that Tommy's failure was my failure.

23 Aunt Bet Comes to Visit

Claire

I'd met Aunt Bet, Will's only sister, when we were in Kansas City, once and briefly at that. Maggie had told me Aunt Bet was entirely different from the rest of that side of the family, and Elmer spoke of his Aunt Bet in glowing terms. After all the pointless arguments and rebellion from John's kids, I was looking forward to seeing a better side of Elmer's clan. Maybe someone like Maggie. No one could equal Maggie. I teared up, thinking of her.

The following Sunday after Tommy took off, we went to Tyrone for our biweekly trip to check on Elmer's folks—and to see Aunt Bet. Frail as she was, she had traveled from central Kansas to Tyrone, determined "to make a last trip to see Will and Mary Grace."

Will greeted us without getting up from his rocker as we entered the house. John's three youngest hovered at the bedroom door; their darting eyes signaled they were either up to no good or had something to hide. I'd bet they knew Tommy had run off. Joyce and Phyllis, the two oldest, vanished into the kitchen.

I heard Mary Grace directing the girls to wash a sinkful of kettles and pans. The protests and banging that ensued brought a smile to my lips. A triumphant look on her face, Mary Grace emerged from the kitchen. She turned and called, "Bet, Elmer's here."

Aunt Bet toddled out of the kitchen, a smile creasing her features. She took my hand first, her dark eyes peering over rimless glasses and piercing my own, as if sensing a kinship.

"Claire. You remember me, I hope." Her voice held a touch of mirth but quavered from shortness of breath. "I was just leaving brother Jim's house in Kansas City when you and Elmer come to visit. Fifteen years ago, you 'spect? But now that you're here, we'll have time to talk."

I assured her I hadn't forgotten that meeting. Elmer had told me her real name was Epsie Jane. Epsie Jane Smith, but the brothers called her Bet. I wondered what sorts of things we'd discuss but guessed it wouldn't be small talk.

She turned to Elmer, grasping his hand with both of hers as she looked up into his face. As Elmer sat on the divan near Will, she greeted each of our boys in turn, driving little Jerry to seek refuge behind my skirt.

Addressing us all, she said, "The train doesn't stop in Larned, so Minnie took me over to Great Bend. I rode that iron rooster all the way here. I love the train. They take such good care of old folks like me. Since Will and Mary Grace have their big sixtieth wedding anniversary coming up, I thought it would be a dandy time to spend a few days together before all the celebration."

I glanced at the boys. Sammy and Dickie simply gazed at her, transfixed by this quaint little lady with puckered lips and visible moustache, her flowered print dress not quite covering the tops of her rolled-down cotton hose. I hoped they'd mind their manners.

Aunt Bet continued with a recitation of bus and train trips she'd made since the Depression ended, mostly to see brothers Joe up at Phillipsburg and Jim and Cart in KC. I was caught by her self-sufficiency and confidence, especially at her age. I wondered how much education she had. She didn't use big words so maybe she hadn't even gone past grammar school. Maybe I was too self-conscious about my limited education.

My mind drifted. I wondered if I should be more independent in expressing my opinions and doing what I wanted, how it would play out with Elmer. Attending church and the monthly Home Demonstration Club meetings were about the only times I did something on my own, besides fixing Blanche Ausmus' hair every two weeks. That hardly counted, except she and I talked about personal things, like in-law problems and what we would do if we didn't have so much to do. In the twenty years Elmer and I had been married, it seemed I voiced my opinions less and less, all in the interest of marital harmony. Or cowardice.

My sister-in-law Grace often encouraged me to express myself, even if no one agreed with me. Not that she was preaching rebellion; rather, why not campaign to come up to Ness County more often to see her and Myrrl on the farm? I had told her Elmer's folks took a lot of attention, being we provided most of the food for them and John's three youngest. Four, counting when Tommy lived with us.

My thoughts were interrupted by Will's gravelly voice. He was getting cranked up about the younger generation—their laziness and disrespect of the elderly—a tired complaint that I usually tuned out. With Aunt Bet there, everyone tried to be polite by letting Will have his say.

I glanced at Elmer. He kept his hands bundled in his lap, seeming content with his father getting an audience for his opinions. Married almost sixty years to Mary Grace, he didn't often get that opportunity. Everybody needed the chance to say their piece.

Unbidden, my eyes swelled with moisture. No one seemed to notice as I quietly got up and swept into the kitchen. I blew my nose, then a few dabs with my hankie, and returned as Will began to wind down.

Aunt Bet interrupted, her voice placid as a swan on a pond. "Well, my experience has been that youngsters won't be getting into trouble if they's got better things to do."

"Exactly right, sis. You can bet the farm on that." Will pounced on her affirmation like a cat on a mouse, though he seemed relieved to give up the floor to her.

She nodded. "One of the best things for kids to do these days is regular attendance at a good church and Sunday school. I've seen that time and again, haven't you, Will?"

Deadly quiet in the room. Religion was taboo, the unspoken subject in that house, but Will's quick agreement with her had boxed him in. He couldn't reverse course without looking foolish. I wanted to shout, or at least catch Elmer's expression. I chanced a quick glance at his hands. His knuckles gleamed white, bunched against his belt.

Aunt Bet continued, oblivious to everyone holding their collective breath. "Too many people think religion is a passel of don'ts—don't have fun, don't try too hard, don't expect much out of this life 'cause you'll get it all in the next. You've heard folks say that, haven't you, Will?"

He stared at her, then coughed and licked his lips. "Yes, I suppose I have."

She laughed, a tinkling bell in the quiet space. "I can't lay claim to living a perfect life, no-sir-ee. We older folks—not just the youngsters—we get so attached to the idea of handling problems on our own that we forget to turn them over to Jesus. Now that's pride."

Elmer found his voice. "Mom, is dinner about ready?"

"Oh! I'll see about the roast." Mary Grace ordered Joyce and

Phyllis to set the table.

Aunt Bet called as she left, "Mary Grace, let me peel those potatoes."

I said, "You stay here and talk with the men. Besides, you're the guest. I'll help with what needs to be done." Elmer needs to hear more from this wonderful aunt of his.

Dinner ready, I went out to escort Aunt Bet in while everyone else trooped in after her. My hand on her elbow, I spoke loudly enough for all to hear. "Aunt Bet, you are such an encouragement to me. I take our boys to the Baptist church in Forgan. They learn a new verse every Sunday. One of these times, I'll be brave enough to sing in the choir, so help me."

With a sly smile, she leaned over and poked Elmer in the ribs, causing him to jump. "Nephew, you might give some thought to going with your lovely family to that Babtist church."

Grinning, he trapped her hand between his. "Aunt Bet, you're as ornery as always."

We had a pleasant meal that blissful day. For years, I'd felt like the prophet Elijah, carrying God's message to that family all by my lonesome. That day, I had an ally. What a gal. I think she rather enjoyed knocking us back on our heels.

I was to shortly learn I wouldn't escape her surprises. While the two girls cleared the table and began washing the pans and dishes, Aunt Bet shooed me out of the kitchen. "You go out in the front room. I want to show these girls I can help around here too."

I'd barely gotten settled beside Elmer on the divan when she again ambled out to address me. "My mind's been failing me, Claire. Almost plumb forgot to say this—I'm so pleased that you, a daughter-in-law, took on the total complete responsibility to prepare the whole dinner for the big doin's for Will and Mary Grace's anniversary."

I felt the color drain from my face. I wanted to speak but couldn't think what to say. I whirled to Elmer and got only a shrug. Where did she get that idea? There had to be an explanation. I stood and just as quickly dropped into a chair. Like a deflated balloon, I was the one all short of breath.

As she disappeared back into the kitchen, Elmer turned to Will. "Dad, what's going on? Is this your doing—this business about Claire fixing a big dinner for your sixtieth anniversary?"

My temples throbbing, I watched the exchange in silence. I wanted to see how or if Elmer would protect my interests from being trampled again by his folks. In the background, I heard the boys playing blind-man's bluff. In the kitchen, the clatter of pots and crockery.

Instead of answering, Will riffled his hand through his hair, pursed his lips, and took a deep breath. "Well, I didn't exactly say Claire would do such a thing. Just that it would be nice if someone would put a little something together for us. Ain't just every day that—"

"And who would that someone be, Dad?" A faint smile played at the corner of Elmer's mouth as he leaned toward Will.

"Well, it could be anybody . . . anybody that would want to do something special . . ."

"Where did Aunt Bet get the idea it would be Claire? Did you suggest she might be a likely candidate to organize a family celebration?"

Will swallowed. "Claire's name come up in the conversation, I suppose."

I'd never seen Elmer badger his father before, but there he was, steadily pushing Will to own up.

"And . . .?" Elmer waited. Getting no response, he said, "So what was it you wanted her to do?"

"Well, I don't rightly recall . . . exactly what . . . Your mother remembers such things better than I ever could." Will stopped, as if unsure how much to reveal of his expectation. Seemingly hit by inspiration, he bellowed, "Mom! Come in here. I need some answers."

Mary Grace barked a reply from the kitchen, which drew a sharp response from Will. She marched into the living room, brandishing a floured rolling pin. In nothing flat, the two of them were woofing at one another, Will declaring she had shamed him into an unseemly expectation of his favorite daughter-in-law. Mary Grace countered with familiar complaints about his laziness, belching at the table, and failure to pick up after himself.

I'd never seen Will stand up to Mary Grace and was enjoying seeing him speak up for himself. Elmer must've felt the same way, as he made no move to intervene. Phyllis and Joyce used the rumpus to slip out of the kitchen, and our three boys and Corky appeared at the bedroom door, intent on seeing what was going on.

Aunt Bet steadied herself at the kitchen entry, her eyes widening. For moments, she watched and listened before

163

retreating. She returned with a dishpan and heavy spoon and commenced banging on the dishpan until Mary Grace and Will quieted. Breathless, she said, "Well, now I know how one stays married for sixty years. Mercy! What brought this on?"

Will started to speak, but Elmer held up his hand and turned to the children. "Outside, all you kids. Scoot. You too, Jerry. Get your coats." When they hesitated, he turned on his growl. "I said outside. Now!" As one, they fled.

Apparently satisfied, Will stood and went into their bedroom, returning with his tin of tobacco. He sat and began stoking his pipe.

Aunt Bet began to giggle. Setting her dishpan aside, she collapsed into the nearest straight-back chair, her body convulsing in silent laughter. Elmer and I joined in, soon followed by Will, who whooped like a Cimarron cowboy. It was even funnier—to me, at least—because Mary Grace seemed unable to allow herself the luxury of laughter, and of laughing at herself.

Then, the thought . . . really, more akin to an idea . . . It came upon me like a slow-moving freight, gradually picking up steam. Claire, this is something that should be done. There's really no one else in the family willing or capable to do it. You want to be taken seriously? You can do this, all the organization and planning, the invitations, getting enough food—we had a good crop year. You'll do it—for Elmer and his folks, for the whole tribe. But most of all, for yourself. To show anyone who wants to ask, can you handle something big? Put a big write-up afterwards in The Southwest Daily Times, The Herald-Democrat, even The Forgan Advocate.

Not many people stayed married forty years, and fewer still, fifty. Sixty was monumental, but that's what Elmer's folks had done. Well, I was determined too. Before it was over, I put together a spread worthy of a potentate to mark Will and Mary Grace's anniversary. That's how Mama would've handled it.

When it was done, so was I, or nearly so. Halfway through the preparations and invitations, I wondered what possessed me to attempt such an audacious undertaking—almost singlehandedly, in fact. Dear Blanche corralled a group of the WMU ladies from our church to help out, thank goodness. The whole affair brought a hundred and six neighbors and family to our farm on a windless Sunday afternoon just before Decoration Day. The spread in The

Southwest Daily Times even had a picture of the honored couple with a write-up just like I would've done it. Because I wrote it up.

A review of the guest registry revealed five names unknown to anyone in the family. At first, I was upset that somebody would pull such a stunt. Elmer suggested I see it as a compliment; they were willing to pass themselves off as relatives in order to partake of Claire Hall's cooking.

Aunt Bet hadn't planned to attend the big doin's. Crowds wore her out. But she said she was coming because I told her what her unplanned pep talk had done for me.

We never saw her again before she passed away that fall.

That dear lady will be one of the first ones I'll look up when I get to glory.

24 The Story of Will

July 1950

Claire

Two stars reflected from our headlights, glowing ghost-like in the road ahead. It was our dog Shep, recently acquired from McCarter.

We were just returning home from another Sunday at Will and Mary Grace's house in Tyrone. A house they would've never had if we hadn't bought it with part of my inheritance. I still bore a grudge over that, God forgive me.

As we pulled in, I saw an old Chevy pickup parked next to our house. Ray Hunter sat on the front fender, straddling the left headlight.

His relaxed pose was deceiving. Though it wasn't unusual for a local farmer to drop in on a neighbor, only an emergency would prompt an unannounced visit near bedtime. No one waited outside on a windless July night for nothing. Hordes of gnats would appear, crawling across and into eyes, nose, and ears. Ray's appearance at that hour meant he'd come in response to some disaster, an urgent need, perhaps a frightening message.

I expected him to call out, perhaps rush over to us. But no, Elmer's cousin was never one to get excited. Ray ambled in with us as we carried our two youngest into the house. They'd been rocked to sleep by the ride home. Sammy trailed behind until Shep thrust his nose into his hands.

Elmer lit a kerosene lamp in the kitchen and motioned Ray to sit. Instead, he paced, as if needing to delay announcing a reason for his late-night call. I quickly got the boys in bed and finished lighting two more lamps. Elmer pulled the gallon jar of tea out of the icebox and placed it and three drinking glasses on the table. "Surprised to see you out in this heat. Edith on the prod? Need a place to sleep?" He grinned.

Ray finally sat, fanning himself with his hat before dropping it on the floor. "Boy howdy, that ice tea looks good." He slugged his glassful down and then lapsed into a fit of coughing.

I refilled his glass as he pulled out his bandana and swabbed his face.

Eyes watering, he said, "No, Elmer, no problems with Edith. It's . . ." His voice dwindled. He rotated the refilled glass in circles on the oilcloth covering. "I just got . . . Earl called a while ago . . . from Tyrone."

"We just came from there." I wanted to shake him if he didn't out with it.

"Yeah, that's what he said." Ray's voice took an unnatural pitch as he looked up at Elmer. "Your dad . . . Will, he's gone."

Will was gone? I tried to comprehend and looked quickly at Elmer. He seemed to have stopped breathing for the moment. I pulled his arm to me, instinctively to protect him. As if I could. He looked as if an arrow had gone to his heart.

Ray took a deep breath, seeming to process his own grief. "Earl said Will, uh, your dad, complained of not feeling well after supper. He got up and went back to the bedroom. That's where they found him." He swallowed and said, "I'm sure sorry, Elmer. Will and I never had a cross word. Always glad to see me. Treated me like I was powerful important."

Elmer stood, still silent. Ray did, too, and squeezed Elmer's shoulder. As he turned to leave, Elmer asked, "How's Mama?"

Ray coughed. "She's in sort of a daze, Earl said. Took her medicine afterward and went to bed after the ambulance . . . after it left. Earl said to tell you he'll stop by in the morning."

Elmer and I stood in the quiet of the house until the whine of Ray's pickup faded. "Going outside." He turned and nodded for me to come.

The night air enveloped us, soothing as it loosened its hot grasp on that July day. Elmer took my hand in his, and we stepped hesitantly until our eyes adjusted to the moonless night. I thought how long it had been since we'd last strolled together, probably not in years. My heart full, I put my opposite hand in his so I could place my arm around his waist.

Never one to speak of his feelings, Elmer lowered the barriers that night. Stopping now and then to gaze at the stars, we held each other.

As one, we returned to the solitary pool of light spilling out the only window still awake. He leaned over to whisper, "I can't

167

tell you how much you . . . how much I feel shielded, protected, by your being with me, Claire. You're still my sweetheart, you know."

"I'll always be your darling."

No tears. Elmer wasn't a weeper. Those brief hours, nevertheless, brought brightness to my soul out of the shadow of his grief.

The Panhandle wind comes like Geronimo, hard and fast. Always unexpected, it promises rain but mostly brings dusters to drive the pilgrims back from where they came.

Those words of Will, like other sage sayings of his, marked him as a thinker. The Dust Bowl years of the thirties proved his point, as dust storms drove thousands from the farms they'd planted on the Great Plains. Whole towns dried up in the face of those years of drought.

Over the previous twenty years, the wind had ruined crops, suffocated livestock, sent blinding storms, and stifled hope for many. Even our drive back to the farm was slowed by washboard roads scoured by the wind. Elmer and I might've given up if we'd had any other place to go.

Asked why he stayed in our dry corner of the world, Will said he would've escaped the unremitting dusters, but "didn't feel right about leaving family."

For whatever failures one might lay at Will's feet, he was "that likable old coot" who bound us together with his tales, his amazing knowledge of history, his sense of humor, and his congeniality. To Elmer, he was Dad, the one who indirectly anointed Elmer as Leader, Provider.

Everyone likes a good story, and few could tell a story better than my father-in-law. That gift induced all sorts of people into doing things for him. Will readily slid out of jams that would've put other men in jail or out on the street. Elmer said men were inclined to trust his dad because Will was "self-deprecating."

Granted, Will made for lively conversation in his homespun way. For a man who grew up in the backwoods of Indiana with little education, he was articulate and well-read. He was generous with what he possessed, which was never very much. In his later years, he and Mary Grace depended on family—mostly us—to meet their material needs. Will was witty, kind to children and dogs, vexed with cats and public officials, and overly indulgent of his offspring. That last trait, I saw as evidence of his primary defect—a persistent and carefree laziness.

The opportunity to spin a yarn brought out a different side of Will. A natural performer, he came across as a combination Will Rogers and William Jennings Bryan in dramatizing a tale. That previous afternoon, as I helped Mary Grace clean up after Sunday dinner, I heard his baritone in the front room. Each retelling sometimes opened a window into understanding the family I'd married into.

Will would sit in his old rocker in the living room and tell stories of his youth to the grandkids lounging on the floor. Variations often came from the questions. The children sat enthralled at his tales of growing up with four brothers and a sister, of almost joining the land rush into the Cherokee Strip, about desperadoes—some of whom he knew—hiding along the breaks of the Cimarron River, about cowboys working the XIT, and legendary U.S. marshals hunting down outlaws in No-Man's Land.

৯৵

I told Elmer I'd get my preacher, Elzay Caywood, to do Will's funeral services. Unspoken was the knowledge that with Maggie gone, no one in his family had the foggiest how to get a parson.

Elmer handled everything else, which meant we'd end up paying the expenses. I didn't speak of it to Elmer. He knew I'd worry about the money, anyhow. That increased my embarrassment—thinking of cost at such a time. I'd unconsciously allowed materialism to stifle humanity. Eyes burning, I bowed my head as words I memorized, words of Jesus, swept over me: *Therefore I say unto you, take no thought for your life, what ye shall eat, or what ye shall drink; nor yet for your body, what ye shall put on. Is not the life more than meat, and the body than raiment?*

On our way to Liberal for the funeral, Elmer said, "Finally got ahold of Durward. He's roughnecking for a wildcatter south of Dumas. Misses his little girl. Can't get off work, but he'll help with expenses. Said he'll send something from his next paycheck. I'm proud . . . of my son."

"He's a prize. I've always seen him as my son too."

"Yeah." I sensed Elmer wanted to say more, but he remained silent.

169

From the Blue Bell School to Skinny White's place, only car noise filled the void. I glanced at Elmer but looked away as if I hadn't seen the line of bright coursing down his cheek.

He coughed and swiped at his face with the back of his hand. At random, he rattled off some of what he'd done to prepare for the funeral. "Earl met us when I took Mom to pick out a casket at Millers. He'll bring her to the funeral home today. Slipped me thirty-seven dollars, to go for expenses . . ." The last bit was for me, to ease my anxiety.

At the mortuary, a surge of heat hit us, radiating off the pavement and sidewalks. My veil stuck to perspiration that formed on my upper lip. I was wearing the same black dress I'd worn to Pop's funeral.

Pop. My dear Pop. Melancholia swept over me like a wave. I gathered the boys to me before entering the chapel.

Sam Miller, the mortician, greeted us. Gracious and organized, he gave a sense of order that was so lacking in my husband's family. One of his assistants took us to an anteroom where Earl and Gertrude waited with Mary Grace. Shortly, my preacher entered. After introductions, he explained how he planned to lead the service. "Does that sound satisfactory to everyone? I'm happy to make whatever changes you might want." He waited.

No response. Everyone simply looked back at him. I realized this family was unused to formality, even tradition, so probably no one even ventured to question the parson.

Finally, Reverend Caywood stood and thanked us in our silence. Taking charge, he looked at his pocket watch and nodded at Elmer. "We can begin when the family is seated." He left the room and proceeded to the front of the chapel, where he sat.

Elmer escorted his mother to the front row, followed by Earl. Besides the funeral home people and Brother Caywood, only Elmer and John's son-in-law, Alfred, wore suits. The rest of the men had dressed up in gabardines or blue jeans and starched shirts; the women, in their "funeral clothes." Thankfully, the undertaker had positioned electric fans around the chapel. Our boys beside me, I joined Elmer by his mother. I wondered if Tommy had come.

After most everyone got settled, a lady in a powder pink dress played two hymns on the piano. Then Brother Caywood came up front to greet the family and read Will's obituary. I was sure they'd be impressed by this down-to-earth man of God. Best of all, he wasn't a shouter. He reminded me of pictures I'd seen of Bob Fenimore, the All-American from Oklahoma A&M.

Elmer looked straight ahead during most of the service, signaling his intention not to be swayed by whatever religious talk the preacher might slip in. From time to time, he'd turn to whisper to his mother. Mary Grace's expression hardly changed during or after the service. No emotion to speak of, except when she couldn't get her sweater off. Elmer helped her, and then she went back to being like she was before. Probably figured she'd shed all her tears during the sixty-one years she and Will were married. Hard times for us, too, during the months and months they lived with us. Mustn't be so critical. My in-laws are grieving.

I remember little else of the service. Outside, a uniformed officer stood at attention beside an idling police car in front of the hearse. Another mark of order. The funeral procession followed the officer out past the fairgrounds to the cemetery on the northwest edge of town.

Eventually, the mourners gathered around. Brother Caywood read from First Corinthians and gave a short talk on the hope of those called by God. Coming like an open furnace of judgment, the wind picked up, scattering his words. No matter. I doubted if the family was inclined to listen.

The relatives withdrew as the morticians lowered Will's casket into the ground. I expected someone would announce what was to follow. Nothing of the kind. They simply milled around as if expecting instructions. Of course. Elmer, or I, was to be in charge. I was tempted to simply let them stumble about, but realized they truly were sheep without a shepherd. I would put something together, even on such short notice, mostly to honor my husband.

John's oldest daughter Bonnie and her husband Alfred came over to shake our hands. I exhaled. How nice. They spoke to Elmer, and as they turned, I saw Alfred give him a bill. I leaned forward in time to hear Bonnie say, ". . . just wanted to contribute—for the family. We know you've done so much, Uncle Elmer and Aunt Claire. We can't stay. Have to get to Amarillo before dark. Alfred has an early meeting Monday morning . . ." Then they were gone.

Elmer said, "Isn't that something? I don't expect her dad to help out." He paused. "I'm glad Bonnie got a fine man. She deserves some happiness."

I spotted Darlene and Louise, Bonnie's younger sisters, and started toward them. A rakish-looking young man stood between them, his head nodding as he spoke. He seemed tense, his lip slightly curled. One of John's boys, surely. Yes, he's the one who came out to the farm, making demands. Bill, the oldest. He must be about twenty-three now.

Then he saw me looking at him and instead of waving or smiling, he ducked his head. I sucked in my breath. Doesn't he want to greet me—his aunt? I stopped where I was. Maybe they were having a private conversation. Though I expected him to look my way again, he never did. I got the impression of separation, perhaps animosity.

I scanned the crowd for Kenny and Tommy. Didn't see them. Knew it was a wrong attitude, but I was glad they hadn't come. I breathed easier. Kenny had been so hateful the few days he'd been in our house. And Tommy, running off without warning. Treating us like enemies, after all we'd done for them.

Elmer's brother Jim and his wife Beatrice approached. By her pursed lips, I could tell she was determined about something. Pulling Jim behind her, she leaned in close so we could hear above the wind. "Claire, Elmer, we have to get back to Buffalo. Our car is none too dependable. I wanted to let you know . . ." She paused, as if to be certain we—and Jim—heard her. "We will send some money to help with the expenses. Right now, I don't know where it's coming from, but that's what we'll do. Jim and I agreed." She turned to him. "Isn't that right, Jim?"

He twisted around to spit, before turning back to us. "That's right. My wife is always right." He laughed hoarsely, then asked, "Anybody seen Bud?"

Elmer shook his head. I wondered how Mary Grace must feel about that.

I wended the hundred feet through the white granite monuments to where Maggie's body lay. The soil had settled, leaving a depression. My throat tightened—the rest of the family seemed to have forgotten, although they had all stood at that very place only four years before. I bent and caressed the grass where the earth dimpled above Maggie's dear head. Maggie wasn't there. Of course, she wasn't. Maggie was at peace, far, far away . . .

They all came out to the farm for a dinner later that afternoon. Once again, Blanche had organized the church ladies on short notice to prepare a spread, and Gertrude brought a bowl of coleslaw. I heard Elmer ask Earl to join us at the Tyrone house the next day.

What was that about? Oh yes, Mary Grace would be alone. No way could she handle John's three youngest. I dreaded going out there . . . to the house we and Maggie had struggled so mightily to get for them. I wondered why Kenny and Tommy hadn't shown up, but respect had never been their long suit.

ை

Mid-morning the day after the funeral, Earl and Gertrude pulled in just behind us at the Tyrone house. No one appeared outside to greet us as we stepped onto the front porch. Over in the next block, a Model A cranked up and roared off into the distance.

Elmer opened the door and we followed. Mary Grace stared at us from the kitchen, as if in a daze. John's three youngest children stood bunched in a tight knot at their bedroom door, silent, watching us. How strange.

"GET OUT OF HERE!"

A man shouting. As one, we whirled toward the source—the main bedroom door to our left. A muscular figure charged across the room and crashed onto Earl, knocking him against the wall. He staggered and almost went down. A grotesque expression on the attacker's face—Bill, John's son.

I tried to comprehend—what was happening? Why?

The living room churned with erratic movement. Earl bounced off the wall, leading with a forearm jab. One foot caught Bill in the groin and he doubled over. The impact caused Earl to stumble.

I pushed my boys against the wall behind me. Elmer spread his arms in front of us, gaping in shock. A whirlwind of arms, elbows and knees sent chairs flying.

Bill's siblings began chanting, "It's our house! It's our house! Leave our house!"

Grappling and spinning, the two fought for advantage. Surprisingly, few punches were thrown. Bill had Earl in a headlock but couldn't hold it.

Earl—fully four inches shorter and twice the age of the young bull—showed a grittiness and strength that silenced the kids. With a quick reverse, he had Bill in a half nelson. From behind, he grabbed Bill's nose with the strong fingers of a man who earned his living working with steel. Earl twisted down, gasping, "Give!

Do you give up, are you gonna give—?"

The younger man fought for control but then lost it entirely. A dark stain spread across the front of his tan trousers. He let out a strangled cry, and then a desperate exclamation. "Yes! Give! I give!"

Earl held the punishing hold a few seconds longer. He released Bill and leaned against the wall, breathing like a machine. With a curse, he rasped, "Get . . . out . . . Get out . . . of here and don't you come back . . ."

The brawl took no more than two or three minutes, but it seemed to have lasted an hour.

Bill, crushed in defeat, seemed to melt away. Joyce, Phyllis, and Corky retreated into the darkness of the bedroom.

Gertrude fussed over Earl. Still puffing, he gave a wry grin. "It's been a long time since I was jumped like that, but when it's happened to you onced, you kinda go on instinct. If you don't, you're gonna get your plow cleaned." He gingerly touched his bruised anatomy. "Young hellion! I shoulda tied him in a knot and hung him on the clothesline."

Elmer's voice had an uncharacteristic tremor. "Bill thought he was going to take over. As if he could've kept it! Even if he'd whipped you and then me, too, I'd've had the sheriff in here. Such a young fool! He plotted all this at the funeral yesterday . . . I'll bet Kenny and Tommy probably were in on it, too, but they chickened out . . . Young coyotes . . ."

Humiliation hit me. I dashed to the west window, peering at Grice's house across the street. They had surely heard the commotion. My sense of relief vanished in a flame of embarrassment. They'd think our family was a bunch of savages.

Mary Grace seemed in a near state of shock. She needed custodial care. I shook my head, knowing what that meant.

Elmer motioned for Earl to come outside, and we headed out, too. Got the kids in the car and told them to stay there. We four adults clustered on the porch.

Thankfully, Elmer already had a plan. He gestured toward the front door. "I'm not going to leave this house for those buzzards. This little farce shows I've been patient long enough. As soon as we get everyone cleared out, I'm going to padlock the place."

Earl winced as Gertrude dabbed at his face. Through swollen lips, he said, "I got a request. One request. I'm gonna read John the riot act. He knew all about this! He'll say he never heard

174

anything about the plot, but you can bet your bottom dollar he knew it was a-comin'. I know where to find him, and you better believe he'll have his kids outta here by Wednesday morning. I didn't take these lumps for nothin', and we better settle it before those other snot-noses try to come in here and take over."

All settled—John would have to find a place for his kids, and Mary Grace would again come to live with her two sons. My chest tightened; was there no other recourse?

One thing was clear. The past few days had turned our world on its ear—once again.

25 Care of Mother and Son

Sammy

Daddy said things were going to be different around our house after Grandpa died. Grandma was coming to live with us, and he expected us boys to behave and help her feel at home. We thought that would be fun 'cause she always seemed so glad to see us when we went to visit her and Grandpa.

When she moved in, Dickie, Jerry, and I had to crowd into the back bedroom. A difference, you betcha. I knew that would be trouble. I'd have to find safe places for my things. It was hard enough to keep my younger brothers from messing up my stamp collection when I had it laid out on the table. Even before Grandma came, Jerry had taken my rock collection outside when Dickie and I were at school, and I never did find all my pretty rocks and pieces of flint. He'd gotten into my marbles and Dickie's too and had scattered them to kingdom come. We told Mama but she said we'd have to put our stuff up. After all, Jerry was just playing, and he was only six years old. So what can you expect? Yeah, a lot of good that did me.

I didn't know where to stash my watercolor paints and brushes, colored pencils, and drawing paper. Finally, Mama let me have a secret drawer in the buffet where I could hide them from my brothers.

The change became a bigger aggravation after bedtime. Being in the same bed as Dickie seemed more like trying to sleep with a sack of snakes. He must've had nightmares, squirming and kicking besides. It did no good to tell him to stop; yelling just woke Jerry up. Then he'd start howling. That brought Mama into the bedroom, wanting to know what was going on and telling us to quiet down or we'd wake up Grandma, in the bedroom next to ours.

About then, Grandma would poke her head in the door, saying she couldn't sleep with all the commotion. Mama tried to be polite to Grandma. She'd apologize and tell Grandma she had things under control and would she just go back to her room.

Then Mama had to get Jerry settled down, which usually took a while. I couldn't go back to sleep because I knew what was coming next—a whispered lecture from Mama. Every time I tried to explain, she hissed, "Hush! It's the middle of the night. Get to sleep, and stop sulking."

So unfair. And I wasn't sulking; I was trying to right a wrong. Before it ended, the whole house would be in an uproar. What was really unfair—Dickie never woke up, and it was all his fault.

I decided if I ever had kids, I'd treat them with respect, and I'd make sure the guilty one got punished.

Pretty often, instead of going back to sleep, Grandma decided she needed something in the kitchen, which was right next to Mama and Daddy's bedroom. I could hear her rattling pots and talking to herself while I was trying to get to sleep.

Grandma messing around in the kitchen set Mama's teeth on edge, regardless the time of day. She said Grandma wanted to rule a kitchen that wasn't hers. Grandma's midnight clatter jacked up Mama's stress level. I would've told her she could solve the whole problem by making Dickie stop kicking like a bay steer. I never did, though, because after one of those night sessions, Mama wasn't in any mood to listen to my suggestions the next morning.

Summer was the best time of year for us boys. It meant we could go without shoes and shirts—except of course when we went to town or to church. Our neighbor Lew Buffalow said we looked brown as Indians, which made us feel proud. Being an Indian or a mountain man was just about the best thing a boy could be.

Not long after Grandpa died, we boys realized Grandma wasn't the same person we knew at her house in Tyrone. Grouchy, I guess. Didn't take much to set her off. Mama reminded us that for the first time in sixty-one years, Grandma had to face life without Grandpa.

Grandma didn't seem to notice us much, either. Lots of times, she just sat in the rocker the whole day, not even braiding rugs. I heard Mama talking with Daddy about how she was acting, but they stopped talking when they saw us boys listening.

We didn't need to hear everything, anyway, so we went outside, Jerry trailing behind. Dickie had been watching wild birds around our farm, and he convinced me there might be a late hatch of kingbirds in a nest far up in the big pear tree. Okay. So we climbed twenty feet or more up that tree, trying to see into the nest. He was more of a daredevil than me, so I let him go first.

Finally, tired out and unable to discover any baby bird life, we descended the old monster and went back to the house. Maybe Mama had something baking. There was a good chance she did, 'cause Jerry had disappeared. Dickie was the best climber, but neither of us was as good as our little brother at being at the right spot when Mama pulled goodies out of the oven.

Nothing going on in Mama's kitchen, so we went into the living room to see if Grandma was in a mood to talk.

She was. Out of the blue, she said, "You boys hadn't oughta be coming into someone else's house without a shirt on. And no shoes either. Don't you have no manners?"

Dickie and I looked at one another. We didn't know what to say. What was she talking about? We knew better than to sass Grandma. Anything coming from a ten- or an eight-year-old could be considered sassing, so we got our shoes and shirts and left without a word. I thought maybe we didn't hear her right.

A couple days later, a hard wind ended our game of marbles out by the windmill. All three of us boys trooped in, shirtless and shoeless, innocent as lambs. Or at least as innocent as goats. Dickie and I set our sacks of marbles down and, using a long bootstring, we marked out a ring for playing marbles on the floor. Then I looked up to see Grandma frowning at us.

"There you go again, you boys," she barked. "Coming into somebody else's house with hardly a stitch of clothes on. Why, that's shameful."

Dickie must've forgot kids were always supposed to be polite to Grandma. He said, "But Grandma, this is our house. It ain't nobody else's—"

"It is too. This is Elmer and Claire's house, and I believe they'd think rather poorly of you boys coming into their house half-nakkid." She usually said nekked, but pronouncing it nakkid meant she was really upset.

Dickie wasn't scared of Grandma. He said, "Yeah, Grandma, it is Elmer and Claire's house. And it's our house too. So that's why we're gonna take our shoes and shirts—"

"No, it's the other Elmer and Claire's house. Don't argue. I know what I'm talking about. It's not your Elmer and Claire."

"The other . . .?" Dickie didn't know what to say.

I sure didn't. But I knew what to do. We had to tell Mama. "C-

Come on, Dickie." As we left the living room and went through the dining room, I hollered, "Jerry, you leave those marbles alone!"

Mama looked up from ironing clothes as we came into the kitchen. "You boys letting Jerry play with you?"

Dickie started to say something but looked at me instead. I said, "Mama, Grandma . . . sh-she thinks there are t-two of you and Daddy. She says this house belongs to . . . the other—"

"What are you talking about?" She set the iron back on the stove and eased into a chair. She kept her voice low. "Boys, sit down. Now what is it about Grandma? What's this all about?"

Dickie blurted, "Grandma says we can't come in here without shirts and shoes 'cause we're in somebody else's house and we shouldn't be like a bunch of savages and—"

"Slow down," she hissed. "Sammy, tell me what's going on."

I explained everything until Mama understood.

She said, "Okay boys, I'll talk to Daddy about this, and we'll handle it. If Grandma complains . . . says anything about this again, I want you to come and tell me right away. No back talk to Grandma, you hear?"

We hurried back into the living room in time to see several marbles roll across the linoleum and under the divan. Grandma sat in the rocker, her mouth open like she was about to bawl us out again. Thankfully, her eyes were closed.

Dickie said something about getting the marbles. Then he tiptoed out to get the broom.

Mama said Daddy had a long talk with Grandma. After that, Grandma never said anymore about our house or what we should do. Mama told us Grandma's mind had been slipping a little but maybe she would get better. She said we shouldn't ever talk back to Grandma but only do what she or Daddy told us to do.

Grandma never did get better, and I wished we could've talked together, like we used to over at their house in Tyrone. Once in a while, Daddy would carry her out to the sandy hillock north of the house, so she could enjoy the summer night when we'd sit out there and look at all the stars like we used to do.

On quiet evenings with no wind, Mama would tell a story. Stories of when she was a girl. We loved those times.

Jerry always asked Grandma if she had a story, and she didn't say anything. Then one particular evening, as the sky skipped with rainbow colors playing hopscotch across the west, Grandma perked up and started talking about when she was a girl. We all edged in closer; even Daddy leaned in. Thoughtful Jerry helped pull her shawl over her shoulders and she began: "Yessir, our family name was Haworth. I was right proud of that name. Born and raised on a farm near Kokomo, Indiana. We used to go to barn dances when I was a girl. Elmer, that was before I met your dad.

"I always liked to do the schottische, and I was good, even if I do say so myself. Anyways, some girl I'd never seen before showed up at one of the dances. I could tell right away she musta thought she was something special. She had red hair like you never seen before, and it was heaped up on her head like she flung it up there with a pitchfork. What a sight.

"Directly, she come over where we was and started making fun of my name. How she learned it I never knew. But she was making a nuisance of herself. I couldn't believe it. Then she says, 'Hay-worth, huh? So, how much is hay-worth tonight?'

"So I told her. I put my hands on my hips and I said, 'It's worth more than that red straw you've got piled up on your head.'

"She backed up like she was snake-bit. Never said another word. Tickled me pink. I put her in her place, for sure."

Grandma sat, her head nodding like she was reliving the whole story all over again. With barely a smile, she pursed her lips for a long time, nodding her head all the while. Now and then, she uttered a little sound, kind of like when the chickens are settling down for the night.

I wished I could've seen what she was seeing, but I knew I never could.

We boys asked her to tell us more, but that was all she said. I could tell she was thinking about things, though. By then, it was getting nearly dark. Sheet lightning flashed across the eastern sky, and we saw Bill Kizer's silo and windmill silhouetted against the sky.

Daddy picked Grandma up and took her back in the house. That was the last time she went with us out to watch the stars.

❧ *Fall 1950* ☙

Then Daddy got sick, and we began worrying more about him than Grandma.

The sore in Daddy's mouth wouldn't heal, and I could tell

Mama was worried after the doctor in Liberal looked at him. So Ray's sister Amy came from Denver to stay with us boys. I hated to think of Mama leaving us, but we knew she had to.

Amy stood with us boys at the front door as we saw Mama and Daddy back out of our driveway and head north, going to Wichita for Daddy's operation. I watched until our Chrysler was out of sight. I felt sick to my stomach, like when I was homesick during the big blizzard. I wondered if Dickie and Jerry felt like me, but they headed back into the living room and began playing marbles.

Amy was nice, and she said she loved us boys. I believed she did, and she always had good meals ready for us when we came home from school. My brothers didn't talk about being lonely, but I could tell. We all missed Mama and Daddy so much.

Finally, Uncle Earl and Gertrude took us boys to see Mama and Daddy in Wichita at the hospital. We all hugged her and she was crying when she said she missed us. Then she took us in the elevator up to the room where Daddy was. He couldn't say anything because his mouth was so sore where they'd operated to get the cancer.

Mama took us past the taxi stand and pharmacy to her apartment down the street from Wesley Hospital. She said we could stay with her until Daddy could go back home. Then she took us to a little café and we each had a hamburger, a cheeseburger, and a malt. It was so good to be with Mama, even without the food.

26 The Waiting Time

Claire

Elmer and I were home at last, together with our dear boys. It seemed we'd been in Wichita for eight months, instead of eight days. The staff and surgeons at Wesley Hospital were positive and knowledgeable, always talking hope and confidence. They had done their best for him, and with the prayers of family and friends in our church and community, all we had to do was wait.

Wait for Elmer's body to overcome the shock of taking a piece from the roof of his mouth. Then begin the process of healing.

They'd warned me Elmer would be in deep pain. Everything hurt him so much. Eating was an ordeal, regardless of the variety of broths, soups, and puddings I prepared. He had difficulty talking, and at night, he whispered that breathing felt like swallowing flaming razor blades. Sleep came only when he was too exhausted to remain awake.

I suffered as well, watching the man I loved hurt so much that it took over his existence. There seemed nothing I could do to help him regain the spring to his step.

Doctor Hilbig at Medical Arts Clinic in Liberal scheduled biweekly checkups to monitor Elmer's progress, and to help him deal with the pain. Most frustrating though, at the end of each appointment, the doctor said we should see improvement the next time we came in. But it never happened.

After Elmer's first examination, Hilbig pulled me aside as a nurse pushed Elmer's wheelchair toward the clinic entrance. "I couldn't have wished for a better doctor than Doctor Melancamp for Elmer's surgery. He's simply the best. But I must tell you, the malignancy was well advanced. His—"

"You're saying there's no hope?" Before I could stop, my voice betrayed the nightmare of dread churning within me. It spilled like vomit upon my fragile fabric of faith. I wanted to scream.

He stepped forward, his voice an even-toned counterpoint to my fear and doubt. "Not at all, Claire. Just to say, Elmer has a long, hard road ahead of him. The speed of his recovery will depend on his ability to overcome fatigue and the shock to his system. He won't feel like eating. You've got to make sure he does." He waited for my assent. "We'll continue to medicate him for pain, but within limits, of course."

"What do you mean? Can't you control it?" There it was again—despair asserting itself.

"I'm sorry. Not completely. Too much morphine, for too long, brings the danger of addiction."

"So he'll have to get over it on his own?" I took a tissue one of the nurses thrust into my hand and pressed it against tears streaming down my face.

"I'm afraid so." He dropped his eyes, then returned to his upbeat manner. "As I told Elmer, the swelling and occasional drainage should lessen shortly. He's not a sedentary man. Probably hates the idea of using a wheelchair, even to move about this clinic. Mild exercise will prevent clots and facilitate healing."

I had tried to prepare myself so I could best help Elmer recover. In those few moments, my helplessness and craven fear, punched a hole in that façade. Unless I got myself together, I'd be more hindrance than help.

Putting a lilt to my voice, I said, "Come on, big boy, we're going home. I'll fix you that homemade soup that's better than what your mama used to make." I held the car door open as the nurse, a heavyset brunette, helped him into the passenger seat.

As I drove us back to the farm, I tried to mimic Doctor Hilbig's cheerful optimism, but Elmer wasn't fooled.

"I saw the doc talking to you. What's he keeping from me?"

I glanced over at him and sighed. "He said we got a rough road ahead, as you have an aggressive form of cancer. But he said they wouldn't even bother treating you if you didn't have a fighting chance—"

"Yeah, that's what it is—a chance."

"We'll take it, big boy. You can make it, I know." Thinking to divert that line of conversation, I said, "Remember, I told you I called reinforcements—Myrrl and Grace, and my sisters. Ethel and Pearl got their families praying for you. Not to mention my church. Can't do better than that." I reached over and patted his leg. "We've never been through anything like this. But we're going to do it. We're in it together, and we'll come through it together."

He didn't respond. The engine cough of our '41 Chrysler broke the silence as I turned at the state line corner. Should've had

Elmer's brother Earl do his magic on the carburetor.

ഹ~ൈ

Once we returned home, I had to face another reality. I had to run the farm until Elmer regained his health.

If he regained his health. I tried not to think of that . . . But the thought remained, an unrelenting dragon lurking behind whispered questions and unnecessary disagreements. Cancer had taken every person we knew afflicted with that dreadful disease. Doctor Hilbig had said, "The best thing you can do is keep a positive attitude. Many people have survived cancer. Otherwise, we wouldn't bother treating Elmer. Don't lose hope . . ."

Would Elmer be one of the "many people who've survived"? We wanted to believe it. Wishing wouldn't make it so. Hilbig hadn't given us names of cancer survivors. I could only think of Maggie, forced to see a quack up at Halstead because she couldn't afford a specialist in Wichita. I wasn't sure our team of specialists promised any greater chance of survival than Maggie's witch doctor. We went in regularly, but the hoped-for healing proved as evasive as midsummer rains.

Elmer had always been the one in charge, from when I first met him working on the Deluxe sales crew. Always a half step ahead of the other crew bosses, he viewed problems as opportunities. That was when he was in his prime. After Wichita, he was barely maintaining. Eating and sleeping were chores he could barely endure.

But me run the farm? I cringed inside at the thought and tried not to panic. Our modest savings went up in the smoke of Elmer's surgery. A mounting debt at Peoples National Bank—we'd probably tapped our limit . . . Mary Grace still with us, her mind going . . . The fall wheat crop yet to be planted . . . Needed to get things buttoned up for winter; temperatures had dropped to twenty-three below a mere nineteen months before . . . Over it all, I needed to be there for Elmer, and for our precious boys, neglected during the medical siege at Wichita. Not actually neglected, Amy looked after them. But it was still too much.

How could I do all that needed to be done?

I wanted to cry. I did cry. One brisk evening after supper, I left Elmer resting in our bedroom and the boys and Mary Grace in the living room. I grabbed my sweater and quietly slipped outside. Awash in tears by the time I got to our sandy hillock north of the well house, I dropped to my knees.

A furry form thrust itself against me. Shep. As if he knew. I cried aloud to the darkling clouds, "God, don't you see this is too much? I'm on the verge of losing my husband because of this cancer and WHAT WILL I DO? And our boys, they need their daddy . . ."

For a long time, I raged and wept and then prayed. Gently aware of a change, I sensed I wasn't alone. Calmly, I began listing my register of fears, needs, doubts, and cares to Jesus. Assured of his presence in that sanctified time, I laid out the insane possibilities that had haunted my midnight hours.

He listened. He heard me. A sense of peace covered me like a mantle. By then it was nearly dark, and I knew I'd be missed. Not wanting to alarm the family, I arose, Shep beside me in the dim light, and made my way back to the house.

ᔕᕽᕽᔕ

The very next month, cousin Ray and neighbor Edwin Eagan came over to plant fall wheat. They had already cut and bound the cane that Elmer had planted months before. I remembered Pop saying: Noble acts prove themselves when we need them most.

When Elmer heard about the planting mission, he voiced an unusual request: "Claire, I don't mind them helping us. I'd do the same. Just tell them I want to watch while they're doing it. Not that I doubt they'd do it right. I just want to have a . . . some sense of involvement in running the farm. Ray'll understand."

I went outside to tell Ray when they brought their equipment over. He said, "No need to explain, Claire. Why don't I come in and have another word with Elmer?"

"Good idea. He's sitting at the table."

He followed me back to the house and stuck his head in the front door. "Hey, Elmer. Claire tells me you want to watch two experts in action." He gave a wide grin.

Elmer waved back at him. "You guys only do as much as you want to. If I wasn't tied to this chair . . ."

"It won't take long. We're glad to help. Claire says she'll drive you over to the field. You can watch all day if you like. Edwin wants to break in his new drill. He won't take offense, and you know I won't. Once he gets a-going, I'll come back over and take a look at your herd. Might want to sell three or four yearling steers. I'll check back with you in a day or two."

185

It seemed every time Elmer had a down day, Ray stopped by to see him, keeping his visits short so as not to tire him out. Edwin hired two high school boys to shock the cane bundles for winter feed. When I thrust two twenties at him, he declined, declaring it was too much and he'd square accounts later. Thank God for good neighbors.

I reminded Elmer about his mother. He'd forgotten her mental confusion and outbursts of anger. Though physically strong, she was easily upset and suspicious of what we were going to do with her. But we had to do something.

With Elmer's assent, I asked Ray to call Earl and have him come and get Mary Grace. Thankfully, Earl showed up the following weekend. After seeing Elmer's condition, he dutifully gathered Mary Grace's old suitcase and pasteboard boxes. Just another chapter of taking their mother to live with him as long as needed. He probably suspected it might be a long time. Of the four adults sitting around our table that morning, he was the only one not needing survival treatment of some sort.

ふ

Fall turned to winter as we kept our appointments at the clinic. Hilbig went through the same ritual each time—a pep talk as he greeted us, followed by occasional blood work, questions about fatigue, elimination problems, trouble sleeping, or weight gain or loss. He asked Elmer what seemed silly questions; then I realized he was checking his memory and ability to concentrate. Elmer passed those tests every time.

I tried not to burden Elmer with concerns about the farm. Sometimes, it couldn't be avoided. I needed his direction. Right after New Year's, I told him we had to see if Chet Naylor would back us through Elmer's recovery. If not . . .

The boys had gone to school, excited to be playing basketball again after the holidays. With only twenty-five kids in school, Sammy and Dickie both played on the team. Elmer settled into his cushioned chair at the kitchen table as if poured there. Slackness in his face and arms betrayed his fatigue.

I intended to be calm but failed miserably. "This scares me, Elmer. I need you with me to make these decisions. I don't mind talking to Naylor—or anyone else at that bank. But we've got to keep the farm running. Will he want me to sell more livestock? I—"

"Now, look at you. You're my gal. Tough Tess." He moved his arm across my shoulders. "You walk in there like you belong. You're representing not just yourself, but the boys and me. Not to mention the hopes of every farmer who put a plow to this godforsaken land. Chet Naylor wouldn't have a job if he didn't extend credit to farmers when they really needed it." He paused to catch his breath. "People's National Bank wouldn't exist if they failed to stand behind folks when the going got tough. Right now, it's tougher than a pine biscuit for us, and we need them to do their part. You go in there just like you did with Deluxe and sell to those big shots behind their shiny maple desks."

Elmer gave me what I needed, a reminder of who I was and what I represented. I went to Liberal midweek with specifics in mind: planning for the next crop year, if and when to sell livestock. Even which cows we'd sell. Chet Naylor listened to it all. When I was done, he gave us what I asked for. I had to sign a loan extension, but it was the right thing to do.

As I gathered my purse and notes I'd prepared to make my case, Naylor asked about Elmer. I sensed he genuinely liked my husband. Maybe I was trying to put a good face on it, but I felt he really cared—not just about whether his bank would recover our indebtedness, but whether Elmer would recover from a disease that could fell anyone.

Afterward, I stopped by the clinic to make a payment on our balance. Doctor Hilbig beckoned me into his office. My body seemed gripped by paralysis. Whatever he had to say, I didn't want to hear it.

Not meeting my eyes, he gestured me to a chair. "Didn't expect to see you, Claire. I was just going to call your neighbor—Ray Hunter, I believe—so they could relay the message to you. Umm, we just got results from the lab tests from your last visit . . ."

My mind practically shut down as Doctor Hilbig reviewed what I had already rehearsed in my imagination. Lymph nodes in Elmer's neck were shown to contain new malignancies. To reduce the chance that cancer might return in the future, he said it would be prudent to completely remove the afflicted areas.

He paused from time to time, patiently waiting for my weeping to subside. When I was able to concentrate and listen, he said he'd already contacted Doctor Melancamp in Wichita. They'd be ready for us and had scheduled surgery the following Monday.

27 Hope and Faith

January 1951

Claire

The second morning after Elmer's surgery bloomed bright and fresh as I left the hotel across from Wesley Hospital. The gurgling fountain at the hospital entrance reminded me of renewal that comes with every spring. Was I foolish to hope? That day, Doctor Melancamp would tell us.

Only one possibility—Elmer's recovery—would justify my hope.

Recovery. Such a magical word. To be able to go back to what was, the way things used to be. The way they should be. Skills of the surgical team and God's healing power had been deployed to vanquish cancer, the adversary.

I tried not to think of such things as the nurses attended to Elmer. My breath caught when I first caught sight of him. His neck and jaw swathed in gauze and tape, hoses and monitors draped over and around him. I touched his hand, unable to stop the tears, springtime and gurgling fountain forgotten.

Doctor Melancamp arrived, unnoticed by me at first. The nurses fled, and we directed our attention to the surgeon, who pulled a chair up within Elmer's line of vision, opposite me. Speaking a few words of assurance to Elmer, he then engaged both of us.

I tried to remember all he said, about his confidence in their efforts, but time alone would tell if the surgery was successful. He reached forward, touching the side of Elmer's face. I held my breath as the doctor continued, "Other than massive excision that might permanently affect your quality of life, Elmer, there is one other option. We could use radiation to—"

"Absolutely not!" I barked at the esteemed physician, and he drew back, his eyes wide. "I'm sorry . . . sorry, Doctor Melancamp. You see, Elmer's sister—his only sister—was diagnosed with uterine cancer, and they . . . her husband . . . took her to that place north of here, to Halstead. I'm sure you've heard of that quack. He literally burned up her insides, Doctor Melancamp. Maggie died a painful death. I wouldn't wish that upon anyone . . ."

The doctor waited for me to run down, his face mournful. "I understand. Unfortunately, while significant advancements are currently underway at other institutions—Johns Hopkins, the Mayo Clinic—in the use of radiation for cancer treatment, it is not as simple or easy to control in every case. Indeed, there's the risk of damaging adjacent tissue and organs. Despite the inherent dangers, I simply wanted you to be aware of that option." He stopped. "I'm so sorry . . . about your loss . . . the grief and pain you must feel over her—Maggie, you said? Very sorry. Please consider that as not an option."

He closed his visit by announcing that after two additional days of recovery, Elmer should go directly to our hospital in Liberal. He would give specific instructions to Dr. Hilbig regarding daily monitoring of Elmer's condition for a two-week period. Dr. Melancamp said that would be sufficient time to determine the success of the surgery, and what measures should follow.

I called Hunters to have someone come for us. Ray answered, saying Elmer's brother Earl had already volunteered. He chose to come for his big brother. That hadn't mattered before, but now Elmer, the protector of the family, needed help. This showed a different side of Earl to me. I pondered that he hadn't backed off when Bill ambushed him at the Tyrone house. He had fought Bill like a wild animal—like he was defending Elmer even then. There was certainly more to Earl than what I had thought.

The first week after our return, the preacher and his wife stopped in to see Elmer at Epworth Hospital. I met them in the lobby just as they were leaving. After greetings, we went to a nearby sitting area to talk.

Brother Caywood said, "I'll be coming back to see Elmer. We had a good talk." He pulled a bulging envelope from his coat pocket. "Glad you showed up, Claire. Some of our church men— George Eagan, Henry Ausmus, Cliff Wakefield, and others—they got together and, well, they collected enough money to extend the telephone line to your house."

I swiped the tears running down my cheeks. "Such dear people. This means so much . . . We've really needed a phone."

"Claire, the people in our community think a lot of you and Elmer and your boys. Henry and Blanche are providing a telephone. We've confirmed the complete cost with Billy Bob. There's enough money left over—it's all here in this envelope—to pay for wiring and plumbing your house."

I tried to absorb all that information "Did you tell Elmer about this?"

"No, I thought you'd want to do that." He handed me the envelope as they arose to go.

"Yes, I will. Thank you . . . Such wonderful people." I hugged them both.

After they left, I lay beside Elmer, half-on and half-off the edge of the bed. I caressed his forehead, his face, and his lips. Then I held the list out at arm's length and read off the names of all the people who'd contributed, starting with Mrs. Ratlief's widow's mite.

On the sixth day, Doctor Hilbig intercepted me as I emerged from the second-floor elevator. He wanted to talk to me—alone.

This couldn't be good. On the verge of collapse, I let Nurse Dorothy steer me into an unoccupied room off the nurses' station. Doctor Hilbig followed us in and allowed me to have my cry, Dorothy's arm around my shoulders. Somehow, I got myself together. Dorothy and Imogene on each side, I sleep-walked to Elmer's room.

Deep breath. Straightening my shoulders, I went to Elmer. I swept aside the medical paraphernalia and gazed down at him. He looked back, knowing something was up.

"Honey," I said. "Doctor Hilbig wants to talk to us. He's here now. Is this an okay time?"

Elmer clutched my arm and pulled my face down close to his. He ran his right hand up my arm and neck, up the side of my jaw and to the corner of my left eye. He whispered, "Got a tear right there, sweetheart. Better wipe that off . . . else I'll think you're . . . you're not happy to see . . . see me."

It was too much. I was a blubbering mess for minutes. My arm swept out to pull a chair beside the bed and I settled into it. Gently, I pushed my fingers through the beautiful gray curls that matted his forehead.

The good doctor told us what we'd individually steeled

ourselves to hear. The medical establishment had done all it could. Which was not enough. He told us that Elmer had three, perhaps four months, and that he'd recommend I take him home . . . for our family to be together.

Already January, that meant April or May.

✎ *Spring 1951* ✎

In the corroded days and weeks following Elmer's return to our farm, neighbors strung the telephone line from Bill and Pearl Kizer's place, east of us. Paul Teverbaugh dug a septic tank and installed the plumbing fixtures that we never seemed to have the money to buy.

At long last, the REA extended power to our house and I brought out the little table lamp I'd gotten in Colorado Springs. I set it on the nightstand next to Elmer's bed where it glowed against the darkness that threatened to defeat all light. I got a list of those who had given even five dollars for the expenses. I'd send every one a thank-you card. Then I'd pay them back—to the dollar.

A squad of helpers—dear neighbor men—took turns sitting by Elmer's bedside each night. When fever overtook him, they lifted a glass of water to his trembling lips or placed cool compresses on his forehead to lessen the pain. Mostly, they came into the solemn house to assure me I wouldn't have to go through this trial alone.

One April afternoon, Elmer whispered to me. "Honey, can you telephone the preacher? I'd like to talk with him."

"Right away?"

"Yes, if he can come out now."

The boys and I were at the supper table when Brother Caywood knocked on our door. He smiled and greeted the boys by name, then followed me into the darkening bedroom. He bent and squeezed Elmer's hand. "Hello, Elmer, it's Elzay Caywood. I'm glad you called me. Do you want Claire to stay while we talk?"

"No, she can finish her supper."

I sat at the table with the boys. From eleven-year-old Sammy to Jerry, who'd just turned seven, they quieted. Only the occasional chink of utensils on plates broke the tide of silence. From the bedroom, Elmer's voice seemed barren and far-away. I could hear only his low-toned words, ragged with pain and fatigue, but it was evident he had made some sort of request.

Brother Caywood's mellow baritone responded, compelling and encouraging. "Let me explain, Elmer, what God has done for you. First of all, he loved you. He loved me, too. We're both sinners, you know." A deprecating chuckle—then the preacher's voice calmed to a personal intimacy, like two friends sharing.

I strained to hear, and got the pastor's words in short volleys: ". . . all born in sin . . . our very nature . . . But God loves us so much . . . forgives us . . . things you said you've done . . . accept his greatest gift . . . Jesus. Jesus, and him alone."

Elmer said something I couldn't quite hear. Brother Caywood's voice: ". . . trust . . . we're adopted . . . You understand and believe?"

Elmer's response came only loud enough for me to know he'd spoken. The preacher, and another inaudible response. I resisted the urge to jump up and go into the bedroom.

Almost too quiet. What were they saying? Another question, which was followed by an overview of creation and the fall of man. The preacher stopped. I heard a soft smack, as of pages of his Bible falling closed.

My pastor emerged from the room. Quiet, as if in awe, he said, "The angels in heaven are rejoicing. Elmer is part of God's family now. He's very tired, so I'll go now. I realize I'm weary, too—it's like I've taken part in a mighty struggle. Please call me, Claire—even at a moment's notice—when you need me."

Sammy

Thursday morning came warm and clear. Only a faint wind, and the unexpected rain of a few days before had left a warm blanket over the prairie. Already mid-June, well past time to put in the milo, but with Daddy as sick as he was, Mama said she couldn't think about it.

We'd just gotten finished with breakfast when we heard the sound of tractors—many tractors, much bigger than our little Ford—outside our house. But those tractors were not going past; a whole line of them had pulled up in front of our house. A knock on the door made me jump. Edwin Eagan came in; he told Mama that "a few of the neighbors had gotten together, and we're here to put the row crop in."

Mama didn't know what to say. Finally, she said thank you.

I was glad. It had seemed like we had fought a battle all by ourselves. Mama said it wasn't true—several neighbors had been sitting up through the night with Dad. I guessed they were on our side all the way.

Edwin went back out and waved the farmers in—Ray Clapp, Kenneth Taylor, Reuel Rushton, Charlie Ausmus, and Lawrence Emrie. Then they scattered. Every place that didn't have wheat or pasture, they planted—all in half a day.

Claire

Doctor Hilbig came out that afternoon, leaving whispered instructions for Edwin and Ray, who stood in the yard like guards before a king's court.

I went in to Elmer, told him he didn't need to worry about the planting anymore, that it was done. The doctor beckoned me out of the bedroom after he'd gone in to look at Elmer. He parsed his words, enunciating them as if pulling a butterfly from a spider web. He said Elmer's systems were near collapse. I spun around and returned beside the man I loved. I caressed his forehead, hot with fever, and then touched both sides of his face, now meager and stricken.

Elmer quivered in an outbreak of pain, which startled me. In the still afternoon light, I saw moisture glistening on his face and realized it was my own tears. I touched his forehead, hot with fever, and then both sides of his face.

Despite my resolve, I slumped beside the bed on my knees, both hands clinging to his right arm, and broke down in uncontrollable sobbing.

"No, Claire," he whispered, lifting his free arm like a feeble flag, "I'll be . . . with . . . . Jesus."

Elmer's words penetrated, and with an effort, I choked off my tears and caught my breath to listen. Elmer seemed to be drawing all his resources to say more. "I know . . . I'll see Jesus . . . Last night, I saw . . ." A faint gesture toward the foot of the bed, then he dropped his arm, exhausted.

I waited, scarcely breathing as I watched his face. He opened his eyes as if asking me to do something. Then I understood and carefully kissed his lips so as not to impede his breathing.

Sammy

At twenty after nine that evening, Ray and Edith came in where us boys were sleeping. Edith woke us up, and led us into the kitchen, bright with harsh light. Mama was with Daddy, but she came out in the kitchen and threw her arms around us.

We went in where Daddy was. Instead of someone telling us

to be quiet, Mama told us to say good-bye to Daddy. We each hugged him, easy like. He had hurt so much, but then he seemed not to notice. Our daddy was past help. Our family was in ruins. Without my daddy, what would happen to us?

He tried to say something. I thought he would smile, but he couldn't. He couldn't say anything.

Mama put her arms around all of us, and we had a big cry. Edith took us back to bed. I fell asleep almost at once.

Claire

Thirty minutes later, on the fourteenth of June, 1951, Ray reached across Elmer's bed. He made a choking sound and quietly pulled the white sheet over the face of his cousin, his friend, his brother. The father of my sons, the man I could not live without.

28 The Hardest Day

Sammy

Daddy was gone. I was numb, expecting that some way, someone would step in and stop the awful emergency from coming true. Eleven was too young for me to lose my daddy. For Dickie, two years younger, and seven-year-old Jerry, it was even worse. All our lives, we'd had Daddy, and then we didn't. We were left only with memories of him, and black and white pictures propped on the top shelf of Mama's buffet.

Mama said that sometime in that hopeless night while we boys slept, an ambulance had carried Daddy away to the undertakers in Liberal.

Blanche Ausmus and Ray's sister Amy showed up as if they'd been hovering to jump in and help. Without anyone telling them what to do, they began washing everything in the room where Daddy had spent the last five months of his life.

Mama was already on the wall phone, cranking the operator to call her relatives up in Kansas and back in Ohio, notifying Daddy's kin in Kansas City and Durward, down in Texas. "Yes, at ten till ten last night . . . Yes, yes . . . Thank you. We understand . . . Services will be Sunday at three o'clock at the Forgan Baptist Church . . . No, but you are invited to the dinner at our house that day . . ."

By the time she got near the bottom of her list, some voiced surprise that Daddy had lasted beyond the first day of spring, as if he shouldn't have prolonged the agony of their suspense. A few—not even shirttail relatives—questioned Mama for not subjecting him to radiation treatments, the kind that burnt up Aunt Maggie's insides, or for not sending Daddy to a big clinic back in Minnesota. As if we had that kind of money. Blanche overheard that. She had a tizzy, said some people were like that, ready to criticize anything.

Dickie and Jerry stayed in the kitchen with Mama, but after listening to the same message countless times, I went outside. I headed back of the house, to my private place—the two big spreading locust trees that marked the southeast corner of where the house set.

I scrunched on the ground under a low sweeping branch, where no one could see me—from the road or the house. A rising breeze brushed leafy twigs against my head, like a gentle hand. All I could really think of was that we were alone. It wasn't supposed to happen. No one else I knew had ever lost their daddy. Losing him was losing everything—what he'd been to us, and what he would've been, watching us boys grow up and being our defender. Would Mama be our protector? She wasn't as strong as Daddy.

I leaned back against a low limb and looked up at the popcorn clouds reaching across the sky. So many things Daddy had been— farmer, animal doctor, horse trader, pig seller, cattleman, weatherman, fixer of things big and small. I saw him in my mind's eye—pond fisherman, bird hunter, scout, traveler, salesman, harvest time beer drinker, and always pipe smoker, storyteller and prankster. He'd been a talker . . . I choked up . . . I'd never hear his voice again.

Mama told us that when he was sales boss with Deluxe, no one was as good a dealmaker as Daddy. Like the time I went with him to a school meeting. Everyone got quiet when he stood up to say his piece. He always had an answer for any problem I knew about.

Daddy said you had to be a man of ideals and convictions; that I'd learn more what that meant when I got older. Mama said Daddy proved it by always standing up for the little man. When Daddy told Brother Caywood he accepted Jesus, he said later he wished he hadn't waited so long to do it. He wanted to tell his cousin Ray about Jesus, but by that time, he was too weak.

He made quite a commotion when he spoke out against people using county equipment for their relatives. When I told him that talk embarrassed me at school, he said you had to do the right thing. Daddy called out some people, so they didn't like him. After he found Jesus, Mama said he'd rather talk about the Lord than catch crooked politicians.

Right then, I didn't care about the crooks in Oklahoma City or Kansas City or Washington. I didn't know what we would do without Daddy.

৵৶

Mama said she wished she hadn't scheduled the funeral for Sunday. What did we care? Any day would have been a sad day.

Our house full of company, Mama thanked everyone for coming and for all the food they brought.

Blanche had organized the church ladies just like always. We were about ready to eat dinner when she looked outside. She hollered, "Claire, come over here. Would you look at that?"

The crowd near the front door parted as Ray and Lila Clapp came in. Ray said, "Claire, could your boys come outside? My boys got something for them." He waved behind him.

Mama turned to me. "Sammy, get Dickie and Jerry. Oh, there they are."

We went outside. There stood Everett, grinning at us, and his brothers Jay and Larry. Everett held a squirming black puppy with brown markings on his chin and legs. "Hey, you guys, we got a present for you."

That bundle of fur and energy fell into our arms while Everett explained. Just weaned, the little guy needed a home, and the Clapp boys thought he'd be just right for us.

Right then, we named him Fido. He was just perfect.

Claire

I'd wondered how I was going to get through the day . . . how the boys would manage. That puppy was God's gift to my boys. They were in a different world with their new buddy.

My dear sister Ethel and faithful Myrrl and Grace were such encouragement during that hardest day of my life. I wondered how I'd get through the funeral that afternoon. Grief is a hard taskmaster, but I couldn't let it keep me from watching out for my boys. All the days, the weeks and months I'd devoted to caring for Elmer . . . I now had to dedicate everything to my dear boys. They were all I had, and I was all they had.

Ethel had gotten the boys' clothes ready; she'd made sure their shoes were polished and shirts ironed. Even laid out an extra shirt for each, knowing about accidents and spilled food from when her four boys and three girls had been little.

I hardly recall anything about the funeral service. Blanche told me afterward that Brother Caywood gave the most stirring sermon she ever heard. After the deacons ushered everyone out but the pallbearers, I drew my boys around me, like a mother hen gathers her chicks. The four of us were crying, couldn't stop crying, as we arose to approach the open casket; we must have been such a mess. I didn't care. It was the last time I'd see the face of my beloved Elmer this side of heaven. For a long time, it seemed, we huddled there, our hearts broken.

Aware of Brother Caywood beside us, I ran one of the verses through my mind: *O death, where is thy sting? O grave, where is thy victory? The sting of death is sin; and the strength of sin is the law. But thanks be to God, which giveth us the victory through our Lord Jesus Christ.*

I wanted to believe that. But victory, whatever form it took, seemed as far away as the moon. I felt only the sting of death and sorrow. And my boys, how would I manage for my boys?

I turned toward the back of the church, emptied of the mass of people who had come to bear witness to our loss. Somehow, we would go on. We had to. That was all I knew.

The four of us, still weeping, turned toward the double doors that framed the brightness of that June afternoon. Outside, scores of devoted people waited for us, still as statues in the afternoon heat. Honoring my dear Elmer. Velma Wakefield said people had come from all over Beaver County to our church.

En route to the Liberal cemetery, Sammy counted sixty-two cars behind us on Highway 64 after we turned north at the Turpin wye. Every vehicle we met on the thirty-mile journey pulled off the highway and stopped, showing respect for Elmer.

Myrrl and Grace were our only overnight guests after we returned home. Their kids had gone back to Ness City with Pearl and Lem. Thankfully, the boys had their new puppy.

Exhausted as I was, I wanted Myrrl and Grace to stay with us a long time. Don't leave us alone. I wanted them never to leave but knew that was impossible.

The following morning, Ray and Edith Hunter pulled in behind Myrrl's blue Ford. Edith carried a small basket as they entered. Rather surprising, as she never went to much trouble cooking. After I introduced the two couples, Edith said, "Got a clutch of eggs from our bantams, Claire. Bet you never had such eggs. Being that the eggs are smaller, they got a higher proportion of yolk—makes great omelets."

"Oh. My boys have never eaten an omelet—"

"I'll fix those boys an omelet." Grace had been listening. "That will be fine. In fact, I'll make breakfast for everyone."

"Nah," Ray spoke up. "Edith wanted to help out a little, so we just brung these little eggs." He looked my direction. "Claire, you let us know anytime you need anything." With that, he turned and Edith followed him out, waving at the boys with their new puppy.

Grace set about preparing breakfast. The boys weren't too sure about the omelet. For a change, I was glad someone else was at the controls of my kitchen. Afterward, the boys went outside to play with their pet. I poured a round of coffee and sat at the kitchen table with those two favorite people in my life.

Myrrl kept clearing his throat. I looked at him, waiting. Finally, he said, "Well, little sister, what are your plans for the future?"

I arose and gathered the basket of sympathy cards from the top of my piano. "First, I'm going to answer all the cards from the wonderful people who blessed us all these months. The ones who prepared meals and sat up with Elmer, those who helped get our phone line in and paid for the plumbing. Look at this—there must be a hundred and fifty cards here, not to mention those who signed the guest books."

"That's great, sis. Umm, I was wondering—do you plan to work in Liberal, or maybe Beaver? Don't imagine there's much in Forgan that—"

"What are you talking about? Work in Liberal? How would I work in Liberal? I've got a farm to run."

"Whoa." My big brother put a hand over his mouth, casting a glance at Grace. "You're surely not planning to stay out here on the farm . . ."

"Myrrl! What are you talking about? I was raised on the same farm as you. I'm not a man, but I've learned a few things since you and I hoed potatoes in Mama's garden . . ." I stared at him, and then Grace. "Why would I want to leave the farm? This is our—"

"I told you." Grace bundled my hand in hers and raised her eyebrows at Myrrl. "You tend to sell your little sister short sometimes."

He shook his head. "I don't think it's a good idea, Claire. You out here all by yourself . . . and this farm isn't . . . well, it's hardly big enough to support anybody. I'd be worried about you."

"You think I can't do it? Well, I can. Besides, this farm is all my boys have ever known. This is their home. I know how to drive a tractor, and so does Sammy. Although I'll wait until he's old enough to manage by himself before I put him out in the field."

"Well, sis, you've surprised me before," he said. "If anyone can, you'd be the one." He sighed and gave me that goofy smile. "Let me pray God's blessing over you before we leave."

❧

Blanche and Henry came by to collect her dishes and a roasting pan just as Myrrl and Grace were leaving. They hurried in and out, apologizing for interrupting. As I watched both couples leave, I realized how much I wanted them—anybody, really—to stay, to stave off the loneliness. But that would be playing the coward.

Friends had warned me not to let the blues get me down. The boys and I would be alone; that was probably why Myrrl doubted the wisdom of us staying on the farm. Pop reminded us to always go to the Psalms when you're feeling low. So I did. They seemed more real than ever before, like David and the other writers went through the same deep valleys as me.

But there we were, just the four of us. Our house, strangely quiet after the hubbub of activity and voices, seemed almost alien, so I took the boys outside to our hillock north of the house. Jerry clung to my hand all the way.

Once we got settled, Jerry said, "Are we going to watch the stars, Mama?"

The older two laughed. Dickie said, "There's no stars in the middle of the afternoon, silly." He looked to me. "We're here so we can talk. This is our talking place, isn't it, Mama?"

By then, all three had crouched in a semicircle around me, looking up expectantly into my face. I almost broke down, looking into their trusting eyes. Feeling tears coming, I ducked my head. At that moment, I knew I had to be strong. "Yes, this will always be our talking place, just like it was when Daddy was here."

"Now, Daddy's in heaven, isn't he?" Dickie said.

Jerry wanted to know if Daddy could see us right then. That started a discussion about heaven, about God, and—from Jerry—a demand to answer the questions so he could have another piece of Goldie Taylor's banana cream pie.

Sammy said, "I don't think Daddy c-can see us n-now, because the Bible says there won't be any t-tears in heaven."

"Yeah, but I'll bet Daddy can see us," Dickie said.

"Let's see if God will show us," I said. "Maybe Reverend Caywood will tell us, too."

More questions followed. I didn't have all the answers, but the boys seemed content with my leadership. A car pulled into the driveway, so we trooped back to the house.

Durward and his wife Wilma emerged from the sedan. They had gone to Elkhart to visit his mother; he hadn't forgotten to stop and see us before they returned to Borger. Arms outstretched, he engulfed me with a hug. Wilma, a striking redhead, was new to us, but she patted my back as I wept and received their comforting embrace.

I invited them in for supper.

Durward shook his head. "I'm sorry, Claire. We can't stay but a few minutes. I gotta be out on the rig at six tomorrow morning, ready to go." He leaned back against the front fender of the car, a breeze riffling his dark wavy hair. "Claire, we didn't get to talk much before Dad's funeral, but I wanted to see what you planned to do, now . . ."

My antenna up, I said, "What have you been hearing . . . about what I planned to do?"

A sheepish grin. "Can't catch you unawares, can I?" His right hand fumbled in his shirt pocket, and he pulled out a pack of Chesterfields. Idly spanking it against the palm of his other hand, he withdrew a cigarette. "John's crowd—and some of the others on Dad's side—said they ain't no way you're gonna make it out here on this little plot of ground."

I stared at him as he lit up. "Do you believe that?" My throat felt dry.

"Claire, I know you. Shoot no, I don't believe that. You're a strong woman."

"Well, why bring up rumors, and hurtful rumors, at that?"

"That ain't all they said . . . and I wanted to put an end to their gossip. 'Cause I think what they're saying is a lie . . ."

"And what else?" By that time, my breathing was shallow, agitated.

"They're saying . . . that you plan to farm the boys out to relatives so you can go work in tow—"

"That's a lie!" I snapped. "A stinking lie. I wouldn't split up my boys. What kind of mother would do that?" I wanted to yell.

Wilma put her arms around me. I heard Durward's voice. "Don't you worry, Claire. I hear another word about that from anyone, I'll cram it down their throat."

The boys had followed Wilma and pressed against my legs. I said, "Oh, boys, your mama's crying again. But it's just because we all miss Daddy. Everything's okay."

201

Durward stood behind Wilma and looped his arm around both of us. "We're not that far away, Claire. It might seem like it, but if you need to talk, you call—anytime."

I knew Durward would even come if I asked. But when the chips were really down, I'd have to turn to the Lord.

29 Cards and Community

Summer 1951

Claire

The basket of one hundred thirty-eight sympathy cards floated like a ship of hope atop my piano. I would answer every one, thanking them for their prayers, kind words, and, for some, their hours of sacrifice. I grabbed a handful off the top and laid them on the dining table. Some were from friends we hadn't heard from in years. I sighed, wondering if they knew how much their words of connection meant to me.

First, thanks to the six neighbors who'd planted our milo the day Elmer died. What could I say? Don't ponder overmuch. They gave of their time and tractors because of our need; any attempt to repay them would diminish their gifts. Over the nine months of Elmer's sickness, there had been dozens of donations—mostly grants of time. I could never make up for such caring, but I would acknowledge it.

It took me all morning to write cards to those six farmers. I shook my head. At that rate, it would take a month of Sundays to respond to the piano list. Besides, I had the necessary work of running the farm. Oh, God, I miss Elmer, my beloved . . .

Tears came, and I didn't try to stop them.

My grief run dry, I arose and looked out to check on the boys. Still playing in the sand pile north of the well house.

Once, when Myrrl and I were kids, we'd gone out in the pasture to bring the milk cows in, and we came across a newborn calf. Its mother lay nearby—dead. I looked between the two animals, one dead, the other barely alive. I remember holding my breath, as if by an act of will I could stop the march of time to keep that calf alive. Impossible. In that lonely moment, I was struck by how time keeps going, whether you're ready for it or not.

I wished to be with Elmer, even for the space of a heartbeat . . . O Heavenly One, can you not grant that? But in the next breath, I looked at the boys playing outside the kitchen window and imagined what their lives would be like if I were gone. Possibly like that little calf staggering about on wobbly legs, without a protector or guide. I couldn't bear the thought.

I went outside and sat on the front step, hugging knees to my chest and wondering what God thought about my faded faith. His universe seemed indifferent, uncaring that Elmer lay beneath the cold sod of Liberal Cemetery. Death—is it not punishment? Spirit of the Holy One, comfort me. A new thought—perhaps it is sacrifice. I shaded my eyes against the unblinking sun, wheeling overhead as it had since time began. No stopping to ponder grief or whisper words of comfort. Life pulsed in the butterflies that besieged the lilac bush, and in the chattering kingbirds darting into the pear tree to feed their young.

Stop it. Brother Caywood had said Elmer is with Jesus. That was true, and I believed it. My emotions said I still hurt. Loneliness, rigid and cold, swept over me like a plague.

For the first time in my life, I felt a fear that paralyzed my ability to think. I couldn't let it rule me. Pick up, get up. There were things to do. My big talk to Myrrl and Grace about staying on the farm had better have legs.

I'd done the things I knew to do. But simply milking cows, feeding the chickens, and washing and re-washing every dish in my cupboard wouldn't support my family. While Elmer was sick, I'd had to be the strong one, caring for him. Before that, we'd faced trials and hardships and a few victories, both working together, building our farm as a place for the sons who eventually came. Now it was me again as the only one. I couldn't muster the will to claim the title of strong one.

Think, girl. Figure what needs to be done, knowing my strength had limits. So did my credit at People's National Bank. Naylor's sympathy wouldn't allow him to extend credit without end. Me being a woman would make it all that much harder too. I said I'd pay back every penny, even though I owed thousands of dollars to try to save Elmer.

The milo planted the previous week would soon be coming up, and it had better be cultivated or weeds would crowd out the new sprouts. We had a knife-sled, harrow, and cultivator . . . in what order were they to be used? Were all needed, and were they fit for use? When to use what? Elmer had made those decisions, and I never asked the whys and wherefores.

And what cows or calves to sell? Ray would know. Better get

204

him over for advice. I'd lived most of my life on a farm, but then I realized there was so much I didn't know. I knew how to perform individual tasks, but strategy was a horse of a different color.

ઝ~ળ

I called Ray, telling him I didn't know if I should sell my calves, and if so, how many. He said he'd be over that afternoon to look at the herd. Whatever the case, I suspected I'd need to present a plan to the bank for eventual repayment. It would help if I either had cash in hand or a sure date for an initial payment. The last I'd looked, my checking account held the grand sum of ninety-seven dollars and fourteen cents—most of it borrowed money I'd gotten from the same bank.

Ray came in, smelling of sweat and dried cow manure and bringing the memory of Elmer. I finished clearing the dinner table as the boys gathered around Ray. Jerry admired his tooled Acme boots and asked for a story. As Elmer's cousin, Ray treated the boys as if they were his own, telling yarns and admiring their latest project, which happened to be Fido.

He sipped from the cup of coffee I set before him and said, "Boys, did I ever tell you about my cousin, Newt Bruffett, that had him a talking dog?"

"Newt who?" Dickie snickered. "You don't have no cousin by that name. Daddy would've told us about any Newt Bruffett, 'cause he would've been Daddy's cousin, too."

"Not necessarily." Ray shot a grin at me, and then turned to his audience. "Boys, I'll explain about cousins later. Now, do you want to hear about Newt's talking dog?"

"Dogs don't talk, Ray," Jerry pulled on Ray's vest. "You're just making that up."

Sammy settled into a chair. "Let him t-tell the story, you guys."

Ray said, "Okay, boys, I'll tell the story and then you decide for yourselves . . . Newt had this old yellow dog that he said was kinda special. I saw it a time or two but didn't pay much attention to it. Old yellow dogs are a dime a dozen. Anyway, Newt finally decided to get rid of that dog. Put an ad in the Herald-Democrat that—"

"What's a Herald-Democrat?" Jerry asked.

"The Beaver n-newspaper," Sammy said. "Just listen."

Ray waited until the boys stopped frowning at one another

and then continued, "All right, Newt put this ad in the newspaper: For Sale, talking dog—only $5. See Newt Bruffett."

Jerry said, "No one believes—"

The two older boys shushed him, and Ray went on. "Well, most people were like Jerry here—they don't believe dogs can talk, so no one went out to Newt's place to see his dog. Besides, who wants another old yellow dog? Finally, a Yankee passing through saw the ad, and got directions to Newt's place. He pulled up and Newt is sitting on his front porch, with the old dog beside him. The Yankee gets out and says, 'You the man with the talking dog?' And Newt says, 'Yep, that's me, and this here is my talking dog, Biff.'

"The Yankee says, 'Well, have him say something.' Newt said, 'You could ask him a question.' So the Yankee starts to say something, but realizes how stupid it would look, a grown man asking a dog a question. Finally, he works up his courage and says, 'Biff, why don't you tell me the places you been?' Well, old Biff gets up, stretches, and starts talking, 'I was born in New York City, but when word got out that I could talk, J. Edgar Hoover had me brought down to Washington, DC. He sent me out on cases all over the country. I helped solve crimes you wouldn't believe, because no one thinks a dog can—'

"This Yankee feller' jumps up and says, 'That's amazing! I can't believe it.' He turns to Newt. 'Now why are you only asking five dollars for your amazing dog Biff?' Cousin Newt said, 'For starters, you can't believe a word he says. He'll claim he's been everywhere, but Biff hasn't been outta my yard since the day he was born. I'd feel I was cheating you if I asked more than five dollars.'

"So there you have it, boys. That's the story of Cousin Newt's talking dog.'"

Ray held a hand over his mouth to conceal his laughter. "I can tell you boys don't believe my story, but it's true—as far as I know."

They just looked at Ray. When they started asking questions, he said, "Boys, get your shoes on. I'll need you to drive the stock into the corral so we can look at those cows.

"Claire, we might oughta figure two or three different options, depending how much money that banker and his loan committee will expect by fall. I'll give you my notions and opinions about how many cows and calves you'll have to sell to satisfy them."

It took a while to head the cows into the corral, but once it was done, Ray looked them all over. He said to definitely cull the bony old black milk cow before she croaked; get rid of those brindle beasts Elmer got in a deal with Johnny McNutt, on and on. By the time we'd talked it over on the way back to the house, I had an idea how many to sell right away, and which ones to sell in the fall after they put on some weight. That would allow me to give Naylor a good faith advisement.

I didn't ask Ray about hogs; Elmer had been the pig expert, so I was on my own there. As far as cultivation of our milo, Ray said I should call Edwin Eagan or maybe Lawrence Emrie for advice.

I hesitated to bother the neighbors, but knew I couldn't blunder about, guessing what to do. If my neighbors would provide the know-how and experience, I'd provide the will.

☙❧

Within the next three weeks, Ethel, then Pearl and Lem, came to visit. I suspected they wanted to investigate Myrrl's report. Ethel was blunt. "Being a farmer's wife is hard enough, but if you stay on the farm you've got to be the farmer and the farmer's wife, mechanic, . . . veterinarian, accountant and planner, nurse and counselor and teacher. I could go on and on. That's a lot of jobs for one person to fill and . . ." She laid her hand on my arm. "While I don't doubt you'll manage, you've also got to count the cost. You'll have to do it by yourself. You won't have another adult to listen to your ideas or console you and encourage you. It'll be you, just you, except when we can come down."

"I know, Ethel, but this place is what I know. It's what the boys know—"

"They can change; they're young. They can adapt, but you're . . . forty-five in August. Once you commit yourself to this farm, it could drag you under."

"I hear what you're saying. It's a big responsibility. Maybe more than I realize. And if I stay, I won't be able to do much else."

"Well, I don't think I'd be that limiting, but staying here does restrict your options."

"Is that bad?"

"I'm not sure. I don't think I'd choose to stay here, on the farm."

"You and I are two different persons. Don't forget that I was the one who flew the nest to spread my wings. I was the one who married a man I hadn't known all my life—a man who smoked and drank, who was divorced, a man who never darkened the door of a church. But he was so much fun and we loved one another. And he was handsome!"

"Oh, that he was."

"Ethel, do you realize the risk a woman takes when she marries a man like Elmer? Women watched him when he came into a room. Some of them tried to steal him—even after we were married. Maybe I was stupid or blind, but I married him knowing all that. Because I was brash enough to think I could hold him . . . believing he wouldn't dump me for some floozy . . . that he wouldn't tomcat around. I took my chances with him, but we had a marriage that was good and getting better. If we'd only had a few more years together." I had to stop, was getting emotional. "Our marriage was far from perfect. His family—oh, my, I've told you all that. Yes, I took a risk with Elmer, and I've never regretted it. Now, I'm willing to take a risk in staying here, on this farm, with my boys."

"Claire, I guess I've been selling you short. Sometimes I just think of you as that little girl beside Pop on the buckboard seat—"

"I've made some dumb mistakes, Harold being the worst. Staying here is risky, but I'm willing to put my all into it. My boys don't need more change in their lives. We better stay right here— same friends, same school and same church, same home."

"Yes, I should accept you're bound to take risks I wouldn't. I've probably been denying that." She paused. "You are who you are, and why should I try to change you?"

30 Perceptions and Reality

Claire

Here I was, not knowing if I was supposed to harrow or cultivate our newly planted milo. When I grew up in western Kansas, everybody farmed with horses. Elmer and I had plowed and planted with a team ever since the Hoover presidency. Over those nineteen years, I learned a lot about farming. By the time Elmer bought the Ford tractor to replace our workhorses, I began having babies. So here I was starting all over again as a farmer.

Much as I disliked exposing my ignorance, I called Edwin Eagan for advice. I needed to learn how to keep our crop from being choked out by thistles, ragweed, sandburs, pigweed, and any other tares that might overcome the new milo plants.

Edwin came up to our house, all seriousness, and asked to look at our farm equipment. The boys and I trooped out to show him what we had.

Sammy said, "I d-drove the Ford tractor lots of times. Daddy let me do it."

Instinctively, my hand went out to push him back. Mechanical equipment presented all kinds of dangers. "No, son, I know your dad let you drive the tractor several times, but not out in the fields." I shot a quick glance at Edwin. "Elmer never had the boys do any of the actual farming. I don't . . . I would never forgive myself if anything happened to one of my boys."

"I understand. Gladys was nervous about Eugene doing field work, and he's at least three years older—"

"Four," Sammy blurted. "I'm eleven, and h-he's fifteen."

"Well, son," I said. "We're not out here to discuss that." I directed Edwin's attention toward the battered drill, Ford tractor, the Shaeffer plow . . .

He looked around and said, "For right now, you'll be needing the knife-sled, harrow, and cultivator. Milo already planted, but I see you've got a two-row planter—"

"Daddy called that a lister," Dickie informed him.

"I see. Well, sometimes I call it a lister too," Edwin said. "You got the Ford. What about that old Case tractor?"

"Don't use it. Have to crank it," I said. "It doesn't have a starter."

"You might find a buyer for it—Charlie Ausmus, Glen Monroe."

We continued talking about our machinery, which wasn't much, compared to some of the big farmers. But we didn't have a big farm either.

Sammy

I couldn't forget why Mama didn't want me to run the Ford tractor in the field. She remembered what happened the last time I drove it back from the Meisenheimer place over west . . . That was the day I almost killed Daddy.

He took me and Dickie in the pickup over to the field where he left the tractor. After he checked the gas, he said to me, "All right, son. Drive straight home, just like always. You've done that about six or seven times, haven't you?"

"This'll be the eighth," I said. "I d-drove it almost twenty-five miles, c-counting the other trips from here."

"Yep, you're getting to be a real farmer." He tousled Dickie's hair. "This cowboy is going to help me get old Ted and Bill in the loading pen. They're the last two horses I'll sell to Ray Amen. Gonna keep old Mable and Diamond and their colts." He gave me a stern look. "Now be careful. I'm depending on you." I always liked to hear him say that. Made me feel big, important. Then he smiled.

The Ford was easy to mount—just step onto the running board from the side, in front of the rear wheel, and land in the seat. Daddy waited to make sure it would start; then he headed out to the main road. I saw Dickie, his face pressed against the rear window, wishing he was me.

I stamped my left foot down on the clutch pedal to put the Ford in third gear while I was going over the plowed ground. Once I got to the driveway, I geared it up to fourth. Hardly anyone ever traveled that road along the section line, but I stopped and looked both directions like Daddy told me to. All clear, so after getting on the straightaway, I depressed the clutch to slip into third gear. My shoe slipped—almost all the way off the pedal. I'd forgotten the clutch pedal was worn shiny slick. Never mind, I got my leg up and back on the clutch and was off. The hand throttle was on the steering column, and after getting back into high gear, I opened it up to full speed.

Heading home, I pretended I was a race driver, except at the corner where I turned south. Less than a mile the rest of the way home, and I was still racing, going full blast. Daddy said the Ford would only go about fifteen miles per hour, but I felt like a big shot, driving top speed.

Once to the barn, I slowed down past the corral, looking to see where Daddy wanted me to park. Then I saw him, in front of the center overhead door of the garage, directly across the road from the house. He stepped to the side and waved me to park the tractor on the uphill slope in front of that door, so I stopped to gear down to second. Once started, I was ready to stop in front of the center door.

My foot hit the clutch pedal but skidded off, and the tractor kept going. My pants leg was kind of holding the clutch down, and the tractor almost stopped. But the clutch came up just a little and the tractor bucked forward on the slope until it nudged into the overhead door. Then it rolled back a little ways.

Pressing down with my leg, my pants leg was still caught on the clutch, holding it part way down. I was afraid if I pulled my leg up, the tractor would ram into the shop door again. Pushing my left leg down as far as I could had my pant leg holding the clutch down, and the tractor began to roll backwards. I was frantic, not knowing for sure what to do.

Daddy saw the trouble I was having and moved in to pull me off the tractor. At that instant my pant leg lost hold of the clutch and the tractor lurched forward.

The big rear tire caught Daddy's leg and he went down. Everything happened so fast. I looked down and that big wheel was going right up Daddy's leg and over his chest.

He twisted his head to the side just enough for the big lug-tread tire to miss his face. The tractor kept going after it went over his shoulder and then it died—a miracle.

I just knew I had killed my daddy. I couldn't move but sat there crying. Then I saw him get up off the ground, real slow and bent over. His face was white as a sheet. He tried to catch his breath. Finally, he staggered over to a sawhorse and sat.

I scrambled off the Ford and ran across the road to get Mama. She came out right away, crying for Daddy. Then she saw him sitting there, and we were all crying, except for Daddy.

He didn't have enough breath for much of anything but pretty soon he started talking. "Yeah . . . I'm . . . I'm okay, I think."

Mama was wringing her hands and looking real close into his eyes. She kept asking if he was all right. Then she set her shoulders and said she was going to take him to Doctor Hilbig at Liberal—right then. I was really surprised when she asked if I was all right.

I cried out, "It was my f-f-fault. All my fault." I cried harder. Was Daddy going to be all right?

Daddy whispered, "No, son. My fault. I should've just reached in and turned the key off. That would've stopped it. Don't know what I was thinking."

"Elmer, I'm taking you to the doctor—right now. You may have broken ribs, ruptured spleen or kidneys, anything. Wait right here. I'm bringing the car over to you." Mama hurried off, and soon she had the car backed up right beside Daddy.

Then they were gone. After what seemed like hours, they were back. Mama said Daddy had no broken bones or ruptured anything. But his entire body was sore for weeks. She said it was a miracle, and she couldn't say enough how thankful she was to the Lord.

Claire

Edwin said cultivation of our row crop was first done with the knife-sled, attached to the Ford with a three-point hitch. A few weeks after knife-sledding the row crop, it would be time to harrow. The Ford could pull our three-section harrow from the drawbar. Then, before the stalks got too high, it was back to the three-point hitch for the cultivator. He said that should keep most of the weeds under control.

Our knife-sled needed new blade sweeps, which I could get from Tedford in Liberal. Simply take one of the old sweeps with me to make sure I got the right size. Also, the blades came with blunt edges and would have to be sharpened by a blacksmith. Ed Jones, west of Greenough School, would be best to do that.

I had no problem with doing business at Tedford or any other farm implement company, but going into an isolated country blacksmith shop . . . I felt my palms beginning to sweat. In my years of traveling sales, I learned that coarse men only amped up their rough language if a lone woman stepped into their den.

Even my father never took me into a blacksmith shop when I was a girl. He said it was no place for a young lady. The very thought of traipsing into that male domain brought dryness to my throat. I imagined it as a dirty, cluttered cave of smoke and fire where local idlers sat around, chewing and spitting, swearing and whatever else such men did.

Regardless, going to Ed Jones' blacksmith shop was what I'd have to do. Then I hit upon an idea. Take the boys with me as kind of, well, protection. Surely the hangers-on who frequented the place would moderate their talk with the boys there.

Elmer had often taken them if they weren't in school. They would return home, full of wild accounts of the flame, smoke, and sound of the blacksmith shop. Occasionally, they'd tell me bits of conversations they'd heard as well. That certainly embellished my image of a blacksmith shop.

First, we had to remove one of the blade sweeps. We located Elmer's big crescent wrenches in the garage. Sammy and I pulled and pulled to loosen the bolts holding the old sweeps, with little success.

Fortunately, Glen Monroe, who'd been a pallbearer for Elmer's funeral, stopped by to see how we were doing. With a touch of lubricating oil and an extender, we finally loosened the bolts and removed the old sweeps. I had already cracked every fingernail but decided to wear heavy gloves if I was going to be a farmer.

As he left, Glen told us to call next time we needed help. I told him I would have to manage on my own, or I'd be calling for help all the time. He just laughed, but I knew he meant well. Grateful for the neighborly help, I bathed my sore hands in warm salt water and used the last of my Jergens hand lotion.

I hadn't planned a trip to Liberal but went to the implement company the following day. Tedford sold me two new pairs of sweeps, blunt-edged as Edwin said they'd be. Instead of dropping them off at Ed Jones' on the way home, I procrastinated to give myself time to think things through. I'd never met Ed Jones, as he and his wife Mary didn't attend school functions. I imagined him as a brawny hulk whanging a ten-pound hammer against plowshares, sparks flying and hot iron sizzling as he dunked his creations into a bath of murky water. His arms and face were likely pitted and scarred from flying bits of molten metal and splashes of scalding water. Probably why he wasn't seen at community gatherings.

Enough delay. I told the boys we were going to the blacksmith shop the next day, and why we were going. Such excitement, enough to lift the pall of grief that had burdened us all.

I couldn't believe how I'd fretted over this simple matter. There'd be so many more like it. I had to face reality. Though I was a mother, I was also a woman alone. Might as well get used to being seen as "that widow woman," and ignore suggestive remarks that were sure to follow in my wake.

Bound in that knowledge, I put on a sensible print dress and draped a light sweater over my shoulders despite the heat of the morning. After all, isn't that how one dresses to go to a blacksmith shop? I took comfort in the jubilation of the boys, who might as well have been going to the circus.

A Studebaker pickup and an Allis-Chalmers tractor sat outside Ed Jones' shop when I parked the Chrysler to the side of the open door. I opened the trunk. "Sammy, Dickie, get those sweeps and bring them into the shop. I'll see if Mr. Jones is . . . is available." I peered into the darkness behind the gaping door. No smoke. No clanging. No nothing. I started inside, pulling seven-year-old Jerry with me.

"Out here!" A man's voice, brisk and flute-like, sounded behind me. I jumped.

"It's Ed Jones," Dickie announced from behind the car.

I turned as a small man came across the road from what was obviously his house. He was scarcely as tall as my five-four and walked with a decided limp. His left shoe was fitted at the sole with a four-inch-high metal lift, as his leg appeared to be stunted. A railroad engineer's cap perched askew over a thatch of white hair. Below that, a placid face with a half-smile. Two of the bluest eyes I'd ever seen stared into my own.

"You must be Elmer's wife."

"Yes, how did you know?"

"Recognized the car. And these boys. Never forget them. I'm Jones." He stuck out a hand. As I took it, I noticed it bore none of the blemishes I'd imagined. "I'm very sorry about your husband, Mrs. Hall. One fine man, Elmer was. We had many stimulating discussions about matters affecting the world."

"Yes, thank you, Mr. Jones."

"Call me Ed. And what have we got for today?"

"Just these sweeps," I gestured toward the boys, who stood

with their implements like soldiers at attention. "For sharpening, if you . . . if you could . . . have time."

"I surely can." He took the blades, one by one. "Would tomorrow noon be sufficient?"

"Yes. Certainly." What a gentleman. I was aware of Jerry pulling on my sweater and turned to him. "What?"

"We want to see what Ed Jones is doing inside . . ."

"Nothing much going today, son," the blacksmith said. "Why don't you come tomorrow noon? You can inspect everything I'm doing." He grinned and waved at the boys.

On the way home, the boys chattered about all the things they were going to inspect. I determined not to let my imagination run away like wild horses in the future.

31 The Acceptance Affliction

Claire

Sammy brought Elmer's big crescent and a box end wrench to me from the garage. It took some straining and skinned knuckles, but we bolted on all the knife-sled blades that Ed Jones had sharpened. Every day, it seemed I learned something new about farming. For sure, it involved more than jumping on the tractor and heading out to the field.

Something as basic as fueling the Ford tractor took more gumption than I expected. Gasoline had to be transferred from one of three fifty-five-gallon steel drums, thence into five-gallon gas cans, and then hoisted up to pour into the tractor tank. One of the barrels was nearly full, another was empty, and the other about half full. Elmer had told me a full barrel weighed over three hundred pounds. That was the rub.

I started with the half-full barrel, tilting it against a sawhorse to fill two gas cans. I dreaded that daily ritual of wrestling the gas barrels. Ray happened by a couple mornings and gave me a hand. He handled them like he was bulldogging a steer.

I understood why Myrrl had questioned my ability to run the farm. Some tasks simply required brute strength. That, or God's intervention.

One hot July day, Sammy and Dickie were helping as best they could as I struggled to tip the nearly full barrel to fill the cans. One held the funnel and the other braced the sawhorse.

We didn't realize anyone had driven up until a guttural falsetto penetrated my concentration. "Claire, hold it there. Lemme give you a hand." It was Glen Monroe. I knew he lived just north of Ray and Edith.

Startled but glad for the interruption, I eased the barrel back to upright and caught my breath. I waited for my arms to stop shaking and greeted Glen. How much help could he be? He was barely taller than me. Some people ignored him, as his wife had a bigger voice and presence, but his down-to-earth manner always put me at ease.

"I'll get on that barrel," he said. With that, he tipped it against the sawhorse while I opened the spout and held the funnel. The boys stepped back and watched.

He filled both of our gas cans, then flung one up to top off the tractor tank. Next, he refilled the emptied can and let me borrow one of his gas cans, which he also filled. "Set those aside for tomorrow," he said. A few minutes to catch his breath then, "You need to git you an elevated fuel tank. Zack Wiley can fill a hundred-and-fifty-gallon tank just as easy as streaming gas into those drums."

"Sounds ideal," I said, "but I got to go cheap. Besides I wouldn't know the first thing about setting it up."

Glen took a step backward, shaking his head. "Claire, you're forgetting you're part of the Baptist Church of Forgan. We'll pass the hat for those in—"

I dropped my head. "I wasn't raised to take charity."

"It's not charity. It's us doing our duty—take care of widows and orphans, like the Good Book says. And Bill Potter can set the posts and frame it up for you. He's handy that way. You won't have to do a thing. Besides, a woman's got no business rasslin' these barrels. One of them rolls off that sawhorse, it could mash one of your boys. Or put you in the hospital. Then where'd you be?"

He didn't know it, but I was about to cry. His logic was making too much sense. "Well, I'll pay it all back."

"We'll talk about that later." He grinned and scuffed the heel of his boot in the dirt. "Good thing I stopped by to see how you all was doing. Oly said she doesn't know how you can stand to be out in the field sunrise to sunset on these hunnerd-degree days. You need to get you an umbrella for that tractor too. Ain't no reason you can't get one at Tedford's. Won't cost much and will save you from heat stroke."

I slapped my dusty bonnet across a front tire. "I'm getting used to it. I've got all the west side knife-sledded. Just have to finish the north part of the eighty east of the house."

"You're doing good." He pointed to a spot next to where my barrels were lined up. "This location suit you for setting up your elevated tank?"

I stood there, arms akimbo, accepting help I didn't want to ask for but knew I sorely needed. "I . . . yes, that'll do."

Glen moved away from the tractor and lit his pipe. "Well, I better scoot. Got my own farming to do. If Bill Potter's not

217

available, I'll send the preacher. Brother Caywood's not afraid to get his hands dirty." He laughed and waved at the boys as he crawled back into his pickup.

ڰﻭ

Bill Potter had come and gone. Earlier, Henry Ausmus and the preacher had delivered posts and framing to support the tank, which Gene Nichols had brought out to start the project. It was a different feeling, being the recipient of other people's charity. Not one I was comfortable with, but I'd already had two close calls of nearly having a barrel roll over me and Sammy. Nevertheless, I was determined to pay back every nickel they'd donated.

I had almost finished writing thank you cards to all the people who'd provided food or help during Elmer's sickness, and those who had sent sympathy cards. Now I had notes to write to the donors for the gas tank project.

The following Sunday after church, I came up to shake the preacher's hand. "Brother Caywood, I'm so thankful for my new gas tank. Could you give me a list of everyone who contributed, and how much they gave? So I can write my thank-you cards, you know . . ."

He smiled as he shook my hand. "Well, I can give you a list of names, which is almost everyone in church. But the amounts? What do you need that for?"

"I'm paying it back—every penny."

That benevolent smile again. "No need for that, Claire. We—everyone actually—gave because we wanted to bless you. Besides, we're blessed by giving to you. Jesus said it's more blessed to give than to receive. If we give only out of an expectation of getting it back, that's not really a sacrifice on our part." His eyes searched mine. "Let us do good for you, dear lady."

"You don't understand. I need to pay it back. I have to. It's the way I was taught . . . to not owe anybody, if I could help it." I caught my breath, feeling light-headed, and reached down to adjust the jeweled pin on my blouse that Elmer gave me on our twentieth anniversary.

"Well, you don't owe us. That was a gift. I'm glad Glen saw fit to alert us to your need. Besides, most people give with the expectation that their giving will remain anonymous, in accordance with Christ's command to not let your right hand know what your left hand is doing. Claire, we're grateful the Lord blessed us so we can pass it along to you." His gaze shifted; someone was behind me.

I sputtered, "But, but the list of names—"

"Clair-ie, if you don't get through the line, the Methodists are going to get all the roast beef dinners at the café." Blanche, mispronouncing my name again.

I didn't need to be coddled and everyone might as well know it. However, it was, after all, still church. I looked for the boys so we could go home.

I reviewed the diminished heap of cards still nestled in the large blue bowl atop the piano. Brother Caywood thought he could hide my obligations from me. Not this time, or any time. I went straight to Velma Wakefield, the church treasurer, and nicely asked for the list of donors for the tank project. She didn't even blink; handed over a carbon-papered list of the names and amounts and I was in business. That list went right into the blue bowl.

I stared at my piano, a Straube upright, for a long time. Pop had ordered it from Hammond, Indiana, for my sixteenth birthday. I loved that piano but with Elmer getting sick, I didn't have anything to praise about for over a year.

That wasn't exactly true; Elmer had accepted Jesus, a mighty hallelujah to send him to glory. Knowing he was in heaven meant everything to me. I wondered why God allowed circumstances to bring such grief. Our preacher said it was because the Fall of Mankind had tainted all creation. What a price to pay for Adam and Eve's failure.

Sammy

One evening that summer, Mama said to come into the living room. After Dickie and Jerry finally got settled down, she sat on the piano bench, facing the keyboard and flexing her fingers.

What was she going to do? A piano was just a fancy shelf to store memories, its top crowded with pictures of distant relatives in cardboard frames, most embossed with Olan Mills Studios. I thought of other parlors. Ray and Edith's piano was so covered with waxy looking photographs, she must have saved them since Hoover was president. No one ever played their piano. Only schoolteachers like Mrs. Cates used pianos for music.

Mama brought her hands down to the ivory and black keys,

like she really was going to do something special. She began to hum. I recognized The Old Rugged Cross and Amazing Grace. She said one word: Chords. Hit it again. Not a tune, but a grand sound, nevertheless. She began to play, start and back up to repeat, until she was satisfied to go on. Then a melody she later said came from a recital, a long-ago performance when she was a girl.

The stirring runs and triumphal melodies seemed magical, transforming our little house into a concert hall, notes ascending and thundering. Dickie and Jerry sat with eyes wide. I probably did too. We were all spellbound by the crescendo of sound. The music overwhelmed our griefs, breaking through the sadness and loneliness.

I didn't want Mama to stop but all too soon she did. She said, "I can't believe how hard that was to make my fingers work right." She laughed. "Wish I could remember the rest. It's a recital piece I played at Jenny Fitzgerald's. Her father was the undertaker. We had iced tea and homemade ice cream afterward."

It seemed like Mama did lots of fun things when she was young. Maybe someday, I'd do things like that.

That evening of music made life seem so much bigger, as if it might hold dreams I could only imagine. I wondered what a person had to do to deserve such things.

32 The Necessary Truth

Claire

I stared at the letter from Merle Lansden, Attorney. It informed me that I was to come to his office in Beaver to probate the estate. Lansden's letter included a list of questions, covering routine predictable matters. One seemed invasive, even unnecessary—the one about prior marriages. Pop had told me lawyer-client communication was supposed to be confidential, but he also quoted Ben Franklin: Three people can keep a secret if two of them are dead.

I was tempted to lie. So I did.

As far as I was concerned, that skunk Harold never happened. We'd had no children—which made it easier to erase him from my past. Elmer would've rightfully mentioned his prior marriage; he had fathered Durward during the bitter year he'd been married to Florence.

If I acted as if I'd never been married before, perhaps that hurtful, hateful chapter in my life would cease to exist. No one needed to know. Not the attorney. Not anyone. I'd never met Lansden, but Elmer told me he was an important man in Beaver County, even exceptional for our neck of the woods. He undoubtedly gleaned general information about us from preparing Elmer's will, and the story of neighbors planting our crops made the local newspapers.

Aside from the annual trek to get car tags, we seldom went to Beaver, the county seat. The town seemed remote, although it was the same distance from the farm as Liberal, and not as big. Maggie had lived in Liberal, and the tug of sweet memories lingered, though it had been five years since she'd gone to heaven.

I figured it might be easier to keep a secret in Beaver County, home of roughly four people for each of its 1,800 square miles. On the other hand, if word got out, the entire county would know.

The receptionist ushered me into a paneled conference room featuring an oak table with six leather armchairs surrounding it. A tall, patrician looking man in his mid-forties entered and introduced himself as Merle Lansden. He immediately expressed his sympathies over our loss and asked how the boys and I were doing.

How nice. I'd expected bankers and lawyers to be cut from the same cloth, unfeeling and all business. "We . . . we're managing," I said. "Our neighbors have been very kind, helping in so many ways."

"I know those people in the Greenough community. Solid, dependable, and willing to lend a hand. Here . . ." He pulled out a newspaper with an article circled in ink. "I saw this in the Liberal paper four months ago." He began reading,

"'Greenough community neighbors of Elmer Hall, who has been ill for several months, recently put in a telephone line to his house. They also wired the house for electricity after the power line was extended to the Hall farm . . .'

"That's an example of what the rest of this country needs—people like your neighbors. Makes me proud."

I dropped my head. "Yes, we couldn't have better neighbors. Of course, I'll repay them for what they spent, even though it'll take time to do it."

He leaned back, eyebrows raised. "I doubt they expect to be repaid, but that's up to you, of course." He paused and withdrew a few documents from his linen folder. "I understand after your husband passed, you read the will at the office of the J. P. in Forgan. Thank you for bringing the property inventory and list of heirs.

"You may already be familiar with the probate process. To assure there are no misunderstandings, let's review responsibilities and actions expected of both of us—you as executor, and me as your attorney."

His fingers steepled, he reviewed the essentials of probate—to determine ownership of assets after a person's death and to transfer the decedent's property to the heirs. Though Elmer left a simple estate, Lansden said it would probably take ten to twelve months to complete the process. So much for a quick settlement of affairs. He ended with this statement: "We'll have to deal with creditors so they can be repaid."

My breath caught before I could speak. "I've got less than a hundred dollars in the checking account. Does that mean I'll . . . we'll lose the farm, to pay off debts?"

"No, not at all." A half smile. "Let me put your mind at ease.

The laws are written to protect survivors at the time they are most vulnerable, during the grieving process.

"I'm here to guide you all the way through the administration of the estate, which will include hearings, schedules and deadlines, clearing title to assets, disbursing assets according to the will, tax returns, and finalizing Elmer's affairs. It sounds like a lot, but it's mostly procedures to protect the interests of the heirs and to assure the intent of the deceased is followed." He paused. "Feel free to interrupt if you have questions."

Lansden paused momentarily, then squinted, apparently looking for something in his sheaf of documents. "I wanted to clear up a conflict." More squinting and shuffling of papers. "The information your husband gave me doesn't jibe with your answers to my questionnaire. Yes, here it is. Elmer stated you had a prior marriage. You make no mention . . ." At that, his eyebrows went up, his eyes questioning.

I gulped and managed to stammer, "Well, you see, as far as I'm concerned—"

"I should say . . ." Lansden dropped his head to peer over his bifocals. "Neither I nor any person acting in an official capacity would have a salacious interest in your marital status, past or present. However, the law—the court system—might have an interest as regards any third party claiming an interest in your husband's assets. Such third party could be a previous marriage partner, unjust as it might be. I'll need all essential information and documents so I can better protect your interest against such claims." He stopped, his baritone thundering the potential of danger to me and the boys.

I gasped. I felt my lower lip trembling, struggling as if to prevent my face from turning wrong side out, like one of those plaster molds Sammy brought home from school for his plaster of Paris crafts projects.

My attorney dropped his eyes, giving me time to regain my composure.

I took a deep breath. "I should restate . . . correct . . . my answer. It should be . . . what is. Not what I wish it to be." A sense of resolve gripped me, and I leaned forward, surprised at the strength of my voice. "I was young. Far too inexperienced and naïve. Far too patient with lies and false hopes. I married this man . . . Harold. We had no children. I tolerated disrespect to the point of betrayal. By the grace of God, I was given another chance . . .

with Elmer, a man worthy of . . ." Then the tears came.

Mr. Lansden sat, unmoving for moments while I had my cry. I became aware of his hand, proffering a neatly folded white handkerchief.

I took the hankie, and he began speaking when my sniffles ceased. "Yes, and I was young once. I made mistakes." A glint of a smile. "I still make mistakes." A pause, then, "So, let's confirm the record to show what was, and clarify that Elmer Hall's heirs are yourself, and your three boys. Are there others?" He looked up.

"His son, Durward, by a previous marriage."

"Ah, yes, Elmer's previous marriage. Was that union officially dissolved?"

I exhaled. I was ready for that one. Fishing into my purse, I withdrew a copy of Elmer's divorce certificate and laid it on the table, smoothing it out so he could see it. "That woman has no claim on the estate. Durward does, in accordance with the will. He will always be Elmer's son. I consider him a son."

"Very well. Let me know if you run across other pertinent records." He pushed back from the table.

I stood. "I'll get a copy of my divorce certificate to you. It's at home."

"Thank you for coming in. I'll let you know regarding meetings and filings. The legal system sometimes moves at a glacial pace." He smiled.

On the way home, I realized I hadn't asked how much this probate was going to cost me. Anyway, I felt cleansed to be up front with the man, although he'd forced me to declare myself. My face burned. I wondered what God thought about me trying to pull a fast one. Try as I might, I couldn't get the Ben Franklin quote out of my mind.

33 The Widow Minister

Claire

Blanche called to say she was coming over for her biweekly hairdo. We never considered it an appointment; more like a time for us to catch up on things. With her, one could expect to do more listening than talking. She never paid me, although she occasionally threatened to. I never asked for payment, but sometimes she'd bring cucumbers, carrots, or a head of cabbage from Henry's garden. Yes, and the loan of an extra crank telephone before we got ours.

Much as I wanted to have someone to confide in about my meeting with Lansden, I knew better than to breathe a word to Blanche about my first marriage. Too easy for her to forget what was supposed to be confidential.

The batch of sugar cookies I'd baked was fast disappearing. Dickie slipped in to get another and said Henry Ausmus' pickup was coming up the road. Shortly, the roar of Henry's muffler signaled he'd dropped Blanche off and she was toddling toward our front door.

We greeted one another and she headed to the buffet to deposit her cardigan sweater and mailbag purse, like always. She sat in the chair I'd set up next to the west windows of the dining room, then commenced with the latest news. "Clair-ie, I tell—"

"Blanche, that's not my name." I didn't try to hide my annoyance.

"Oh, sorry. Claire. Well, as I was saying, you're getting new neighbors a mile north of you. Glen and Oly Monroe's youngest daughter, Roberta—the one that got hitched to Arthur Durbin—they're moving into that vacant house Kenneth Taylor owns . . ."

She went on about how she didn't know how Kenneth could farm all the land he had and yet keep buying more. I tuned that out, waiting for her to talk about something else or give me a chance to speak. Eventually she ran down.

"Blanche," I said. "Last Saturday morning, I was just leaving for Liberal when a couple driving an old flivver pulled in, said he

225

was Wayne Williams and he—"

"Wayne Williams! My stars, Claire. I hope you didn't let him in the house. That man will talk a courthouse statue to dust."

"Well . . . I didn't. Told him I had business in Liberal and didn't want to be late. It was embarrassing, having to treat a visitor so inhospitably."

"Don't feel poorly about him. He's not dangerous, just a terrible waste of time. Attends some little holiness church out in the sticks. He fancies himself a minister to widows and orphans. Probably reads the obituaries and looks for the unsuspecting to descend on."

"Blanche, that's . . . that's harsh. Is he really that full of himself?"

"You've got that right. Actually, I believe it's the man's social life. But if I was you, I'd be planning how you're going to get rid of him when he shows up again. Because he will. Mark my words."

"Uh-huh," I said. "Oh, I met Elmer's attorney last week. Have to settle the estate, you know. I wasn't—"

"He's your attorney now. I hope you got one that won't try to buy his ranch off your dime. Who'd you talk to?"

"Merle Lansden. He—"

"Lansden? You got a good one. He was Speaker of the Oklahoma House of Representatives back in '44. Got tired of the politicking and set up a lawyer business in Beaver with Goetzinger. Word was he might be up for a judgeship. How you going to pay him, Claire, if I might ask?"

"Oh my. I guess he'll have to get in line. Elmer said he had a solid reputation, but I doubt he knew how much. So, you think he's a good attorney? That is, one you could . . . could trust?"

"You got no choice, Claire. He's your lawyer. What's to trust? You got secrets?"

"Oh! Secrets?" I dropped my comb and bent to pick it up; my breath caught. "Sure, I've got secrets, like everybody else. That's why we . . . why you come over, so we can swap secrets." I tried to laugh, but it came out more like a gasp.

Blanche slipped out of the chair and went to my telephone. Before she rang Central, she said, "I'll let you do the talking next time, sister, so you can share your big secrets, okay?"

"Oh, you bet. As if I haven't told you my life story from the time I was hatched."

With our milo harvest and the six head of cattle I sold in October, I made my first payment on the mortgage and set a little aside for Christmas. If I could only hold down expenses. The old Chrysler was getting harder to start every time I went to town. I was embarrassed to think of going back to J.C. Naylor to ask for money right after I'd waltzed into People's National Bank to give him a check.

Every winter brought snowy days that made it miserable to get out to the field where we'd shocked bundles of cane for cattle feed. The weather already getting nippy, the boys and I took the tractor and trailer out to the west field to get a load of cane fodder to stack in the barn. Some of the bundles were so heavy that Sammy and Dickie could hardly handle them. Working together, we managed to get a big load on the trailer and brought it in. Ray and Edith were waiting for us. Sammy parked the tractor and trailer, and I greeted our visitors. Dickie and Jerry grouped around Edith. I saw she'd pulled a lizard out of her apron pocket.

Ray waved me over to the corral. "I was hoping to take a gander at that young heifer I doctored for pinkeye a week ago."

I joined him and we located the animal. The boys separated her into the holding pen and Ray looked her over. "That eye has cleared up real good. We caught it in time before it could spread to other animals. Unusual for livestock to get pinkeye in this cooler weather."

As the boys turned the heifer out, we walked back to the house, settling on the front steps in the afternoon sunshine. I said, "Ray, can you take a look at the car? It's harder to start with cold weather coming on. Elmer kept things running but I hardly know where to begin."

He pulled out his pipe and scratched a wooden match on the concrete step. "I'm not much of a mechanic. Could be the plugs or carburetor. Anything Elmer couldn't fix, he'd have Earl do it. Why don't you ask Earl to check it out?"

"No. Not asking any of Elmer's brothers for anything. I've always gotten along with Earl, but no. Don't want to get that family thinking they can pick up a free meal here—"

"Earl ain't like that," Ray said.

I dropped my head. "It's not him. It's his woman Gertrude."

The boys having gone to unload the feed, Edith came over to

join us. "I don't know what Earl sees in that woman. She ain't happy unless she's got something to bellyache about."

Ray gave a knowing grin. "I always thought Earl had good sense. Since he teamed up with Gertie, I may have to revise my opinion." He raised his eyebrows. "You say none of Elmer's kin been around?"

I looked at my nails, split and rimmed with dirt. "Durward and Wilma are the only ones to check if we're even alive. They come up from wherever he's working in the oil fields. But the rest—me and the boys could slide off the edge of the earth and they'd never notice."

"Durward's reliable, always has been," Ray said.

Edith said, "Your people still up in Kansas? Don't they come to see you?"

"Myrrl and Grace—usually with their two youngest, Evelyn and Gary—they've been down twice since the funeral. Wish they'd come more often. We don't get much company. They don't know how lonesome it can be. Everything I do is for my boys, but sometimes, I just need a grownup to talk to. Someone who knows my history, my heart . . . You understand?"

Edith jerked her hand up and laid it on my arm. Surprised me, as she wasn't one to show emotion. "We do, Claire. Ray and I are here for you, much as we can. But your own blood, they's the ones you need. In fact, we're going over to Harper County today, to see Ray's aunt and my cousins. Before they forget us too." She laughed, a self-conscious wail that wafted between us.

Ray started, as if awakened. "Well, we best get going, Claire. Have the boys keep an eye on that heifer, just to be on the safe side."

They got into their pickup, and with a wave, were gone to see their relatives. The wind stirred dried leaves eddied up against the barn, and I realized the boys had gone out to get the four milk cows in. They'd said what a good cow dog Fido was.

I went in the house to get supper started. Cornbread and beans, the boys always liked that. Thinking again about the car, the only solution I could come up with was to talk to Naylor at the bank.

I'd just finished ironing the boys' good shirts when I looked outside to see Sammy and Dickie crossing the road, each with a full bucket of milk. I'd meet them at the milk house after they put the milk in the cream separator. They took turns cranking the separator, and when they were done, I'd collect the bowl, tank, and spouts for washing while Jerry brought the fresh cream into the house. The two older boys alternated—one took the skim milk back across the road for the hogs, while the other fed the chickens and closed the chicken house.

Our tasks seldom varied from day to day. We all knew what we had to do, and we did it. I was proud of my boys. I wished Elmer could see them, becoming young men. He would have been pleased.

Tomorrow we'd go to church, always a blessing to sing the hymns and hear what Brother Caywood had to say. I had much to be thankful for.

December 1951

Sammy

Sometimes Dickie's friends came home with us after church, but not this Sunday. Mama said we were going to make Christmas decorations, so not to invite them that day. With Christmas less than three weeks away, we began making stars and angels to put on the raggedy tree Mama bought at Ragsdale's in Liberal.

Fido and Shep began barking outside, so Jerry ran to the door. He hollered, "It's a man, all dressed up like he's going to church. His wife—she's coming too."

Mama dropped the red construction paper she was cutting into strips. She got up from sitting on the floor to see. We weren't expecting anyone. The second she peeked out the side window, she about choked. "Oh, my stars! It's Wayne Williams. Oh my, oh my!" She started to the door, then turned around two or three times, wringing her hands. Of course, all of us jumped up to see this Wayne Williams.

I tried to ask Mama who he was, but she seemed not to hear. I couldn't understand why she was upset. He wasn't any taller than me. Looked harmless, and no question that I could beat him in a footrace. His hair was oiled up with Brilliantine and combed straight back, like a city slicker. He wore a blue suit with white shirt and a red necktie. It took them a long time to get to the front door because his wife, who was taller than him, moved like a turtle. He had her by the arm and was talking to her as he helped her up the three steps to our porch.

Mama was saying she wondered if she had to invite them in

229

but we boys knew she would. She'd let anybody in our house because she didn't want to be considered "uppity." She always said that. Although once she made Dickie's friend Richard Nance go back outside and scrape his feet because he had cow manure on his shoes.

I checked Wayne Williams' shoes when he came in, all a-smiling. Mama greeted them pleasant like and pulled out chairs at the kitchen table. No cow manure, but one of his brogans had lost its lace and it kinda flopped when he walked.

Wayne Williams nodded his head a lot. I could tell he was a talker, just the way he acted. He said, "Mrs. Hall, we just wanted to come by and tell you how sorry we were about your loss of Elmer. It was Elmer, wasn't it?" Instead of sitting in the kitchen, he pulled his wife toward the dining room, like they planned to stay awhile.

We just had straight-back chairs in the dining room, so Mama motioned them into the living room and they sat on the couch.

Wayne Williams began talking again right away. "My father had a brother named Elmer. We never saw him much because he took up with a schoolteacher, but I guess they made a go of it although Aunt Eunice swore she'd shoot him if he ever came around again. Say now, isn't it awful that we haven't had but thirty-hundredths of rain since September fifth?" He didn't wait for an answer but took a quick breath before beginning again. His voice was high-pitched, like a plow that needed grease. "As dry as it is, the whole country is going to blow away unless we get some rain. We must've seen twenty fields sending topsoil all the way to Nebraska." The whole time, his wife—who had buck teeth and wore glasses—said not a word.

Mama was finally able to interrupt him to say she was going to bring coffee. While she was gone, I was afraid he would ask me questions because I was the oldest. What could I say to someone who never listened to anybody else?

Pretty soon, Mama returned and Mr. Williams began talking a blue streak again. "Isn't it awful that Truman fired General MacArthur? You know, that reminds me of my second cousin, Rupert. He found—you won't believe this—he found not one, but three military buttons and a 1923 fifty-cent piece in that field north of Forgan where they used to play baseball. I'd bet there's real money to be found out there . . ."

On and on. I could hardly stand it.

He told about the time his uncle's aunt's third-youngest

daughter got the hiccups and it took three days to get them stopped. Jerry said he hoped that never happened to him.

Dickie and I both glared at our little brother: Don't encourage him! We'd been taught it was impolite to leave the room when company came. After a while I wished Mama would tell us to leave. We'd been sitting two and a half hours, but there was no sign Wayne Williams was letting up. Mama would try to say something once in a while, but he just bulldozed right over her. Not aggressive-like, but when she made a peep, his voice took on an urgent tone like he just had to finish what he'd started.

Finally, Mama stood up, saying we had four cows to milk and would he like to help. He was still talking so she said it louder. He glanced down, seeming to notice he was missing one shoestring, and said he and his wife—he finally said her name was Minnie— had to go home so they could prepare for a trip to the Beaver Sandhills, which was only six miles from Forgan. What kind of preparations would that take?

Mama practically pushed them out the door. She watched until they were gone before she turned to us. "Boys, I've been wishing for more visitors. I need to be thankful I don't have more like that. You're all I need. After chores, we'll have milk and cookies and finish up those Christmas decorations."

34 Thieves

Spring 1952

Claire

Sammy burst through the door, eyes wide. "Mama, I c-can't fill the tr-tractor. No gas coming out of the hose."

I got up from bandaging Jerry's scraped knee, gave him a kiss, and turned to Sammy. "Are you sure? Zack Wiley just filled that tank two weeks ago. Let's go see."

Shep and Fido followed us as we crossed the road. Another pleasant morning—no wind.

I took the hose spout off the spike we'd pounded into the support post and thrust it into the tractor tank. Squeeze. Nothing. I muttered, "Strange. Like it really is empty." Squeezed again. Same result.

Dickie climbed on the tractor seat, grabbed the steering wheel, and pretended to drive. "I talked with old Zack when he brought out the gas. Said he used to trap bobcats down by Beaver River. That's what I want to do. After I get some traps first."

I didn't have time for bobcats and traps. "Well, I paid him $41.80—220 gallons. He said he filled it up."

"Mama, look!" Dickie jumped off the tractor and pointed to the ground. "Tracks. Tire tracks, like a truck. See?"

I tried to take this all in. Things weren't right. No one would steal from us . . . never had. But sure enough, off to the side from where we parked the tractor to refuel it, dual wheel tread marks. Who would do this? No one we knew would do such a thing. Everyone knew we were all alone. A chill crept up my back.

That's why we were targeted. News article in the paper about Elmer's funeral . . . farmer in the Greenough community . . . widow and children. It all made sense. I tried not to think of scoundrels like that. But they were out there, someplace. Could've come from the next county.

Trying to be nonchalant so not to frighten the boys, I said, "Looks like someone's been taking our gas. Probably came in here

Saturday, when we went to Liberal. Or maybe yesterday. Everybody knows we go to church Sunday morning and evening."

"Who, Mama?" Sammy said. "Who would st-steal from us?"

I shook my head and shrugged. "I don't know, son. Let's call Ray. See what he says."

৵৶

Ray came right over. One look at the tracks, and he said, "Anyone who'd steal from a widow woman oughta be strung up. Snakes like that—they'll be back. I'll tell you what, Claire, before you put another drop of gas in that tank, you need a lock on it." He took his leather gloves out of his hip pocket and smacked them across his opposite palm. "While you're at it, call Bud Campbell. The sheriff needs to be out here, helping folks that needs it 'stead of sitting around the domino parlor."

I felt sick about the whole affair. Nausea boiled within me. I scrimped and saved to give the boys a decent Christmas. The more I thought of it, I realized thieves might've been taking gas out of the tank right along—possibly more when we went up to Dodge for Christmas with my sister Ethel. Since we only used the tractor during winter to bring in feed for the cattle, we hadn't caught on until they got greedy and drained our tank.

Ray was tied up the next two days helping his son-in-law work cattle, so I called Glen Monroe. He came over and installed a lock on the hose spout. I called Zack Wiley and told him I needed a half tank of gasoline. Couldn't afford a full tank right then. After I explained the problem, he said he'd be right out. A hundred twenty-five gallons came to $23.75.

I sighed. Those new shoes I'd hoped to order from Sears Roebuck would have to wait. I'd take my old Mary Janes to the shoe shop next time we went to town.

I called Sheriff Campbell and explained what had happened. He came out later that day, and I took him over to the scene of the crime. No luck. Chickens had scratched out the tire tracks.

He gestured toward Shep and Fido. "Your dogs always this friendly?"

Dickie said, "They're good dogs—good cow dogs. Shep is a fighter, too."

"Yeah," Sammy said. "He whipped B-Bill Kiser's big dog. And Fido is really quick. Quicker than a sk-skunk."

Sheriff Campbell pushed his Stetson back on his head. "But

they ain't much as guard dogs, are they?"

The boys and I looked at one another. Finally, Dickie said, "They bark if a coyote comes around . . . or a skunk, in our chicken house."

The sheriff turned to me. "Any chance your dogs might've known the thieves?" He spat on the ground. "Just something to think about."

৯৵

Ray came over a couple days later. I saw him get out and, first thing, go over to look at our gas tank. He stepped up on one of the sawhorses to peer at Glen's handiwork, then came to the house as I went outside to meet him.

"Hello, Claire. Just wanted to make sure your tank was secure. Glen did a better job putting that lock on than I would've." He shook his head, taking a seat on the front step. "Got no use for scum that would steal from anyone. From you, a widow, they gotta be pretty low. If I had any idea who it was. But I don't." He paused. "You might oughta lock your house too."

"Oh, we lock it every time we leave, and at night too. Got a skeleton key and a latch."

"Good. Crooks get pretty bold over time. 'Spect we oughta lock our house when we go to town, 'specially overnight to Harper County. Edith says we don't have anything worth stealing, but you never know . . ."

"I've only got the few things from Mama and Pop. Jewelry and ceramic pieces," I said, "They're precious to me. Not worth a great deal to others, but I'd be heartbroken if I lost the pretties I got from Mama." I did a mental calculation of anything else we might have of value. "Oh yes, there's Elmer's shotgun and the .22 rifle. Don't know what they're worth . . ."

He removed the Stetson and ran his fingers through his hair. "Crooks got connections. They'd find someplace to hock them guns. Keep 'em outa sight, just in case.

"Say," he said. "What about your garage? You keep it locked when you're gone? Elmer had a passel of tools in there."

"Oh my." I felt a throb in my forehead. "There's a padlock on the man door, but we haven't been careful about locking it when we go to town."

Ray lurched up. "Why don't we take a look? Here come your boys. I'll bet they remember what their daddy had in his garage."

234

As we crossed the road, I explained to the boys what we wanted to do. Sammy ran ahead and opened the north sliding door, admitting a flood of morning sunlight to the interior.

Sammy and Dickie swept toward Elmer's big workbench like nails to a magnet. In the hubbub of jabbering that followed, they called out about missing tools: large and small crescent wrenches, a set of box-end wrenches, three pipe wrenches, several saws and drills, three hammers, a set of punches and chisels, screwdrivers, a sledge, block and tackle, a car jack, woodworking tools and clamps. Took everything but the vise, which was bolted to the workbench.

I felt sick, crushed by the loss of tools that Elmer had acquired over the years, instruments and devices the boys could have received from their father's hand. He made most of his own repairs, attending to the multitude of tasks required around a farm. Unlike stealing the gasoline, this theft was personal.

Ray stared at the empty shelves, hooks, and slots, struck dumb by the travesty of wanton greed. Softly cursing to himself, he turned to me. "Claire, I should've come over and helped you with this. I knowed Elmer had lots of tools, but I never would've thought anybody could be this low. Really heartless. Filthy weasels is what they are.

"I should've done it for you and the boys. For Elmer too, even though he's gone. You had so much on your mind. Couldn't expect you to think of all this. It's a crying shame, and I'm just . . . I'm just sorry."

My three sons gathered in a semicircle before us grown-ups. "It's okay, Mama," Sammy said. "Not your f-fault. We didn't know p-people could be so mean."

The other two grabbed me, one on each arm, and hugged my waist. "We still got you, Mama," Jerry said.

For weeks afterward, the boys made it a point to run over to the fuel tank after we'd been gone, looking for vehicle tracks. Once, they spotted tracks from a dual wheeled rig; another time, evidence that a car or pickup had swept in, probably to see if we'd locked the tank. It left me with a simmering rage—that scum, as Ray called them, could be so unfeeling as to target us.

As if that wasn't enough, I got the letter, postmarked Lansing, Kansas. Encased in a wrinkled envelope with a scrawled return address written in pencil, I could barely make out the name. Some numbers and the single word: Maclaren.

For a moment, I stopped breathing. That was Maggie's married name when she was married to Maclaren, the alcoholic. Maggie had raised their two kids by herself after he left for good. Beautiful little Gracie with the china blue eyes of her mother. Elmer had given her away when she married Duane Grounds from Hooker.

My eyes misted, thinking again of dear, sweet Maggie. What a saint. How I missed her.

Gracie had become Grace, a charming and beautiful wife and mother. She and Duane visited us a few times before Elmer took sick; they probably attended Elmer's funeral.

But the letter I held wasn't from Grace. It was from her handsome rebel brother, Billy. Bill. Bill Maclaren.

During the last years before she died, Maggie mentioned several times how hard it was to keep up with Bill's activities, that he'd fallen in with a rough crowd. Picked up for petty crimes, he spent a few nights in jail. Then he was arrested for serious offenses—burglary, grand larceny. For that, he'd been sentenced to the state pen in Lansing. It broke Maggie's heart, to know her son would be spending years with hardened criminals. She wrote him but seldom got a response.

She never quit praying. After all, he was her son. Her little boy, now a man, had gone his own way. She said he seemed to be addicted to taking what wasn't his, as if he was a thief at heart.

I knew I had to open the letter, if for no other reason than it was from Maggie's son. Fetching my paring knife from the sink drawer, I slit the end of the envelope. A sheet of lined tablet paper lay inside. It, too, looked as if it had been crumpled, then smoothed out. I laid it on the table, my temples pulsing.

The words, replete with cross-outs and misspellings, announced that Bill would be eligible for parole in six months. The parole board would consider his request sometime before that. He wrote how bad it was, penned up like an animal. He'd made up his mind to go straight, to stay away from the bad crowd he'd fallen in with.

What he needed most was a job and a place to stay. Just for a short time, until he got his feet on the ground. That would impress the parole board when his case came up for a hearing—for them to know Bill had a place to restart his life.

That was precisely why I wanted to keep my boys on the farm. Give them a place to stand, a firm foundation to launch from, where they could spread their wings and someday go out into the big world.

I didn't want to think of that. The world wasn't just big; it was sometimes dark and uncaring. I drew my hand to my mouth, gazing out the window where the boys were playing, so innocent and trusting. Oh, Jesus, you know how weak I am, how fearful and foolish and full of doubt. You've entrusted these wonderful sons into my care. I can't do this alone. I need you, Jesus. So much.

Bill's last words mentioned how much he'd respected me and Elmer, how his mother loved us and that she would've wanted him to connect with me, because she knew I'd do right by him. He said he was sorry to hear Uncle Elmer had died, and could he hear back from me soon.

I stared at the letter. Bill was locked up because he was a thief, taking things that weren't his. Just like whoever had been stealing our gas. And Elmer's tools. I was plenty mad at those lowlifes. I'd never sympathized with thieves. But this was Maggie's son.

What if it were one of my boys? I couldn't imagine one of them stealing. No, they never would. Elmer was a better father than Dick Maclaren had ever been. I never asked Maggie why Bill stole. Maybe she didn't know why. A mother would never think that of her child. Not if she loved them. But Maggie had had to come around, accept that her boy was a thief.

What would I want others to do if one of my boys were ever in such a mess? How awful. And I owed Maggie so much. She'd been my strength, loving me through the trials and heartaches of losing Kate, and then Pop, of dealing with life.

It struck me that God has a strange sense of humor. Except this wasn't funny. The week before, I was thinking just like Ray—anyone who'd steal from a widow and her kids oughta be strung up. Now, there I was, being asked to take in a thief.

Maybe Bill really has changed. He said he had. Of course, saying and doing are two different things. At the very least, he'd respect me and the boys, because of all I'd done for his mother. Yeah, at the very least—I'd hope so.

Life is never easy. It would be better if it were black and white, like when I was a little girl, living with Mama and Pop on the farm. This wasn't that clear, because I didn't know if Bill had changed. Maybe he didn't know if he'd really changed.

I folded the letter, put it in the envelope, and stowed it in the top drawer of my tall kitchen cabinet, where I kept important papers. I would have to think and pray about what to do. In the end, I'd have to decide.

35 Night Visitors

Summary 1952

Claire

A letter from my attorney made my face burn. It was nothing, really. Simply a notice to heirs and beneficiaries to be published in The Herald-Democrat regarding the final hearing on Elmer's estate. It was also a reminder of when I'd tried to hide the truth from Lansden. My attempt to look good had gotten in the way of doing good and being good. Not an actual lie, just an omission of fact, and it had suited me at the time. But it was outright hypocrisy. I didn't like that about myself but didn't know how to fix me.

The letter went in the top drawer of the cabinet with the other important papers. Bill McLaren's letter, still on top, reminded me I hadn't given him an answer. Rereading his letter, it looked like he needed a job more than a place to stay.

So much trouble, all the details of helping someone else. How ungrateful, Claire. Think of all the trouble the neighbors went to for your sake. Life is made up of parts, a few big events interspersed with hundreds of situations. Like harvesting our wheat crop, what there was of it. Another detail that needed attention.

The lack of moisture all spring had generated dust clouds and dreary hot days. I knew the wheat was thin, the heads small, but we needed what we could get. Sammy said Bill Kizer, next door to the east, had finished his harvest. I called Kizer to see if he'd cut ours. He agreed and brought his self-propelled Baldwin combine over the next day.

Thankful to have that task attended to, I began baking biscuits while Jerry and Dickie labored over the butter churn. Midmorning, we heard the sound of a combine.

It was Kizer. He hopped off his machine and met me and Sammy at the front yard. "Claire, I don't think I can help you. That wheat's too thin. Not worth cutting."

239

I tried to comprehend. We needed that wheat. "Not worth cutting? You're not serious. I know it's not as good as yours, but I expected something out of—"

"I won't charge for what I got—maybe twenty, thirty bushels—but there's not enough to warrant running my machine through it. I cut across what looked to be the best stand. Just ain't there, Claire. Where do you want me to dump the wheat I got in my bin? I don't think you'd have enough to bother trucking it to Floris."

Sammy said, "I'll open the south g-garage door. He can put it in there." He took off toward the garage.

I stood there like a deflated balloon as Kizer climbed back up on his machine and wheeled it toward the garage. By the time Sammy had the garage floor swept, Bill had positioned the big gray monster and started auguring our wheat harvest onto the concrete slab. It made a mound about three feet high. About the way I felt.

He edged the Baldwin away from our garage, then gave me a half-wave as he turned onto the road to head back to his place. I didn't wave back.

Five minutes later, a loaded wheat truck rolled past our place, probably on its way to the Floris grain elevator. Dickie said it was Arthur Durbin, driving one of Kenneth Taylor's new Chevrolet tandems. With wheat selling for two-ten a bushel, that load was worth over five hundred dollars. I was of a mind to get in my car and force him off the road, climb in Taylor's shiny new truck and take that load of wheat to Floris for myself.

Then I remembered the Chrysler wouldn't start without a jump. A new battery would cost more than the car was worth. I wasn't even equipped to be a second-rate truck thief.

One look across the road tipped me over the edge. "Sammy, shut that stupid garage door before those chickens eat our entire wheat crop!"

Dickie started to ask a question, until he saw my expression. He hurried off but stopped when I said, "Did you finish churning the butter?"

"Oh," he said. "It's just about done."

Which meant, of course, that it wasn't done. "Would you like some just-about-done macaroni for dinner?" I said.

He dropped his head, tousled black hair covering his forehead. "Okay, Mama."

We were in a pickle, and I had no idea what to do. Had to do something about the car, regardless whether I wanted to be a horse thief or just a plain mom. I'd already planned how to spend the money from our now nonexistent wheat crop. Edwin had looked at my forty-acre wheat field a month ago. He opined it might make ten or twelve bushels per acre, which meant I might gross $800 to a $1,000, if wheat prices held at two dollars a bushel. Those numbers had been reduced to chicken feed, based on the assessment of Bill Kizer and my hens.

I returned to a quiet house to prepare biscuits with macaroni and cheese. So quiet, and I knew why. Once I had put the food on the table, I looked around at my three boys. "My dear sons, you are so precious to me. I didn't act like it this morning, did I?"

Jerry chirped, "No, Mama, you acted like you were mad at the whole world today."

"Yes, and I'm sorry. I just expected we'd be able to take some wheat to town and get a little money, but . . . well, you boys saw what happened. Kizer said it's not worth bothering with." I met the eyes of my three. "We'll get through all this. You'll see."

I wondered if I was wrong to always try to put a brave face on things—on everything. I'd learned that from Pop. Maggie, too. They both called it faith.

After supper, it was Dickie's turn to help me with the dishes when a blue Hudson sedan pulled into our yard. Not close to the house, but nearer to the windblown tamarack by the road. Shep barked a couple times, but his tail wag signaled friendliness. Fido, not a barker, simply stood, watching. Obviously, the visitor was unsure, as any normal person had a right to be.

So was I. People seldom went visiting in the country after eight o'clock. At least I could step outside and let them know the dogs weren't a threat. Maybe these people were lost.

As I emerged from the house, the lone occupant was just then getting out of the Ford. Then, like standing at water's edge before a big wave hits you, I knew.

I stopped mid-stride, every cell in my being frozen. The figure pivoted around his car door, both hands in his pockets and his chest puffed out. Just like Harold.

Because that's who it was—my ex-husband.

I wanted to scream. I had sheltered my boys from the knowledge of my previous marriage, and here, the crumb had shown up, a hundred and fifty miles from Ness City. To take over, to insert his presence into our lives, take advantage. I didn't know why, but whatever it was, it wasn't going to happen. No way would he sully the memory of their dead father with the knowledge of the greatest mistake of my life—him!

A quick glance behind me to make sure none of the boys had followed me out. I marched toward the bearer of that familiar leering smirk.

Sammy

Dickie and I watched from the kitchen window as Mama headed toward the visitor's car. "Who is it?" he said.

"How would I know? She d-doesn't even know who it is."

"She acts like she knows him."

"Yeah, like she's t-telling him where to go."

"Maybe he asked directions."

"I guess so. She's pointing north."

"Now, she's pointing at his nose. Oh, now she's pointing at the house."

"Oh, l-look at her face. Sh-she's mad."

"Mama's mad." Jerry climbed on a stool to join our watcher's group. "Oh, she's really mad. She's kicking dirt at him."

"He did something really bad, and Mama knows what it is," Dickie said.

"He musta been awful naughty." Jerry got down off his stool. "I'm going outside so I can hear what they're—"

"Don't go out there!" we both yelled.

Jerry stopped, eyes wide and mouth open. Dickie ran over and grabbed his arm. "Don't you go out there, Jerry. Wait for Mama. She'll tell us all about it, okay?"

He still seemed unsure, so I went over to help Dickie. We nudged Jerry back to his perch. By that time, it was almost all dark, and Mama and the visitor guy were like paper cutouts lit by our big yard light. Then the guy got in his car, fishtailed it away from the tamarack, and headed north. She stood there the whole time, hands on her hips, until he was out of sight.

When she started coming toward the house, we hustled back to the living room, like we'd been playing marbles the whole time. Of course, Dickie and I knew Mama would find out we'd been watching her. Anybody with a gabby little brother learns that pretty quick.

Claire

I was wringing wet by the time I returned inside. That louse. That despicable, pompous nothing. He hadn't changed a bit. Determined I wasn't going to let that encounter affect my boys, I resolved not to tell them about Harold. He was history, and he would stay that way with my sons.

Jerry and Dickie asked a few questions about the mysterious visitor, but I deflected them with the explanation that we all needed rest, and we could talk about it later. That seemed to satisfy them, but Sammy's silence told me he knew more than he was letting on.

Two nights later, Shep commenced barking about midnight and wouldn't shut up. He was on the west side of the house, out near the road. It came as an insistent woof, like he sensed or saw something beyond the reach of the yard light, which was mounted on a pole next to the road. Jerry was asleep beside me, so I slipped out of bed, careful not to awaken him. Putting on robe and slippers, I crept to the dining room window, which was cracked an inch to admit cool air. A moonless night, so the illumination arc of the yard light spread only to the fuel tank and dimmed short of the garage.

Shep stood halfway across the road, facing the loading chute. Fido was a critter dog, and if the intruder had been four-legged, he would have been after him. Which meant this was a two-legged trespasser.

I knew without a doubt who it was. Harold, come back to intimidate me. Well, I was having none of that. Grabbing the flashlight, I eased outside, down the steps and through the two lines of Chinese elms in our front yard that paralleled the road. Fido joined me but stopped at the light pole. I stepped into the pool of brightness, my shadow arching ahead of me like water spilled from a can on a flat surface. There being no wind, my slippers made little scrunching sounds as I crossed the road.

Shep began barking again, an angry wail interspersed with deep-throated growls when he saw me. I continued his direction, and he moved beside me as we left the clarity of the illuminated area. My eyes probed the shadows behind and under the elevated fuel tank, beside the parked machinery, toward the loading chute which reared toward me at the south end of the garage. No movement, no sound but my breathing. Even Shep was quiet.

At that moment, the realization I was being watched drove a dagger of terror into my throat. My breath caught. I felt I was going to faint.

Harold the intimidator, I was not afraid of. But nothing about the situation confirmed that's who it was. How stupid. I was fifty yards from the safety of my front door. Scarcely able to breathe, I almost collapsed out of stark terror. Willing myself to turn, I began walking, step . . . step . . . step, back the way I'd come. It took every bit of willpower I had not to twist around to face what I knew was surely coming after me. And even more not to bolt. My only companions, the scratch-scratch of my slippers and Shep, who then decided not to wait for me.

Even as I ascended each of the three steps to our front porch, I expected a restraining hand upon me. Once inside, I struggled with the skeleton key in a frenzy of shaking and whimpering until I twisted it into locked position.

Turning, I slumped into the nearest chair in the unlighted kitchen, gasping and trembling, my body bathed in sweat. "Oh, Jesus, thank you, Jesus . . ." Over and over, I said the words until peace finally came.

God had stayed the hand of whoever, whatever. It may have been Harold. Very likely it was not. I didn't want to think about who. What God did was show me how reckless I could be, how my foolishness had endangered not only me, but the boys as well.

The next morning, I did two important things. First, I wrote Bill McLaren, telling him I'd check with farmers in our neighborhood, to see if any needed a field hand. Dependable help wasn't easy to find.

I didn't tell him that I might sleep better, knowing a man was on the premises.

The next big thing I did was to call Edwin Eagan and ask if he'd see if my wheat field was worth cutting. We could sure use that income.

Edwin didn't bother looking at my wheat ahead of time; he simply drove his green machine—a new John Deere—and cut the entire field. To most farmers, the seven bushels per acre wouldn't have been worth the bother, even at $2.14 per bushel, but we weren't most farmers.

I surmised Kenneth Taylor never knew it, but that $600 kept me from having to hijack one of his new wheat trucks.

I was anxious to see how the situation would pan out with my nephew Bill. Pop would have understood, but I knew Mom would have turned over in her grave if she thought we had a relative in the Kansas State Pen. I couldn't imagine her reaction if I'd told her he was moving from the penitentiary to our house.

36 Brand New

Claire

I raised the shade over the kitchen window. The branches on the tamarack scarcely moved in the thin morning light. Nice to have a calm day. I glanced back into the depths of our house. The boys had better get moving to feed the livestock before the school bus arrived. Only two cows still giving milk; I'd finish that afterward.

Just then, I saw movement far out in the pasture. I stared to the north, then called back toward the bedrooms, "Boys! Come quick. Look. Look at that."

In a moment, all three had gathered beside me. "Look." I pointed. A coyote loped across the flat grassy area of the pasture beyond the narrow lane north of the barn. Then he reversed direction. He was chasing a jackrabbit, usually a fruitless task, and the old jack had a good lead. Elmer said jackrabbits could run thirty to thirty-five miles an hour. We had never seen a real live chase before.

The rabbit circled back north, instead of continuing east where he could've dived under our pasture fence and then across the road to our field. The racers repeated their circuit twice more. Each loop, we could see the coyote gaining. It was clearly a race of life or death—possibly for both, as the drought had taken its toll on everything alive.

None of us uttered a word, like we were all holding our breath. Finally, Dickie whispered, "Mom, he's gonna catch him."

Indeed, he was. The jackrabbit's oval path kept getting smaller and smaller, giving the coyote the advantage of angling across the rabbit's course. None of us said so till afterward, but we hoped the rabbit would escape. Alas, the coyote surged, and with a lunge, pounced on his victim. There was little struggle; the rabbit gave his all, which was not enough.

The coyote paused only long enough to secure the rabbit in his jaws, then went in a sideways half-trot, his head held high to keep his bounty from dragging on the ground. Eventually he disappeared over a rise to the northwest.

After finishing chores, I called Ray and Edith and asked if they could come over to give the old Chrysler a push one last time. Edith wanted to know why but I told her she'd see.

❧

The Chrysler ran well once it started, and that was the rub. I contemplated how to approach my banker. Every time I saw Naylor, I expected him to tell me they couldn't loan me another dime. Didn't know what I'd do if that happened.

En route to Liberal, I thought about the coyote and the jackrabbit—both desperate for survival. The rabbit might have gotten away if he had dived under our pasture fence instead of repeating the loop. The four-strand barbed wire fence would have slowed the coyote, for sure. It made me wonder—were we pursuers or the pursued? Things seldom get better by doing the same process again and again. I barely had enough in our account to make the last loan payment. With the drought hanging on, we were barely making enough to live on.

Something had to change, or we couldn't remain on the farm.

Anyone looking in from the outside might think our life was simple. Eat, sleep, do the chores, send the boys to school, and go to church. Yeah, that, and survive.

Often the most well-meaning folks didn't understand the small complications of being without. I recalled how nice for Oly Monroe to take Sammy and Dickie, along with other neighborhood kids, to Vacation Bible School in Forgan. Before returning home, she took the gang down to Virgil Adams' store for treats. The kids trooped in to order maple bars or ice cream—except for my boys, who didn't have a nickel between them. They sat in the car. Oly, always a talker, was gabbing with other grown-ups and didn't notice. Not the first day, or the second. She was so embarrassed when the awkward situation came to light. Sammy never said a word to me until later "because we don't have much, and I didn't want to worry you, Mama."

It made me want to cry. My dear sons—protecting me. It was true—we didn't have much—but I would've done something to keep my boys from being left out.

I wondered what other farmers in the neighborhood thought about us, me and the boys still hanging on. Like maybe a collective holding of their breaths, expecting us to disappear down a badger hole or be blown to Nebraska with the next big dust storm.

Ray and Edith, along with Henry and Blanche weren't indifferent—they knew what was going on without feeling sorry for us. I couldn't have accepted pity. Edith got a little nosy sometimes, but Ray often stopped in—to "see how them boys is doin'." Maybe he felt obligated, being Elmer's cousin. Or maybe he assumed we'd pull through because Elmer always had.

Edwin Eagan could always be depended on to stop by two or three times a month, suggesting better ways of doing things, or telling us what needed to be attended to. Good thing, because I was uncertain about machines and tasks Elmer would've known about instinctively—best time to plant or cultivate. I had my sources for repairs but didn't always know where to get parts. Sometimes, Edwin casually checked our equipment. Especially after the front wheel of the Ford fell off when Sammy was cultivating row crop. It nearly pitched him off the tractor.

Sammy walked back to the house, and together, we pondered what to do. Edwin would know. I called and he said to pack the wheel bearings with axle grease. He came up and showed us how to do it. After a few tricks like that, he probably shook his head in wonder. I supposed he viewed the boys and me as lost sheep.

The wind churned a pile of tumbleweeds across the road, making me swerve and bringing me back to reality. Claire, stop being so morbid. You're just feeling sorry for yourself.

It had been so dry. Over the previous eight months, we'd had only four-and-a-half inches of rain. Most fields were blowing, sending our topsoil to Dakota or Texas, depending on wind direction. As I pulled into town, I chastised myself for dwelling on the negative again.

I'd booked an appointment with Chet Naylor, and parked in front of People's National Bank with a few minutes to spare. Not sure if the Chrysler would restart, I left the engine running. Anybody who wanted to steal that car could have it.

My footsteps echoed in the polished granite mausoleum known as People's National Bank as I approached Marie, the dowdy blond receptionist.

"Hello, Claire. Mr. Naylor is expecting you." She smiled and motioned down the hardwood hallway I'd walked many times before.

My banker pushed aside files stacked on his desk and nodded for me to have a seat. "Claire, it's good to see you. How are you and the boys doing?"

"Well, thanks for asking. All three are at Greenough School. Since the consolidation, we only have the grade school, but we've got a basketball team. Sammy's a sixth grader, and Dickie is a grade behind him. They both get to play. We win some games too. Jerry just started school." I paused to catch my breath. "We're getting along."

"I'm glad to hear that. How are things with your farm?"

"It's been dry, as you know. I may have to sell some cattle." I studied his expression for a hint of alarm. "At any rate, I intend to make my payment, one way or another."

He ran a hand across his face, stroking his chin. "I have no doubt you'll manage. The drought has put everyone on edge. Every farmer and rancher we talk to is concerned we might be returning to the dirty-thirties. I hear sand has drifted over some of the roads west of town. If we don't get rain, it'll get worse.

"But you didn't come in to talk about the weather. How can I help you today?"

I took a deep breath, giving him the spiel I'd prepared. Without ceremony, I stated my need—sufficient cash to purchase a dependable used car of any make. I didn't tell him the Chrysler was idling in front of his bank at that very moment. Visions of Dillinger and Capone flashed through my mind. What if a policeman . . . I jerked and almost leapt out of my chair.

Naylor must've seen the panic in my face. "Is anything wrong?"

I began to relax as I realized no policeman would be dumb enough to think our old Chrysler was a getaway car . . . "Oh. Oh, no . . . For a minute I thought I'd left the stove burner on . . . I'm sorry." I tried to paint on a serene smile. "We just got a propane stove and I'm getting used to . . . Sorry, I just have so many things on my mind. Please, go on."

He nodded in what I took to be a sympathetic expression. "I understand. You've got quite a burden. Have had, ever since Elmer took sick. Uh, let me make a call—should take just a couple minutes." He picked up the handset of his desk phone and dialed. Then, he swiveled his desk chair around and began talking.

My face burned as I realized how silly I must have appeared to a man who'd walked me through every financial crisis since Elmer was diagnosed with cancer. I'd been late on my last two payments, and he could cut me off for additional loans. I wondered if he'd say no that day.

Replacing the handset into the receiver, he said, "Why don't you go to Hood Chevrolet? Ask for Les Hood. Tell him what you need. I've explained everything. He's a square guy and won't try to pull a fast one. Bring the paperwork back to me—today, if you can. He'll set you up in a nice, dependable car." With that, he stood and extended his hand.

I exhaled, clutched my purse with a trembling hand, and shook his hand. I couldn't believe how so many answers to prayer managed to fall into my fumbling grasp. A long time ago, Maggie had reminded me God is always ready to pour out his love on us.

Maybe that really was true.

The boys were already home from school when I pulled into our driveway in a 1950 two-tone green Chevrolet Deluxe coupe. The dogs barked at the unfamiliar vehicle, which drew the kids to the front door. When I got out, they didn't move but simply stared, their mouths open.

I said, "Why aren't my sons coming to greet their mother? Here she comes home in a new car, and you're not even excited about it!"

All three sprinted toward me in a tumult of laughter, hugs, opening car doors and windows, questions, trying out seats, looking in the trunk, and more hugs. They couldn't have been more pleased than if I'd ridden in as the Queen of Sheba. My boys hadn't known much of anything brand new. I never dreamed that getting something as basic as an almost new motor car could mean so much.

That little green car—complete with fender skirts and a working radio, an engine that started every time, and a heater that heated—it seemed to say we were going to make it. We would pull through.

37 Nephew Rescue

Sammy

We boys didn't know much about our cousin Bill McLaren. We'd only seen him a few times, at Aunt Maggie's. Nobody wanted to talk about him. I asked Mom why.

Busy rolling out pie crust dough, she paused, then sighed. "Bill was locked up, put in prison, because he took things that weren't his. Several times, he took things." She turned back to her breadboard, as if the discussion was closed.

Taking off my glasses, I lowered my voice. "Is he c-coming to live at our house?"

Mama didn't say anything, and I didn't want to interrupt her pie-making operation again. She finished crimping the edge of the crust her own special way all around the edge of each pan. Finally, she said, "Bill won't be staying here—maybe a night if he comes. Would give us a chance to do a good deed—in Aunt Maggie's memory." She put two apple pies and a pan of extra pie dough in the oven. "Bill's getting out on parole, if I can find him a job. He—"

"How you gonna give him a job, Mama? We don't have no money to pay him." Dickie puckered his lips. "I don't want him here. He might take my arrowhead collection."

"Or my marbles," Jerry called from the living room, where he was playing with his train of wood blocks.

"You're b-both wrong," I said. "Mama has to find him a job first. Then he'll come. And he'll stay where he works. Isn't that right, Mama?"

She looked up. "Jerry-berry, you don't have to worry about him taking your marbles."

"He better not take my arrowhead collection," Dickie said. "It's valuable. Ray said it should be worth a lot of money someday."

She opened the oven door. "This pie dough looks ready."

Questions were forgotten in the rush to get a share of the baked dough, sprinkled with cinnamon and sugar. I savored my piece. Guess we boys will adjust, like we always do.

251

Determined to get work for Bill, I asked several farmers at our church. Each said they'd think it over. No commitments after three weeks left me wondering if I might've been too quick to agree to help. My promise had made it my burden. As the last strains of "Just as I Am" wound down after Brother Caywood's sermon, I looked for Floyd Nichols, chairman of the deacon board. Close to retirement, he wasn't a likely possibility, but he was my last hope.

I greeted others as everyone streamed toward the church exit, and timed my departure to intercept Floyd. A greeting, then, "Floyd, would you be needing a field hand this summer?"

"Hello, Claire. Your boys are young to be working away from home, aren't they?"

"I'm asking for my twenty-two-year-old nephew. He needs a job. Wants to build up savings, so he can get established on his own."

"Twenty-two years old? What's he been doing before now?"

No use beating around the bush. "He's my sister-in-law Maggie's boy. You remember, I asked for prayer for her before she died of cancer. She was my dearest friend."

"Yes, I recall. And her boy, you say? He ever work on a farm?"

"I'm not sure. He's . . . I should tell you that Bill—that's his name—he got in trouble with the law after his mother died . . . Things went to pieces—"

"What's this about him being in trouble with the law?"

"Bill fell in with the wrong crowd. Got picked up by the police. Eventually, he was sent to the Kansas state pen for theft. Caught with a truckload of grain—and a truck—that wasn't his. He's served fifteen months but will be released on parole if he can show he's got a bona fide job." I took a deep breath, expecting him to interrupt me again. "As I said, Maggie's death really affected the family. His father was an alcoholic, left them years be—"

"So this boy . . . Bill, he stole. He's a thief. Property crimes." Floyd started edging away, then turned back. "Claire, I don't know why you—with all you got to bear—how you got to be selected as caretaker for this troubled young man. Surely there are other family members who could, and should, step in and shepherd him. For sure, it shouldn't be you. I'd rethink your involvement, if you still have that option." He paused again. "That's not answering your question, of course, and I feel poorly about that. But I can't have a fellow like that around my place. That's the way I see things."

I couldn't utter a response and stared as Floyd backed away. I wanted to sit. Right there in the narthex, at a chair in the corner. Had to think. About Bill, mostly. Floyd's phrase, "a fellow like that," needled me more than his turndown. Had to admit I didn't really know what my nephew was like. I hadn't considered not providing a landing for Bill.

I needed to think about what I'd gotten myself into. It shouldn't be me? If not me, who else? Bill was family.

His sister Grace was family too. Her husband Duane worked for an oil company. Maggie told me Bill had banged up Duane's car and failed to pay for repairs. He hadn't repaid money Grace loaned him without Duane's knowledge. Plenty to set him crosswise with anybody, let alone his brother-in-law.

The only other option wasn't an option. Maggie's husband Lee. Bill wouldn't have the brass to ask him for anything. Lee had called him a snake in the grass. He said Bill was nothing but trouble. Maggie grieved over conflict between the two. From what she told me, Bill and Lee had come to blows once or twice.

It came down to the fact that Bill didn't have many bridges left to burn, and what he had, he'd burnt them all. There was no one else but me. He hadn't done anything against me—yet.

I took a deep breath. I didn't have to be my nephew's rescuer. He could very well serve out his sentence, get what he deserved. Bill had been a thief, no question about that. Maybe he reformed. I remembered Brother Caywood saying it was only by the grace of God that none of us really got what we deserved. Maybe I could show some grace, not be so judgmental.

Other than Blanche having me cut her hair, no one asked much of me. I hated to admit it, but if anyone asked me for a favor, I'd feel obligated to say yes. Obligated. I'd been on the receiving end for so much. Neighbors and friends had been doing something for us ever since Elmer came home from that second surgery. I didn't want—couldn't bear—to say no.

Floyd Nichols' blunt statement that I should have refused my nephew brought a slew of questions swimming in my brain, like newly hatched minnows looking for something to glom onto before they could traverse the floods and flows of life. He insinuated I hadn't thought this through. And if I had, I'd been rash, foolish, unthinking. I'll set him straight on that. Thinks I

253

can't see beyond the end of my nose, just because I'm a woman. He'll find out.

Floyd didn't see family bonds the way I did. The idea I had the right to refuse Bill's request never entered my mind. If anyone asks for a piece of bread, you don't send them away with a smile and a handshake. At the heart of it, Maggie had always been there for me, encouraging, praying with me, insisting I depend on Jesus—good times and hard times.

Helping Maggie's son would honor her . . . It would also help me erase the debt I owed the farmers who planted our crops, the men who sat by Elmer's bedside for nights on end, for the neighbors who saw to it that we got a telephone, indoor plumbing, and electrical power in our house. Brother Caywood said I didn't need to repay those people. To do so would rob them of the opportunity to show compassion. Okay, they showed compassion, so why not pay back what they spent? I'd feel better about it.

Bill knew nothing of all that. He'd never know. So why was I doing it? No one was keeping score.

No one but me.

But if anyone was watching, they would know Claire Hall always paid her debts.

౸౸

After Floyd Nichols shot down my hopes, I didn't have the nerve to ask any of the other farmers at church if they wanted to hire my prodigal nephew.

Two weeks later, Clifford Wakefield approached me after Sunday school. A kindly man, about six-foot-two, he habitually bent down to speak to others. "Say, Claire, I been thinking about that request for your nephew. Got any takers yet?"

I gave a shaky laugh. "Nothing yet."

"Seeing's as how you're willing to stick your neck out for someone in a pinch, I figured I could offer this nephew a chance to redeem himself. Besides, good farmhands are hard to find."

My knees felt wobbly. "Cliff, that would be wonderful. He hasn't had the best examples to follow. I think he'll make it with a new start."

"Shouldn't be any problem. I'll make it clear—any shenanigans, he's gone. Just let me know when he'll be available. I could start him tomorrow."

I felt like giving Cliff a hug, but Velma had come over to join the conversation. Besides, we were right there in church. Still feeling light-headed, I realized how much my rescue effort had weighed on me. Seemed like the job hunt was more for me than for Bill. Now I could tell the boys we'd be able to do good for someone else. Just like Jesus taught. They thought it was okay, as long as they didn't have to give up their bedrooms.

I wrote Bill he could tell the parole board he had a solid offer of employment. They could contact me for particulars. Once he knew his release date, he was to tell when and where to pick him up in Liberal. No way could I go to Lansing. That was clear across the state, up near Kansas City. Trailways provided bus service to Liberal, or he could take the Rock Island.

I ended my letter with a statement that we were helping him because of all his sweet mother had done for me. He could sleep on our couch the first night. Afterward, his home would be Cliff Wakefield's bunkhouse.

Three weeks later, a letter with the now familiar scrawl appeared in our mailbox. Bill wrote that my letter arrived in time for parole board action. They'd scheduled his release. He'd travel by bus and would arrive in Liberal at the Trailways station. Said I could pick him up. He gave the time of 5:10 a.m., August 10th.

He didn't ask me. Just said I could. Certainly not the best time of day. I'd have to get up with the chickens. School started the following Monday, and the board had hired a new teacher. Parents were expected to clean and help get the building ready for classes, which put Bill's arrival right in the middle of everything. To add to the complication, they fired the school cook, so I'd have to pack lunches for the boys until that got straightened out.

I called Wakefield, who also served on the Greenough school board. He offered to pick Bill up, when I told him the hour of his arrival.

"No, Cliff, I'll take that responsibility. He's my nephew, someone I haven't seen for a long time, and I want to greet him." I didn't tell Cliff I was peeved by Bill's presumption. I wanted to meet him face to face and clear the air right off the bat.

Cliff said, "That's up to you, Claire. Just trying to save you the trouble. You know about the school cook situation, I suppose. Mothers will be fixing box lunches, like they used to."

"Thanks for the offer. I'll get him over to your place as soon as he gets his baggage together." A thought hit me. "Doubt he'll have the clothes for farm work . . . Maybe I can find some of Elmer's old work clothes, although he's smaller than Elmer was." My forehead pounded, rejecting the idea of parceling out any of Elmer's personal items to anyone else.

"I can rustle up a pair of work boots, whatever he needs . . ." He paused. "We'll let you know the date for school cleanup. With McCall's field blowing dirt north of the school all last month, we may have to take a scoop shovel to the gym floor. We'll see what kind of worker the new teacher is. He's a young fellow, just out of college, but seems smart as a whip. His old man is Pack Hibbs, county commissioner for District Two."

"We can only hope." I didn't tell Cliff I hadn't thought too highly of the board's previous hires. This new whip-smart teacher was probably more of the same. I wondered if my boys would even be qualified to attend Forgan High School, much less college.

I pulled in beside the Trailways sign a little before five. The place looked deserted, and the bus was supposed to arrive at 5:10? I checked the watch Elmer had gotten me in Wichita, several times in fact, over the next hour as I waited. Still no bus, no ticket agent, nothing. Grim as a judge, I started up the Chevy and headed home.

What was up with Bill? Sent me wrong information, that's what he did. Maybe he wasn't coming at all. I didn't know what to do. No word from him. And Cliff was expecting me to deliver a farm hand to his front door. A fine kettle of fish. After a while, I decided not to stew about it. I knew one thing—Mr. Bill was going to get an earful when I got ahold of him.

At 4:30 the next afternoon, I received a call from my nephew. "Aunt Claire, where are you? I'm here at the bus station, waiting for—"

"Where were you yesterday morning? You said your bus was arriving yesterday at 5:10. I got up at four in the morning so I could be there on time. Nobody was—"

"Five-ten? No, that's when my bus left Kansas City yesterday. It—"

"Well, that's the only time you gave me. How was your departure time going to help me know when your bus arrived? That's the only time written in your letter—5:10 a.m. You gave me wrong information, so you'll just have to wait."

Silence. Then, "Well, when are you going to come and get me?"

I'd come on strong, but I didn't care. "I'll have to get the boys to do the rest of the chores. If I leave at five, I can be up there by half past. Good-bye."

I banged the earpiece in the cradle. "Such lack of consideration." No apology, but that didn't surprise me. I heard the door open. Jerry had just come in. "Son, you tell Sammy and Dickie I've got to go back up to Liberal—to pick up Bill. I should be home a little after six, and I'll fix us a good supper then."

Wide-eyed, he said, "Okay, Mama."

"And make sure you gather the eggs after you do that." I gave him a hug, realizing I probably had thunder in my expression.

Wind was a-blowing up a good sandstorm by the time I got to Liberal. Not the best time to be out in the weather. It didn't surprise me that the station waiting room was closed. Ticket agents weren't paid to pamper stranded travelers. Casting about for signs of activity, I saw a figure separate itself from the shadowed entry and approach my car, head down against the gale. A pile of tumbleweeds bounced across his path and he looked up just enough so I could see his face.

It was Bill, squinting against the wind. I gestured for him to open the passenger door and put his bag behind the seat. He flipped it in and swung in beside me, muttering about the weather. I glanced at him as he got in. A ruggedly handsome face wiped clean of expression. Average build and height. His brilliantined black hair had been swiped across his forehead by the wind, and he finger-combed it back in place. Even that didn't disguise the brutal haircut. Ill-fitting jeans and jacket with white crew neck undershirt—probably prison issue.

"You're finally here." His attempt at a smile didn't reach his eyes. He let the wind slam the door shut. "I always forget the cyclones in this country."

"Actually, you're finally here," I said. "I was here yesterday." I waited for a response. Hopefully, an apology. None forthcoming, I turned to face him, my arms crossed. "I wished you had shown consideration to tell me when you were going to arrive. I came up here yesterday morning. Early, so you wouldn't have to wait. It's your fault you had to sit here this morning."

He swelled up like a toad, lips in a firm line, and began drumming on the dash with his fingers. Probably wasn't used to being confronted that way, and from a woman, to boot.

I started the car. "All right, I've had my say." Waiting a moment longer, I said, "And yes, it's been a dry year." How typical. We talk about the weather, when we should be working out our differences. He kept his head turned to the side window for the first five miles.

My attempts at small talk were met with curt answers, so silence reigned for most of the forty minutes driving back home. What should I talk about with someone who's just been released from prison? Family came to mind. I said, "Have you been in touch with Grace and Duane? Ever hear from them?"

"Yeah, I heard from Sis a couple times. Uh, maybe, yeah, several times. Duane and I never hit it off."

Yes, I can imagine. "Does she know you're . . . out . . . on parole?"

"Not sure. Like I said, Duane's got his opinions and I've got mine, so I, well, I'm starting my life over. Finally." Nothing more.

I waited, then asked if he'd ever done farm work.

"Nah. But it can't be too hard. I can do whatever they expect. I've done lots of things."

"Clifford Wakefield will be fair, and he's got a big farm. Doubt if it will be complicated, but farm work is hard. Long hours, monotonous, out in the heat and wind a long—"

"It's out. Out of the joint. That I will like."

"Oh. Yes, I suppose so." Over the last hill before the farm. "There's our place. I'll fix supper. You bring your things in, and I'll set you up to sleep on our couch. Imagine you're tired from that long bus ride. Tomorrow morning, I'll take you over to Wakefield's farm."

No response. Bill hardly spoke to the boys. Not once did I hear a thank-you.

I felt like I had been babbling. But I was exhilarated to have vented my true feelings. Maggie would've been proud of me. Enough of being taken for granted.

38 Out of the Storm

Claire

From our mailbox, I crossed the road and went inside. I dropped
the Sears & Roebuck catalog on the kitchen table and set out a can
of hominy. Flouring pork chops for dinner, I realized I'd been so
preoccupied thinking about the catalog, I hadn't noticed where the
kids were. A quick dusting of my hands, and I returned outside.

From the top step, I looked all directions, aware the air had
become dead still. Then I saw them out north, just where the
narrow lane broadens to the main pasture. Beyond them, perhaps
a half mile away, was a sight that made my blood run cold.

A wall of frothing dust was headed toward them from the
northwest like a freight train. It seemed to have emerged out of
nowhere. Just like dusters of the nineteen-thirties, it extended
southwest and northeast as far as the eye could see. The boys had
seen it. Appearing like stick figures from where I stood, they
started running toward home. Sammy and Dickie grabbed eight-
year-old Jerry, practically dragging him. Too late—the blanket of
darkness engulfed them before they'd gone fifty yards.

The wind suddenly came alive, sending every tree into a
frenzy of movement. The afternoon sun glowed eerily atop the
cloud of boiling dust before it blipped out as the churning storm
swept over our barn, over me, over everything. I screamed,
despairing they couldn't hear me. Heart thumping, I gasped a
ragged whimper.

I dashed across the road, jerked the south corral gate open,
and charged around the barn, panting and yelling. Sand lashed my
face as I stumbled toward the eight-foot-high windbreak which
Elmer had built five years before. Lord, don't let them lose their
way. I hugged the end post of the windbreak, the other hand
shielding my face as I searched through roaring darkness for my
sons. My sons!

It seemed like an eternity before dim shadows emerged out of
the gloom. A moving figure, then more. Not them, but three cows,
driven by the wind. Minutes later, the boys appeared. They

staggered toward me, heads down, Shep and Fido beside them.

Arms entwined, we surged toward the barn, its dusky profile promising a haven. Once at the west wall, we crab-walked along it until we could slip around the southwest corner, out of the blast. For brief minutes, we huddled, catching our breath. My little men waited for instructions.

I yelled, "Stay together, and move over to the fence." I nudged our cluster east along the south wall.

"Mama, we c-can't see the house," Sammy hollered.

Decision time. We could wait inside the barn, but the storm might rage three hours or three days, and even worsen. My back against the planked wall, I pulled all three into a semicircle. "Look at me and listen. Keep ahold of one another. Don't let go! Jerry, stay between us—hear? We're going to the house. I'll lead. We have to stay together."

I approached the big corral gate, hinged off the barn's southeast corner. Eyes squinted against stinging sand, I pushed the gate open and we edged out—out into the unchecked fury of the monster storm. Away from the barn, howling wind sucked breath away. Faces averted from its lash, we crept forward. The dogs leaning against our legs, we stumbled across the road. Finally, a welcome bump against an elm whipping in front of the house. Still together, we knew where we were and tripped up the front steps, Shep and Fido crowding behind onto the enclosed porch as we went inside.

Loose flashing chattered like a telegraph key gone crazy. Whorls of dust sifted in around every window. No power, so no lights. I lit a kerosene lamp.

Feeling as if I'd held my breath for twenty minutes, I heaved a great sigh, releasing the balloon of tension within. Abruptly, I sat, staring at the film of dust on the kitchen table until breathing returned to normal. When I lifted my gaze, it was to look at those three faces once again arrayed in a semicircle facing me.

"Thank you, Lord, for bringing us to safety," I said.

Jerry said, "Mama, I'm hungry."

I arose and drew the three into my arms. "You're such brave boys." For a minute longer, I held them. I said, "Let's get something to eat."

That storm howled well after dark, finally exhausting itself around midnight. I arose and lit a kerosene lamp. After letting the dogs out from the porch, I carried the lamp to the back bedroom to check on my boys. Standing in their bedroom doorway, I watched the rise and fall of their breathing bodies. A prayer of thanks for those dear sons, and I returned to my own bed.

Sunrise bloomed quiet, not a breath of wind. Going out to the front step, I set out scraps for Shep and Fido and surveyed the damage. Two-foot-high sand dunes ridged from north of the barn across the road and past the house. Chinese elms in front habitually bent away from the prevailing southwest wind, but now stood rigid, almost bare, as if in shock. The storm, coming out of the northwest, had broken branches from every tree, leaving spiked limbs as reminders of its ferocity. Thankfully, I'd gotten into the habit of parking the Chevy in our stout garage. Otherwise, I could only imagine what might've happened to the car.

By that time, several cows ringed the stock tank, quaffing their thirst before heading back to pasture. Hopefully, all our livestock had sheltered behind the windbreak or barn. I didn't want to think of losing any. Better have Sammy get up and make a count.

Out of the quiet, a meadowlark greeted the morning, just as Dickie appeared behind me. I turned. "Listen, son. How do you suppose those birds manage to survive something like that?"

He put his arm around my waist. "Birds know when a storm's coming. My teacher last year said they can tell by the air . . . pressure or something. So they go looking for a safe place out of the wind, next to the ground."

"Oh." I looked at him, so earnest. Growing up before my eyes. Tears forming, I quickly said, "Go put your shoes on. You want to count our cows, or do you want to help me wipe dust out of the kitchen while I fix breakfast?"

"I'll go count cows." Off he went.

❦❧

Cliff Wakefield called on a Thursday. As soon as he identified himself, I responded, "Okay, what's Bill done? You want me to come get him?"

A chuckle. "No, Claire, your nephew probably doesn't have a future in running a farm, but he's working out. Has a lot to learn.

Not as strong as I hoped he'd be. He's pretty soft, probably from lack of exercise, but he'll toughen up if he sticks it out."

"What a relief," I said. "Has he given you any lip?"

"He's been respectful, mostly. Hard to read. Doesn't show much emotion. He found out we go to church in Forgan, so he's raring to go. I guess you'll see him Sunday."

"What a surprise. He never said anything about it to me."

"Yeah, we'll take him—if he gets up in time . . . Anyway, what I'm calling about is to remind everybody about school cleanup day tomorrow. The big blow last week dumped half of McCall's field in our school. We get a good turnout tomorrow, that building will be all cleaned and ready for opening day next week."

"We'll be there. Me and my boys."

"Good. You'll get to meet our new teacher. Leon Hibbs. Wife's name is Maxine. Nice looking couple, although she looks like a teenager. As part of his pay package, the board agreed to fix up that southwest classroom for living quarters the way they want it, just like teachers before them. They'll be moving middle of next week."

"Will she be cooking?" I wondered how long I'd have to be fixing lunches.

"Not interested. We offered a hundred a month, but no dice." Cliff paused. "I got a few more calls to make. We'll see you tomorrow."

഻഻

Eighteen adults and kids showed up for cleanup day, including the new teacher and his wife. Right away, he came over to meet me and my boys. I was impressed with that.

Standing only a couple inches taller than me, sandy hair and blue eyes, he looked little older than a high schooler. His poise and the authority in his voice said otherwise. "Hello, I'm Leon Hibbs, the new teacher. Welcome to work day at Greenough."

I told him my name as he fished a typewritten list out of his pocket. "Yes, I've got you right here. You and three sons, I believe . . ." His index finger tracked down the paper he held before him. "Yes, grades seven, six, and third grade."

I wondered why he came to our little country school of twenty-two kids. Maybe I'd find out. He made a point of introducing himself as "Mr. Hibbs" to Sammy and Dickie, and even Jerry, who ducked his head in embarrassment. Such a difference from previous teachers. Treating each student as an important person.

Noticing that Sammy and Dickie carried boxes, he asked, "What do we have here?"

"Fried chicken," I said. "And a couple pies. Most people brought something, I imagine. That's the way we do things here."

"Very nice," Leon said. "Sammy and Dickie, why don't you take those to the lunchroom? Then report to that group over there to join a work crew." He watched them leave and then excused himself to greet the Isaacs, newly arrived.

For a country school, Greenough was impressive, particularly with its red brick façade and indoor gym. The former high school library had been transformed into the only classroom for all eight grades. Sammy said his teachers bragged that not many elementary schools had such a book collection. That's what he liked best.

Work day was fun as I watched my boys engage their friends, most of whom they hadn't seen all summer. My eyes misted over, seeing how they handled themselves. So much more self-assured than I was at that age.

Most older kids helped with cleanup. Even though Mr. Hibbs met for an hour with the three board members, we finished by early afternoon. Then it was time to eat. My pies and platter of fried chicken disappeared in a hurry.

Afterward, Leon and Maxine came where I was sitting with Henry and Blanche Ausmus. He said, "Claire, that fried chicken and those banana cream pies were yours, weren't they?"

I ducked my head, but Blanche said, "Young man, you'll never get better fixings than what this lady puts on her table, and don't you forget it."

He grinned at her. "Well, Mrs. Ausmus—"

"Call me Blanche. My granddaughter Diane—Charles and Avis' girl—will be starting here next year. Charles is a board member, but I guess you know that already, being's that they hired you for this job teaching our kids."

Leon smiled and tried again. "Yes, Blanche, and as bus driver, basketball coach, part time janitor, and whatever else needs to be done around here. Thanks for helping on our work day. I'll surely remember everything you told me." He gave a broad wink to Henry.

Afterward, as everyone collected their cleaning equipment,

Cliff Wakefield asked if I had time to talk for a minute. He motioned toward the library/classroom. I followed him in, wondering if one of the boys had messed up something. He sat at the teacher's desk, and I sat at a student desk, with the inscription TH loves GD carved in the top.

Cliff said, "Leon looks to be the kind of teacher we've been trying to get at Greenough for years, wouldn't you say?"

I ducked my chin. He's surely not asking for a teacher endorsement from me . . . What's this about? "Well, I just met him, but yes, he pitched right in to help. Seems real friendly . . ."

"Of course, he just met you too. But he made a recommendation to us. Strong recommendation, in fact. Don't know why we didn't think of it. You know, we need a cook. So, Leon recommends we hire you as cook for our kids this school year. We'd pay you a hundred a month, same as what we offered his wife. Could you manage that, with running your farm and all?"

I heard the quaking in my voice. "The boys are helping with the farming, but . . . Could you repeat that?"

He did.

I said yes. I could hardly wait to tell the boys. A hundred a month. We could all get new shoes.

39 A Boy's Best Friend

Sammy

Fido was just a mutt, but as far as us boys were concerned, he could've been pedigreed. Our small but determined friend with the black plumed tail was very smart. I had read about dogs like him in Albert Payson Terhune's books and knew we had a special pet. He had such personality, like he was almost human.

By chance, we discovered Fido was a real scrapper. Not big enough to take on a coyote or a big German shepherd, but he had a warrior's heart, a fighter's intelligence, and lightning quickness. We learned this one May evening when Shep set up a racket down by the locust trees south of the house. He kept barking, so Dickie and I headed out there, Jerry hollering for us to wait. We soon caught a whiff of the trouble—a skunk, probably come to ravage the henhouse.

Shep had experience with skunks, none of it good. Overall, that was okay, since it kept him out of range of this tough customer. Two years before, a skunk had sprayed him right in the eyes. It must have hurt terrible, the way he scrubbed his face onto the ground, snorting in frustration and pain.

This time, Fido took charge. With lunges and feints, he kept the skunk off-balance. It never could get in position to spray him. Just as the little chicken-killer rotated left, Fido dodged right and had him by the nape of the neck, shaking the life out of him.

He did it all, without getting any stink on him. We boys were proud of him. Good thing old Shep wasn't too smart, or he would've been jealous of all the attention we heaped on Fido.

There was more to come with Fido. Late afternoons, Dickie or I walked out in the pasture to bring the milk cows in for evening and morning milking. Contrary beasts, they'd often try to escape. The dogs were great helpers in herding the cows back to the barn. With Fido, it was a breeze. Instead of running at the head of a cow, like silly old Shep did, he nipped at her heels, driving her the right direction. He acted by instinct, like a border collie.

One summer evening, Fido showed his courage and fighting

spirit against a deadly enemy. Dickie and I both went out that time to bring the milk cows in. We found them a mile from the barn at the far corner of the pasture, on the back side of a hill. Cutting our milkers from the main herd, we headed back. Halfway there, Shep and Fido spotted something moving off to the side. Both dogs began howling and growling in a way we'd never heard before. Right off, we ran to see.

They had jumped a big rattlesnake, and he was mad. Its body was big around as the calf of my leg. Coiled up and his triangle-shaped head moving side to side, he was ready to strike. There must have been sixteen to twenty rattles on his tail, and they sounded like evil itself, warning us to stay away.

We scouted for clods or sticks to use as a weapon, but no luck. Only sagebrush and buffalo grass, and we were too far from the house to get the rifle.

Shep stayed well out of range of the rattler, barking ferociously. He knew that snake was mortal danger. Not Fido. Half Shep's size, he dodged in and out, daring the rattler to strike. It lashed out, a flash of death. Fido was too quick and avoided the wicked fangs time and again. Afraid he would get nailed, we called him to back off. He paid us no mind and continued harassing the viper.

I was almost in a panic, fearing for our little buddy. Dickie and I crouched back, knowing we couldn't do anything but watch and hope.

Fido must've sensed the killer snake was tiring. Suddenly he attacked. In a flash, he grabbed that rattlesnake just behind the head. He began shaking the writhing body in a fury of rage. I just knew the head would imbed a fang in Fido's shoulder, but he had him just right. That enemy was done for.

Fido knew exactly what he was doing. Our mouths and eyes agape, we stared as our wonder dog dropped the lifeless body of the serpent and backed away. Panting, he sat on his haunches, eying the writhing body until he was satisfied it would strike no more.

What a show. We hurried the cows home, eager to tell Mama about our champion.

≈•≈

Fido was special in another way. He linked us back to Daddy in a way nothing else could. We had gotten him the very day of Daddy's

266

funeral. That's why I felt Fido was so special.

Everything about our lives measured back to Daddy's forevermore absence. Not only was he our father, he had been our protector and leader. I wondered if we could really feel safe again.

Mama said she'd be mother and father to us, even though she knew it wouldn't be the same. She'd do the best she could, and God would have to do the rest. From the beginning, we believed that. How could we not? She'd proved herself in so many ways. She was our hero.

There were times out on the school ground when I wished I could've said, "My dad will take care of you." Who's going to lay off if you threaten to sic your mom on them? I figured that's why thieves raided our garage, and why we had to put up with occasional bullying at school. I didn't want Mama to interfere, anyway. I needed to take care of myself.

And what's a widow going to do? Equipment breakdowns and car trouble might happen anyway. Sometimes, I kind of expected bad things to happen. When I talked to Mama about such things, she said for us to have faith, that God would take care of us.

I tried to believe that but figured there was only so much God was going to do.

The biggest hurt came one July evening after church—we always attended church twice on Sundays. Church was our social life, so I didn't mind that. My thoughts went to people I wouldn't see till the following Sunday, especially the Forgan girls.

Cresting the hill a mile south of our farm, my eyes immediately went to our yard light. Sure enough, it glowed alone at the center of the moonless dark, straight ahead. Directly west, yard lights from Rushton's and Henry and Blanche's place beamed like searchlights. Biggest of all and only three-quarters of a mile east of our house, an oil drilling rig draped in lights top to bottom rose like the Eiffel Tower north of Bill Kizer's barn. That oil derrick was like a beacon of hope to the whole community, giving us optimism that maybe someday a driller might strike oil on our property.

As we got closer to home, Mama broke the silence. "What's that beside the road, there? Sammy, what is it?"

I thought first it was a shadow, but then could see it was an animal, stretched alongside the road, directly under our yard light.

Bigger than a skunk, perhaps a badger? No, something familiar, but very odd.

The truth hit all of us at once as Mama stopped the car. It was Fido. He was lying, not rising to greet us, his head down in an unnatural angle. I piled out of the car, heart in my throat, and knelt beside our pal. Dickie and I both reached to touch him, but he didn't move. Tears and cries from all of us. His body was stiff. Lifeless. A pool of blood—his blood—stained the sandy ground under his head.

Heedless of our clothes, Dickie and I picked up the body of our dear little friend. Not sure what to do, we carried him toward the house and laid him to one side of the front step. So lost in grief. Heartbroken, we crumpled to the ground, crying beside his body.

Weeping, Mama put her arms around us. "My boys, oh, my boys. I'm so sorry. So sorry." She let us cry some more, and when we finally stopped, she said, "Come in the house. That's all we can do tonight. I'll get an oil cloth to put over him. We'll bury him in the morning . . ."

"Who would do that?" I cried. "Run over him and l-leave him. How could they do that?"

Claire

I put the boys to bed, one by one, praying with them for comfort. I told them I was sure we'd see Fido in heaven, because he was such a good dog.

Thankfully, they slipped into a slumber of emotional exhaustion, much like the night their father died. Sleep not coming, I put on a housecoat and sat at our dining table in the semi-dark room, mind refusing to function and my heart in a deep cloud.

My heart was broken too. It was like when I knew Elmer wasn't going to get well. But this heartache was for my boys. They had lost so much in their short lives. Now this—the loss of their buddy, the one who had been a special comfort to them from the very day we buried Elmer. Making it worse, the callousness of whoever did it—ran over him and drove off, thoughtless and uncaring, leaving Fido lying in the road.

The more I thought about it, the more unfair it seemed. I forgot my grief. A wave of anger rolled over me. Something I'd felt from time to time but never given enough serious thought to think where it came from or what it was directed at. Now, it seemed freeing to name what it was.

I was mad. Mad at God. Where was He in all of this? Hadn't my boys suffered enough? Hadn't we all? Losing those we loved, beginning with Kate, followed by Pop and Maggie in the same year. Then Will, the boys' grandfather and teller of stories. Finally, their father. Now, to cap it off, the pet they adored, left by the side of the road with his life crushed out of him.

Now I could understand why Elmer railed at a God who seemed so distant, so uncaring, during those lonesome dark nights and rainless months of the thirties when we couldn't grow anything. The chickens were barely able to scratch bits of food out of the dirt, and we couldn't even do that.

God, can't you see my boys are hurting?

I wanted to scream at him, shout in his face, "What have these boys done to deserve this? They're just innocent children!"

A pulse of cool air brushed across my face from an open window. The hoot of an owl sounded, giving voice to how isolated and alone I felt at that moment. I arose, pulling my housecoat about me, and went outside, sitting on the top step where I could lean against the porch. I would give God a piece of my mind. In the mottled brightness of our yard light, I could make out the form of Fido, under the oil cloth.

Crickets sang to one another at the south end of the house, where my little garden struggled against the hot plains wind. But I had come out to say my piece. I pointed to the silent form on the ground. "See there, that was their buddy, their pal. You know what they've been through. Why didn't You do something? Don't You care?" I was determined to vent and continued ranting until I ran out of words.

Hearing my voice, Shep came over and sat beside the step, one side of his face shadowed by light filtering through the elms. I stopped and placed a hand on his head. "Shep, silly old dog, you're probably sad, too. Lost your buddy, as well."

He leaned against me, as if understanding. I scratched his head for a moment. I resumed complaining to God and Shep turned again to me, maybe wondering what I required of him.

Suddenly ashamed of my impertinence to the One who had borne me through the past months, the years of grief and hardship, I stopped. What did I desire from Him?

Tears streaming down my face, I arose, leaving Shep and the

269

unseen owl to continue their vigil over my sons' little pal. I returned inside, unable to answer my own question. What do I want of You, God of all Creation?'

Probably, I should be asking—What more do You require from me? But I didn't ask that. I was afraid the answer might be more than I could bear.

40 A Church and Its People

Claire

According to Cliff Wakefield, my nephew planned to attend Forgan Baptist Church Sunday morning. He told me when he stopped by the school lunchroom to hand me my first paycheck as cook. Nice to hear. If it happened, I'd be asked to stand with Bill when Brother Caywood welcomed visitors. It would be a real poke in the eye for the naysayers who counseled against helping my needy nephew.

That Sunday, Vivian Nichols, Floyd's daughter-in-law, fell in beside me as I headed upstairs for morning services. "Claire, I so enjoy having Sammy and Dickie in my class. They always come prepared for Sunday school, get there on time, and they behave themselves. You've done a good job with your boys."

"Well, I try to be a good mother." I squeezed her hand and smiled. "Thank you, it's nice to know we're doing something right, isn't it? My boys enjoy having Gary and Billy come out for Sunday dinner too."

"They say no one can fix fried chicken like Claire." She hesitated at the top of the stairs. "Oh, I don't suppose you've met the new high school music teacher, Mr. Byers. Nice looking man. Fern says he has a wonderful voice. She also mentioned he's single." Vivian raised her eyebrows and gave me a knowing smile as she went to join her husband.

I stood stock still in the foyer, my good mood suddenly dashed. That was the third time one of the church ladies had dropped a none-too-gentle hint about the single music teacher. Why don't people mind their own business? Elmer's only been gone three years—three heartbreaking years!—and every Tom, Dick, and Tillie is trying to make me forget him. As if I can ignore the needs of my boys, as well.

Someone bumped my elbow. Embarrassed to be impeding traffic, I headed to my pew, in case Bill did come to church. It would be a positive sign he was serious about turning his life around. That, and changing his circle of friends.

Jerry and Dickie both joined me halfway back on the far left side. Sammy sat in back with his friends. I turned to my right in time to see Cliff and Velma enter. Sure enough, Bill sauntered behind them. I almost couldn't believe it. I motioned for him to come over and sit by us, so we could claim him as ours. After all, he wouldn't have been there, much less gotten out on parole, if I hadn't made all the arrangements.

Smiling, I stood, again beckoning Bill to sit by us. He appeared not to see me, waltzed in like he owned the place, and parked on the right side, in the very front pew. He didn't look around, just sat there with his head glued straight ahead. I didn't know what to think. Apparently, no one else did either, though I heard whispering behind us.

Dickie said, "Mama, why's Bill sitting up in the front row?"

I whispered, "Maybe he'll come back here, when he sees us."

Practically nobody ever sat in the front pew. Only little kids slipped in there occasionally, and then just to show off before their mothers collared them. Murmurs nearby indicated that was the assessment of this newcomer. How could I introduce Bill, with him sitting way up front? Most everyone in church knew Cliff Wakefield had hired my nephew. It nettled me for Bill to display such conspicuous behavior, coming in church without a lick of sense how to behave. Showing off was almost as bad as getting caught in your neighbor's hen house, in most people's minds. I imagined the pointed remarks from those quick to criticize. If I had my sister Ethel's nerve, such talk wouldn't bother me. My face felt hot.

After the Sunday school superintendent's report and a hymn and prayer, Reverend Caywood asked if there were any visitors. Silence. Finally, the preacher looked at me. "Claire, I believe you have a visitor."

I stood, my hands clammy on the pew in front of us. "Yes. My nephew . . ." I sent a limp gesture toward Bill, as if that might prompt him to stand. He remained seated. Clearing my throat, I raised my voice. "This is . . . He's Bill, working for Cliff Wakefield this summer. Bill Maclaren, my nephew." He remained as immovable as a post, so I sat, my eyes blurred with embarrassment and irritation.

The rest of the service continued in a haze. Mr. Byers, the high school music teacher, sang a solo, which I only half heard. From our location, I couldn't tell if Bill was asleep or listening to what was going on. By then, I didn't much care.

I was mad at both Bill and God for ignoring me. Besides Bill's insolence, God had let Fido get run over the Sunday before.

Brother Caywood said if anyone thought they were immune to any Bible command or admonition, they were sadly mistaken. Sooner or later, he said, every Christian could expect to suffer hardship, even persecution. His words began to get under my skin, the more he went on.

I felt unappreciated and misunderstood. Not exactly persecution, but Bill's obstinance made me look like a fool—another hardship in my book.

Still flustered over my nephew's lack of cooperation, I found myself wondering if Aunt Priscilla might've been right. She forever questioned parts of the Bible everyone else took for granted, such as, "How can a loving God allow evil in the world?" And "Why should unbelieving heathens go to hell?"

Mama said we couldn't choose not to obey particular commands in the Bible, even the parts that upset us. It's all God's word, whether we believe it, or even understand it. I accepted that from her, because after all, she was my mother.

Now, here was my preacher, droning on about respecting the sacred text, that we couldn't pick and choose what parts we wanted to trust him for. He said we might have to endure extended pain and grief, while other folks were apparently getting a forty-year picnic in the park. He ended his sermon with the reminder that it's not for us to question our Heavenly Father, and yes, who can know the mind of God?

Brother Caywood must've studied under the same Bible teacher as my mother. None of them said a word about when God doesn't hold up his end of the stick. Shouldn't God cut a person some slack when the innocent—my boys, for instance—were mistreated or suffered through no fault of their own? Surely there was a limit to how much anyone had to endure.

The preacher didn't say if grief and loneliness had an expiration date. He didn't offer a word about needing care and understanding, rather than people trying to tell you how to run your life. I wanted to shake my fist at him. Ethel would've put him in his place. No way would I ever draw attention to myself like that. So little did the people in my own church know how hard it was—what I'd been through, losing Pop and Maggie—both in the same year—then left alone with three little boys after Elmer died.

There was just so much a widow could bear. The more I heard, the hotter I got under the collar.

I'd have a straight talk with the preacher, right after the third and final repetition of "Just As I Am." I glanced across at Bill. He seemed to be taking it all in. On second thought, it might not be a good idea to lay out my complaints about God and the Bible in front of my infidel nephew. I'd already told Velma we'd take Bill home with us for Sunday dinner. No way I could change that. I'd have my talk with the preacher another Sunday.

ے۔ٯ

Church is a place where everyone is accepted, though not to run other people's lives. Much as I liked Vivian Nichols, I decided to avoid her for a while. I needn't have bothered.

The following Sunday, Itha McNabb made it a point to remind me the new music teacher was single, as if that was vital information I needed to manage my life. I didn't reply, just added Itha to my avoid list.

A week later, Blanche followed me into the ladies' room as I went to freshen up between Sunday school and church. She waited behind me as I checked my makeup at the solitary mirror. "Claire, I was thinking of having a few of the adults over some evening this week for supper. Would Thursday suit you?"

"That sounds nice. What's the occasion?"

Looking past my shoulder, she dabbed an imaginary spot on her cheek. "Just a time to get acquainted with the new people. You could bring a salad, if you like. Say seven o'clock?"

"Blanche, what new people are you talking about?"

She began rummaging in her purse. "Well, there's . . . some I noticed. I started a list, if I can find it."

Hands on my hips, I turned from the mirror to face her. "Blanche, we've been friends a long time, partly by not putting one another in awkward situations. Could we still do that?"

She ducked her head, her face coloring. "Sorry, Claire. I'm just a silly old woman."

"You're not that. But you're not the only one trying to manage my social life. It's almost enough to make me stay home until the busybody epidemic at this church runs its course."

"Oh, Claire, that sounds awful, like people don't respect you for having good sense."

"Yes, that's how I feel too." We grinned at one another, and I went upstairs to see if my nephew was coming to church again to maybe find salvation from his errant lifestyle.

Bill didn't disappoint, perching in the front pew like an exhibitionist, bound and determined to show everyone how religious he was. He avoided the preacher afterward, head down as if deep in thought.

Each time he attended, I brought him home with us after church for Sunday dinner. While I tried to bring the conversation around to the sermon or the Bible, Bill acted as if church was on Mars. Started bragging that he might decide to roughneck on a drilling rig, that men working on the neighboring Kizer well made big money. I wondered where that came from.

His alternate ploy to avoid talking about anything meaningful was to go outside and smoke. By midafternoon, he was ready to go back to Wakefields, to rest up for the work week. So much for bonding with our family.

The fourth Sunday was different. Bill sat up front, but in the third row. That still isolated him from most of the congregation, so who knew what he was thinking? After dinner that day, I determined to ask him what impressed him about Brother Caywood's sermons. I just might ask him if he'd ever prayed the sinner's prayer, if I could figure how to say it.

As things turned out, I never got the chance.

We'd just finished the roast beef dinner I'd put in the oven before we left for church. Sammy and Dickie asked if they could hunt rabbits over at the Flanagan place. I said yes, but be back by five. That would give me a good chance to talk with Bill.

That idea went in the ditch with his sudden announcement. "You don't need to take me anywhere this afternoon. A friend is coming out to pick me up."

He avoided my eyes and his tone seemed a bit too casual. I stared at him. "Is this one of the old friends you told me you were going to avoid?"

His face colored. "No, it ain't."

"You don't need to be so snappish. I'm just going on what you told me about your intentions. Who's this friend, if I might ask?"

"Name's Blackie. He's a roughneck on the drilling rig over east."

I didn't ask how he came to meet this Blackie. The boys, busy harrowing milo to the east, had mentioned there had been all sorts of trucks and people going in and out of the Kizer place since

Standard Oil started drilling over there.

Unfamiliar vehicles drove past our place, which made me nervous. "That's fine," I finally said. "Not trying to pry. So, he'll take you back to Wakefields?"

Just then, Dickie came out of the bedroom, with the .22 rifle in hand. Bill said, "What you doing with that? You're pretty young to be playing with a rifle."

Before he could answer, I said, "Elmer taught the boys how to handle a gun. They know what they're doing."

"I can hit a rabbit across the road from here. Done it before," Dickie said. "We got a twelve-gauge shotgun too, but I don't shoot it much. Them shells are expensive."

Bill held out his hand. "Here, let me see—"

"No." The word came out sharper than I intended. I started over, in a flat tone. "No, Bill, you don't want to even touch that rifle. Not any gun. The letter I got from Kansas Department of Corrections made that very clear—you'd be violating your parole if you so much as handle a firearm. Surely you knew that."

He stared at me, eyes narrowed, his jaw clenched. "You got to be kidding. I'm not going to shoot anyone. We're here in your house, for crying out loud."

I swallowed, struggling to inhale. "Dickie, put the rifle up—now."

My son looked back at me, his mouth open. "But Mama, you—"

"Do as I say. No backtalk!" I waited for him to move, then turned to Bill. "Yes, I know where we are. But that letter was very clear . . . I don't want my boys or me to be a party to sending you back to Lansing, for—"

"You're treating me like one of your kids, you know that? One of your little kids! Well, I'm not gonna take it, you hear?" He stood, sending his chair skittering back from the table.

My breath caught. Was he going to be violent? Standing, I swiveled my chair between us, and spoke in a level voice. "I can't believe you're so rude, Bill. I'm not being unreasonable. In fact, I'm trying to protect you. You violate those rules, they could have you back at the state pen." What was the matter with this selfish young man? Such disrespect . . . I was aware Sammy had just entered from outside, like he wanted to say something. I turned to him.

"M-Mama, there's a tr-truck out front."

Bill clammed up, but he was out the front door and through the porch in a flash. I breathed a sigh of relief and followed him as far as the porch door. A swarthy man in his mid-thirties was easing out of a beat-up Hudson pickup. He ducked his head when he saw me, then sauntered halfway toward the house when Bill called him over. Smooth as glass, Bill acted as if we'd been talking about the weather. He introduced the man as Blackie. I could see why. His dark features were crowned with a mop of black hair, which fell over his forehead and across his left eye. He stared at the ground, like he had something to hide.

The boys crowded behind me, watching, as Bill got in the pickup. Without a wave or a look backward, they headed north.

Sobered by the exchange, I realized I was shaking. The thought struck me—Bill might be dangerous, if his previous reactions were any kind of an indicator. I was glad to have him off the property. It seemed futile, trying to relate to him. He'd shown his true colors that afternoon. Made me wonder if I'd see him at church again. And that Blackie. Not the kind of person I'd want near my sons.

No surprise, Bill didn't show up for church the following Sunday, or the one after that. Cliff and Velma said he'd gone someplace both weekends, but they never saw who picked him up. I could've bet a dollar to a donut it was his friend Blackie.

I finally got a chance to talk with Brother Caywood after Sunday evening services. By that time, I'd cooled down and decided not to make an issue about being upset. More important was my nephew getting his life straightened out. I asked the preacher if he could speak to Bill, even if he had to drive out to Wakefield's to do it. He promised he would, that very week.

On the way home, I shared with the boys that Brother Caywood was going to see Bill, and we should pray that God would get ahold of his life.

Glass. The floor of our enclosed porch was covered in broken glass. Obvious where it came from. The dining room window that looked onto the porch was now a gaping hole. I was bewildered. The boys murmured among themselves. We had just come home from Sunday evening church. This was as bad as arriving home and finding Fido's body alongside the road.

Anxious to determine the extent of the violation, we entered through our unlocked front door and crept from one room to another. Dickie opened the main bedroom closet door. "The guns! They're gone! Rifle and shotgun, both gone." He began to cry in anger and frustration. "Bill did it. I know he did."

I gathered my boys around me with both arms, and let them cry. "We can't be sure who did it. But I'll call Cliff. He'll tell us where Bill was this evening."

Cliff answered on the first ring. He listened while I told him our story. No idea where Bill was, but that he'd collected his pay that afternoon, and was going someplace to work on an oil drilling rig. A man in an old Hudson pickup had come by and they drove off together.

After the sheriff came out and dusted for fingerprints, Cliff replaced our window. I wondered if we'd ever see my nephew or the guns again.

41 Two Letters

Summer 1953

Claire

Two letters arrived mid-August. One maybe good and the other maybe not. I fretted about them for a week, then decided I'd better talk them over with my attorney. Went in the day after Labor Day. When the receptionist approached to say Lansden was ready to see me, I opened my purse for the third time to make sure they were both there.

Pleasantries over, I handed him the first letter. "I'm uncertain what to do about these. This one's from Chet Naylor, my banker at People's in Liberal." While he unfolded and scanned it, I felt relief at being able to share my concerns with another adult. I'd mentioned them to Sammy, and he listened, but what could he say? Finally, I said, "Naylor has bent over backwards to help us, even before Elmer took sick. Now I wonder if he's changing his tune."

Lansden took his time to study both the transmittal letter and a summary of my account. Finally, he spoke. "I know Chet Naylor. Decent man. I'd guess his board is leaning on him." He paused. "You're behind on your payments. Paid only two hundred last year. Did you tell Naylor you were going to be short?"

I stared back at him. My mouth felt dry. "Well, everybody knows there's been a drought. Can't grow much of anything . . . I can't remember what I said. What was I supposed to do?"

He drew a hand across his face, as if trying to massage a reassuring answer. "Yes. Of course, he knows this dry spell has made it hard for every farmer in the southern plains. And making a partial payment . . . that's not unheard of. It seems unusual for the bank to pull back on extending credit, after sticking with you all this time."

"The weather looks like a repeat of the thirties. Our wheat crop was . . . not much." I bit my cheek and swallowed. Wonder if Lansden doubts my ability to manage the farm. "I could sell the cattle. We've got twenty-five head. Ray—that's Elmer's cousin—cautioned against it. Said it's hard to build a herd back up once they're all gone. I don't want to sell. We depend on getting a new calf in the spring from every cow, including the milk cows. Other than what we use, I've been able to sell extra milk to Greenough School, and the separated milk goes to feed our young pigs."

He leaned forward. "You're doing a lot with what you have. Your banker know all this?"

I let out a huge breath. Good to hear someone praise my efforts. "Well, not likely. I don't tell him everything. In fact, I don't talk much to anyone about my business." I chewed my lower lip. "It wouldn't surprise me if the big farmer who tried to buy the place out from under us might be the fly in the ointment, hoping I'll default."

His eyebrows went up.

I explained. "Fifteen years ago, we'd been renting the farm, with the understanding from Federal Land Bank we'd have first shot at buying the place when they put it up for sale. Unbeknownst to us, this land hog—what I call him—tried to undercut us. He would've succeeded, had Elmer and I . . . well, not to brag, but we put our sales skills to good use, and got another banker to lend us the down payment, without collateral. Just in the nick of time."

Lansden leaned back in his leather chair and squinted. "I see. So, you beat out this . . . uh, opportunist, rather than the other way around. Good for you." He paused, appearing deep in thought. "Federal Land Bank, you say? Send me that land sale contract, if you will. They had some unusual conditions in their loan documents. Allowed them to buy up failed farm mortgages and refinance them at lower rates during and after the Depression.

"Now, you mentioned another letter?"

I drew the second packet from my purse and handed it to him. "This might help. Elmer met an oil man in Wichita several years ago, E. J. Bergenthal. I don't know much about leases, and he's asking if I'd be interested in leasing mineral rights. I'd like for you to . . . research, do what you do, so I don't get skinned. Elmer was very high on Bergenthal. I met him once, when he came out to the farm in his big car—a Cadillac, I think it was. Seemed very nice, but Elmer did all the talking with him.

"How should I follow up with Bergenthal? I can't take chances, not when my sons' futures are at stake. The farm is all we have. We lose it, we've lost everything."

"I understand, Claire, you've got . . . have had, a lot coming at you. I'll look into all of this. And," he pursed his lips in a half-smile, "I suggest you hold off a few days before responding to Naylor. Like I said, he's a good man, but we'll not let his board push you around. Maybe a phone call will get their attention." His gray eyes twinkled. "That might be just the ticket."

I wanted to laugh, but only allowed the relief of a deep sigh. "I feel better now. There's so much I don't know."

He waved his hand dismissively. "We're all ignorant, just on different things. You did well, bringing these issues to my attention. In fact, I'd be glad to discuss any questions about your business operations, since you don't seem to, uh, have other confidantes you're comfortable with. I'm impressed with your good judgment, but it's always wise to have a sounding board. Now, is there anything else?"

I brightened. "Yes. Almost forgot to mention, the Greenough school board hired me to cook hot lunches—paying me a hundred a month. Already got new shoes picked out from the Sears catalog for the kids and myself. I hope to make an extra payment on that mortgage with People's Bank."

Lansden stood and extended his big hand to shake mine. "Claire. I'm pleased to see good things coming your way for a change. And I heard Leon Hibbs is teaching at your school. One of our own. Grew up in Beaver, brilliant young man. Greenough School couldn't do better. A great opportunity for your boys."

I sang all the way home. After supper, I'd sit at my old upright piano. The boys and I would have a great time singing. I could hardly wait.

I sent the Federal Land Bank contract to Lansden the next day, with a short note. I wrote that neighbors said Standard Oil was down to 5,700 feet on the Kizer well, but so far, they hadn't struck anything but salt water.

Every farmer in the neighborhood had been hoping for something to give stability, predictability, maybe hope. With less than sixty dollars in my bank account, I wondered what financial security would feel like. It had been so long since I could be undisciplined, even so complacent I could go into a store and get something I wanted, whether I needed it or not. It seemed reckless, even foolish, to entertain such thoughts, but an oil boom would be good for everyone in the community.

Lansden's offer to listen and discuss my business decisions was such a relief. I needed to talk to somebody I could trust, who could help me see the overall picture. Didn't know what I'd do if the drought continued. I wished Ethel or Myrrl lived closer. That would never happen, so why think of it? My appeals to the Almighty had become more wishing than praying. Pop always said we had to let go of our problems so God could answer them. My cook's wages would keep bread on the table . . . Can't give up our herd. Losing the farm would be next.

I chastised myself for being so negative. Tight as money was, I couldn't spend it on long-distance telephone calls. Instead, I wrote Ethel, saying I hoped we could spend Thanksgiving with them in Dodge City, that I had a lot to talk about. Too bad that was two months away.

✥

I expected a quick answer—or at least some instructions—from Lansden regarding the mineral rights lease. He'd always been prompt about other matters. A week passed, then two. I had trouble sleeping. Staring at myself in the mirror, I noticed bags under my eyes. Then Ray and Edith stopped by with word that the Kizer well was down to 6,100 feet, with scant production. A dry hole. The three of us cried the blues over that, which didn't help matters.

Finally Lansden's letter arrived, suggesting we meet the following Tuesday morning. I drove to Beaver, not knowing what to expect.

Merle Lansden recapped his exchange of letters with E. J. Bergenthal and with a man I'd never heard of, a Bosworth T. Doolittle, of North Platte, Nebraska. "Claire, I'm very pleased to tell you that Elmer's faith in Mr. Bergenthal seems justified. He hadn't heard of Elmer's death but asked me to express his condolences to you. He held your husband in high regard. Said Elmer had visited him twice at his home in Wichita, when Elmer took your oldest boy there for allergy treatments."

"Yes, Elmer told me. They hit it right off."

"That was evident in my phone calls and letters to him. He said he's been leasing land around the Greenough community for fifteen to twenty-five dollars an acre. For you, he's offering a ten-year lease of subsurface mineral rights on your farm, with a

282

first-year signing bonus of twenty-five dollars an acre. But there's a hitch that—"

"For all 400 acres?" My body seemed all-atremble. "That's . . . that's $10,000!" I wanted to jump across Lansden's desk and give him a hug. "We could almost be debt-free with—"

"No, Claire. Wait a minute." Lansden held up his hand. "I said there's a hitch. This Doolittle from Nebraska . . . Let me explain." He ripped a blank sheet from a lined tablet and slapped it on his desktop. "Remember, I cautioned you about unusual stipulations in Federal Land Bank contracts? Briefly put, it's this . . ."

Scribbling numbers and boxes across his lined sheet, he began explaining, pausing occasionally to check if I was still with him. "This Nebraska Doolittle acquired a quarter of the mineral rights to the Eagan place when the farm was foreclosed by Federal Land Bank. That proviso remained when you bought the property. Doolittle acquired those rights for fifteen years, with the stipulation that his one-quarter ownership of mineral rights would continue if oil or gas is discovered on any portion of Section 22—where your house and the Kizer place set—during that period."

Lansden stopped and looked at me. "You understand all that?"

I nodded, "I think so."

"Well, Claire, it looks like you've got a significant decision to make."

He pulled out a signed lease form from Bergenthal, and turned it toward me. "First, if you agree to this lease within the signing period, you'll receive three-fourths of the signing bonus—$7,500—as soon as they cut the check. The other $2,500 will go to this Doolittle.

"Now, if you choose not to sign the lease until Doolittle's fifteen-year share expires next year, you'd get all of any signing bonus. However, there's no assurance Bergenthal will be able to offer those terms at that time."

He reviewed the dates and amounts he'd sketched on his sheet, pointing to each as he named it. Watching my eyes to assure I understood, he continued, "So far, the Kizer well is a dry hole. However, until Standard Oil plugs it, there's the possibility it could be considered a producing well, continuing Doolittle's rights to any mineral revenues. The lack of production on that well is a good thing for you." He paused again. "Understand all that?"

"I . . . I believe so. I'd like more time to think about it before I decide."

"Of course—within the signing period noted . . . umm, November 10. Call me if you want to discuss it further, or if you have questions. I'm here for you, but rather than push you into a decision one way or another, I'm purposely withholding my opinion."

I felt my nails digging into my palms as I rose to leave. I wanted advice, not playing games. Yet only God held the future in his hands. Prayer for wisdom was what I really needed. I'd ask my siblings to do the same. Lansden might not understand my delay for those reasons, but that's all I knew to do.

I took a back road home. Swatches of sage sweetened the air, so I pulled the car up to a deserted house surrounded by a grove of elms. Abandoned by a forgotten family during the thirties, the place looked forlorn, the front screen door gently tapping the frame against the wind. I wanted to raise my hands and call out but satisfied myself by ambling among the trees.

The immensity of the open sky and the empty plains held me, lifted me as if by God's hand. I dared not turn to look, for no one can see God and live. Unaware if he set me down, I didn't want to know if my Lord or imagination had carried me. I only knew I felt uplifted in that moment.

42 Double-A Advice

Claire

Seven thousand five hundred dollars. Sounded like a lot, and it was a lot. Not quite enough to get us out of debt. The extra twenty-five hundred would just about do it. I could almost taste it. Pop's quote of the old saw gave me pause—the one about a bird in the hand being worth more than two in the bush. Yeah, and that one about caution being the better part of valor.

Once I decided that was the way to go, my mind cleared, and I began thinking of my next task, which was really more delight than duty. Blanche's daughter-in-law, Avis, had become a confidante and friend. She was coming over for me to fix her hair. Outspoken, Avis frequently tested my presuppositions and biases.

I never knew what she might come up with, and she didn't disappoint. After she settled into my old ladder-back chair in the dining room, I draped her shoulders with a towel and began wetting her hair. "Oh, that feels good, Claire." A big sigh. "You know, for once my mother-in-law is right." A pregnant pause, as if she wanted to say more.

Innocent as a lamb, I couldn't resist. I knew Avis thought Blanche to be an unbridled bore, talking through her hat most of the time. "Oh, well, yes, Blanche is right about some things, for sure. Uh, what's she right about this time?"

"She's right about you, Claire."

"Is that so? How's that?"

"How long have you . . . When did Elmer pass away?"

I had an idea where this was going. "Twenty-six months ago. June of '51. What does that have to do with anything?"

"She told me about your nephew—how things kinda backfired. Why'd you take it upon yourself to straighten out his life anyway?"

For a second, I was tempted to grab her hair and give it a pull. "Umm, I figured I could do something for him, and I wanted to, so I did. Is that bad?"

"Not at all, Claire. But Blanche thinks you, being a widow and with your boys to raise, shouldn't have taken on the added burden of—"

"I didn't have a choice. Bill was up for parole and, basically, I was the only one he could turn to—"

"The only one? I can't believe you're that gullible."

Whoa. Another temptation to give her mane a good yank. I took a deep breath. "His father was an alcoholic. He abandoned the family, so his mother, Maggie, raised him by herself." I finished wetting her hair and divided it into sections. "He fell in with the wrong crowd, and his worthless friends were . . . worse than worthless. By the time they locked him up, Bill had lost everyone's trust . . . Maggie died in '46, a few months after Pop. Bill gypped his sister and her husband every chance he got. Got so bad, they wouldn't let him in the house."

"That still doesn't mean you had to come to his rescue."

"We don't know what it's like to be in prison. The least I could do was give him another chance at making something of his life." I felt a lump in my throat. "Especially when I consider how dear Maggie was to me. She would've done the same for me, if our roles were reversed."

"But look at the grief he dealt you. Breaking into your house, taking those guns. That sounds scary to me. He wouldn't have done any of that if you'd had . . . a stronger presence . . ."

I stopped and leaned around to look her in the face. "What are you trying to tell me?"

She peered through a section of wet hair. "Your nephew wouldn't have pulled those stunts if you'd had a man in the house. That's what Blanche said, and for once, I agree with her."

"A man in the house? And just like that, everything's hunky-dory?" Arms akimbo, I glared at her. "What am I supposed to do, pick a man off the street? What if—"

"Oh, Claire, I didn't mean to put it that way. But you been a widow over two years. How long do you plan to remain single? You're still a young woman. As much trouble as a man can be, they're handy to have around the house . . . Oh, Claire, look at you. I'm sorry."

I couldn't stop the tears. Frustration, grief, plain old-fashioned hurt—it all came bubbling out. I didn't try to put words to it.

She waited until I had my cry. "That was thoughtless of me, Claire. I can only imagine the trials you been through. I was just . . . Well, I wanted to encourage you to, to resume living. I want things to be easier for you and—"

"Avis, I can't suddenly stop being a mother simply because it's handy to have a man lounging around the house. I can't, I won't, remarry until it's right for my boys. And for me." I grasped successive swatches of hair and began snipping. "I haven't even thought about marrying again. It seems treasonous, disloyal to Elmer's memory, to the life we had together. Not to mention I haven't seen any single men around here I'd look at twice."

"So, you haven't kept your eyes shut all this time." A cheesy smile. "Blanche said the high school music teacher is handsome. Doesn't he go to your church?"

"Out of the question. Doesn't understand young people. Word has it that the brats put sugar in his gas tank, if you can imagine. Ruined the engine on his car. Anyway, if he grates on the high school kids, what would he be like with my boys?"

"Oh, it's awful, that school kids would do such a thing." She sniffed. "Well, there's other men . . . John Hiebert's a widower. Attends Bethel Church where you used to go . . ."

"Avis, you—oops! Took off a little too much there, but you did want a haircut. You got me distracted." I giggled.

"Claire, what are you doing to me? Let me see that mirror."

I snatched my little hand mirror off the buffet and thrust it at her. Smirking, I said, "Looks like the beginnings of a pixie cut, don't you think?"

"Maybe so, but I'm not exactly a prairie nymph. My bathroom scales gave me a surprise this morning . . . Don't you breathe a word of that to anyone!"

"I won't if you back off your matchmaking crusade."

"All right, Claire." She finger-combed her bangs, maybe to see if they were even. "You know there'll come a day when the boys won't need you. They'll be all grown up, planning their own futures. I hate to say it, but they might even forget all you've done for them. When that time comes, you'd best have a man in your life."

"All well and good, but that doesn't mean I have to shine around that music teacher right now."

"But you're all alone, out here by yourself. Suppose your nephew's buddy decides to pay you a visit the middle of some lonely night . . . I'm not trying to scare you, Claire, but a lot can happen in the time it takes for anyone to get over here. We're as close as anyone, and it's a mile and a half from our front door to yours."

I chewed my lower lip. "Kizers are a half mile east . . ."

"You'd never call them. You said Bill and Pearl haven't stopped in to see about you—not once. Less than a mile away. You'll ask for help from someone you're not afraid to call in the dead of night." She sniffed. "Charlie'll come, even if I have to kick him out of bed. But Claire, you'll have to make the call. Don't mince around, even when you're not sure if you got an emergency." She inhaled and shook her head. "Don't know why I didn't have this conversation with you before now."

Avis would never win any popularity contests, but I granted she was thinking of me and the boys. I didn't like being told how naïve I was. Too trusting with Bill, just because his mother was a saint. His pigheadedness is what got him into trouble with the law in the first place. Foolish for me to think he'd changed his old habits. And then bringing that scary friend of his, Blackie, out to our place. That nearly scared the liver out of me.

As much as I hated to admit it, the naysayers at church were probably right, albeit for the wrong reasons. My stubbornness almost got us in big trouble. I hadn't thought about bad apples, alert to prey on someone vulnerable. My innocence could have set us up as easy pickings for any predator. That wouldn't have been a threat if Elmer was here.

Stop it. Elmer is forevermore gone. I have to move on. But what did that really mean? The boys were my life. I had to give them a solid foundation, so they could launch out into their own destiny, regardless how Avis or anyone else saw it.

I supposed she was only thinking about having a man around the house. The thought of that kind of commitment brought bile to my throat. Looking out for the boys required they be first. Me last. I did wonder if that was the way it should be.

Avis got under my skin, but Kay Hunter's sister Amy made me break out of my shell. She'd looked after the boys when I took Elmer to Wichita for surgery. After she married the widower Henry Amen, she insisted I drop the boys off at their fine home on North Grant Avenue anytime I shopped in Liberal. From their reports, it sounded like she stuffed them with strawberries and shortcake with whipped cream every time I left them there.

Amy and Henry were sitting in their porch swing when we stopped at their house one late summer afternoon. While Henry took my troop to the back yard to show off his new lawn mower, I followed Amy to the kitchen.

She put a teapot on to heat. "Your boys are so much fun to have around. It's like having grandkids."

I smiled. "You're going to spoil them. You don't have to give them dessert every time."

"I'm glad I can do it. Henry dotes on me, and we can well afford it. For the first time in my life, I don't have to watch my pennies. Those boys have had to do without so much, I'd like to spoil them a little. Henry got out the View-Master last time and we had a scenic tour of the Grand Canyon and Carlsbad Caverns."

"They haven't had to do without, but I hear you."

"My own kids disappointed me so much, so I missed out on having a normal family. Loving your boys is my way of making up for that."

That's what she said, and I believed her. I believed her too when she told me how special Henry always made her feel. I knew Amy put up with a lot from her first husband, a drinker.

Amy changed the subject, rather suddenly, it seemed. Her gentle alto voice always made me pause to listen. It had a husky tone to it, close to a whisper, as if she was confiding in me.

"Claire, I can't tell you how much you impress me. Working so hard to keep your boys together on the farm. You're such a special lady, and I, uh, I believe any man would think you're . . . special, too. I'm not trying to unduly influence you, but have you considered . . . having a man take care of you?" She looked at me, blue eyes twinkling in embarrassment. "Oh, the water, it's—" She jumped up and turned off the burner under the teapot, then filled our cups.

I waited as she dropped tea bags in both cups. "What's this? You been talking to Avis? No, of course, you don't even know her. My neighbor."

"No, I don't know any Avis." A deep breath, and she resumed. "But you've seen how Henry treats me—like a queen. Me, and I'm just a country gal past sixty. Look at all I got, a man who thinks the world of me, this fine house. Claire, if you'd told me God was going to bless me with all this three years ago . . . ." She chuckled self-consciously.

I just sipped my tea.

"Anyway, Claire, as sweet as you are, any nice-looking man would love to spoil you. Might even get one with a little money besides." She looked at me over her steaming cup. "You deserve some fun in your life. We—Henry and I—have a friend we think you should meet . . ."

"A friend? I've already got friends—you and Henry, Ray and Edith, people at—"

"Wipe that smirk off your face, you silly woman. You know what I mean. A gentleman friend. A very nice man that Henry's known for years. I only met him in May when he stopped by on his way from Amarillo. He's a widower too. Lives in Anthony, Kansas. We told him about you. We both think you should meet him."

"You both? Sounds like you hatched this plot some time ago. Anthony? That's the other side of Alva. Must be a couple hundred miles from here. I don't think any man in his right mind would travel half a day just for introductions. He—"

"Well, Floyd would. I had an old snapshot of you, and he must have stared at it for five minutes. 'Mighty fetching,' he said."

"You're barking up the wrong tree, Amy. I'm sure he's nice if you say he is, but I've got other fish to fry besides hooking up with an old guy looking for someone to press his shirts and clean house."

"Oh, he's not real old. I'd never pair you up with an old coot who has one foot in the grave. But . . ." Amy blushed. "We took the liberty of telling him sometime next month would be a good time to meet you, and he's . . . he's all set to make that half-day drive. I hope you'll . . . Oh, Claire, have I put you in a bind?"

I stared at my dear friend. "No, Amy, you put yourself in a bind." Then I chuckled.

She laughed too, kind of weak-like, halfway between hopeful and embarrassed.

I wondered what I was going to do when their friend showed up. Maybe have him slop the hogs.

43 One Sure Thing

Fall 1953

Sammy

"Just pitch it here. I'll hit it." Dickie waved the bat like Eddie Matthews, the Braves slugger, or at least he thought he did.

I gave a high kick and fired the ball toward home plate, a flat rock laid on the ground in front of the garage. Dickie swung late but connected, sending the baseball foul down our imaginary first base line. It headed toward the weed-lined road ditch. "Get it. It's over there," I hollered at Jerry, our only outfielder.

He ambled toward the mass of thistles that filled the ditch. Dickie and I waited . . . and waited. "G-Go help him. He'll never find it, the way he's looking."

"You help him," Dickie said. "You're closer."

I ignored him. It was hot. "You're the one that hit it. D-Didn't you see where it went?"

Jerry shaded his eyes. "It's not here. I can't find it."

"Oh, for P-Pete's sake," I said. "Guess I'll have to look, since you're so h helpless." I hustled to the roadside, peering into heaped tumbleweeds as I skirted the ungraded road edge. "Dickie, come and help, or w-we'll be out here all day."

"That was a good baseball. The whole St. Louis team signed it," Dickie said. "Stan Musial, Red Schoendienst, Haddix—"

"I know, I know. It's a good ball," I growled. "And it's the only baseball we got. I told you we shouldn't have pl-played with it. Should've used our old softball, but no, you wanted to use the baseball Floyd gave us. Now look at—"

"That softball is like a dead cat. No shape to it at—"

"But we can't lose that b-baseball. Floyd said it'd be worth a lot of money someday. So, look . . . over there. Don't just follow me around." My brothers weren't much help. Finally, I jumped in the ditch and started pitching dried tumbleweeds every which way. That got old in a hurry, as their little spikes poked my hands, and still no baseball. Within minutes, Jerry wandered back to the

291

house, and Dickie just stood looking down at the ditch. "Come on, you g-guys, help find it."

It was no use. The sun was getting hotter, and Kenneth Taylor came roaring by in his new pickup, coating us with a layer of dust. "Okay for now," I said. "But we gotta come back and find that ball. It's the only one we got, and it's s-special. Mama said he gave it to us because he likes us."

"He gave it to us because he likes Mama." Dickie kicked a dirt clod.

Afterward, I returned a few times to look for that ball. Nothing. I suspected we'd never find it. What would we say if Floyd asked about it next time he came to see Mama?

There were other things to worry about besides that ball. Like would we have to move to Anthony, Kansas, where Floyd lived?

Mama said not to worry about it. She actually said, "You boys do your chores like you're supposed to." Which was really no answer. Maybe I better not ask, so I wouldn't put ideas in her head. It was plain Floyd really wanted Mama to marry him. I tried not to think about that, because I couldn't imagine anyone taking Daddy's place. Not even a nice guy like Floyd.

I didn't want to talk about Floyd Tade, but Dickie brought the subject up. "Do you suppose Mama would make us move to Kansas, if she marries Floyd?"

His question made me sick to my stomach. "Wh-what do you mean? She hasn't even said she's gonna m-marry him."

"Well, I know he's not a farmer, so he sure wouldn't stay here. Always wears a suit and tie, like he's a big shot." He chunked a rock at a tree but missed.

"Yeah, not a farmer—no c-calluses on his hands, and kind of chubby. Probably doesn't know how to drive a tractor."

Dickie hooted at that. "And he says he's taking Mama out for dinner. Dinner." He wrinkled his nose. "Doesn't he know it's supper, when you eat at night?"

"That's what town people call it—d-dinner. M-makes them sound sophisticated."

"Yeah, but what if we have to move to where Floyd lives?"

"We don't know," I said. "We don't have to move if Mama doesn't marry him."

"And what if she does?"

"Let's not make up p-problems until we have to."

Claire

Avis had reawakened a fear that hovered in the back of my mind since the early thefts after Elmer's death. Nothing since, except for the burglary of the guns. I tried not to think of the bind we'd be in if someone showed up for an unsocial call. Now, we didn't even have a gun on the place, except the old single-shot .22. I couldn't imagine how to make our place look fortified, and less inviting for bad people. Aside from keeping everything locked up when we were gone, the only other measure was having a man around. Which was what everyone else was thinking, according to Blanche.

Being so fixated on keeping things going, I hadn't thought about another man. Didn't let myself think that way. Elmer would always be my one true love. I couldn't imagine marrying someone else. For one thing, it would mean a big change for the boys. What man would want to take over our farm? Any guy worth his salt would already have his own place. He'd expect us to move to his home, among his own people. That would take the boys away from the only home they had ever known. Reason enough to stay on the farm.

No word from Amy for over a month, which was actually a relief. Besides, I had no time for social affairs. The boys and I talked about keeping our place tightened up, protected. Not much else we could do, as everything cost money, always scarce.

Ethel always made me feel secure. Maybe because being twelve years older than me, she was both like a mother and a sister. Thanksgiving with her and Ed in Dodge City became a tradition for us. Three or four of their kids, all grown up now, would sometimes stop in too, so there was lots of food, laughter, and stories. Their four sons had served overseas in World War II. All came back safe, with tales of close calls, weather extremes, and scary nights.

Driving up to Dodge, I visualized talking with Ethel about, well, everything. Although she and Ed weren't rich, their hillside house in an established neighborhood featured upholstered furniture, carpeted floors, and framed prints on the walls. It reminded me of Pop and Mama's place in Ness City.

Ethel was about as wonderful a sister as anyone could have. A registered nurse, she had a manner about her that breathed trust and competence. Capable yet elegant, she'd put on a little weight after bearing seven children, but she was still a handsome woman. Ed Mauch knew he had a winner when he won her hand, and he utilized all of his modest talents to make her happy.

Hugs all around when we arrived at the house on Mulberry Street. Ethel gave individual attention to each of my boys, asking about their school, and what hobbies they were pursuing. Sammy gave her his colored-pencil drawing of quail in flight, and Ed set the boys down to a new picture book from their daughter Vada's honeymoon trip to Mexico.

Thanksgiving dinner was a spread out of the Saturday Evening Post. Later that evening, after the other guests had departed, Ethel and I went into the kitchen to talk. Pushing a cup of coffee in front of me, she said, "So, let's talk about those letters you told me about. What's this about a Nebraska Doolittle?"

I explained the contract claim and choices I needed to make.

Ethel divided two pieces of carrot cake on saucers. "Sounds like you got a good lawyer."

"Oh, he's a very smart man, but first he wants to hear what I want to do. Then he'll give his opinion about the oil lease . . . Oh, this cake is so good." I cut another piece with my fork, savoring the icing. "What it comes down to is whether I should wait and maybe risk everything for an extra twenty-five hundred dollars."

"Fair enough. What's your plan?"

I pushed my shoulders back. "Sign the lease. Get the first seventy-five hundred so we can get control of our lives for the first time in three years."

She scooted her chair around beside mine and slipped her left arm around my shoulder, pulling me close. "Little sister, you've proved you can do it. Taking over the farm after Elmer's cancer treatments, and all alone out there on that little farm. You deserve to trust yourself. Pop would've approved."

Yes, Pop. His name brought a cloak of silence. I thought of his wisdom and encouragement, how he overcame so many obstacles in his life. Finally, I said, "Determination. Pop taught us to persevere, not to quit. That's the way we're made, all five of us. If we kept going, we'd always have hope. Now, I'll see this through. All the way."

"I knew you would. Now what's this about you seeing a man?"

"Well . . . not a lot to tell." I took a breath and fingered my bead necklace. "It's nice to dress up for something besides church.

He's taken me out to nice restaurants, in Liberal, Meade. His name is Floyd Tade. Met him through Elmer's cousin, Amy. A real gentleman, he treats me like a lady."

"And . . ."

"I just don't know, sis." I looked away, my breath shallow.

"Well, do you like him? I mean, really like him?" She leaned toward me. "How do you feel about him?"

"Confused. Not sure if I'm ready for anything permanent. The boys and I have worked so long and hard just to make it, to survive on the farm. This oil lease gives us real hope."

"Sounds like it's not the right time for romance, Claire. From what you just said, you first want to finish what you started."

I sighed. "Never connected it that way, but yes, I've got a job to do—for my boys—before I share my . . . my heart with someone else."

Her eyebrows went up. "For the boys? What about for you? The boys will be gone one day, making their own plans—"

"But it is about me. Simple unschooled, uneducated, ignorant me. I've never admitted it, even to myself, but I need to do this for me, Ethel. Pop, for all the wonderful, blessed things he did . . . for me . . . he stopped me at ninth grade! Said a woman doesn't need more education. You know that's how he was."

I stopped to catch my breath, suddenly angry. "The woman is supposed to find her fulfillment at home, in the kitchen, in the bedroom, motherhood, church, while her husband goes out into the world to slay dragons, build empires, fight battles, and make a name for himself.

"Pop wasn't too excited about your going to nursing school, but you went anyway. He cut our schooling short, so Myrrl and I could help on the farm. Didn't make that much difference to Myrrl, because he intended on being a farmer all his life. I wanted to be in charge of my own destiny. But how could I, if I couldn't even finish my schooling?

"So now you know, my dear sister, the whole reason why I've been, well, hell-bent on making a go of it on our farm." I took a deep breath. Neither one of us said anything for a long minute.

A burst of laughter from the living room echoed what really mattered.

44 The Widow

Claire

The preacher, a thin, balding man in a rumpled suit, arose and stood behind the chapel pulpit, shuffling sheets of paper as if uncertain what was next. He finally selected one sheet and began reading. The obituary. Yes, about time. It's almost over.

Shouldn't have come. Didn't have to. No, not right. I knew I had to attend that funeral, simply out of respect for Durward. Elmer's son, but my stepson, and a man I loved—almost as much as my own sons.

Durward, Wilma, their two little ones, and his older daughter Sandra Lee sat in the front pew. Other relatives filled the second row. Other than Durward, Wilma, and Sandra, I hoped no one else knew who I was.

When the boys and I entered the chapel, our eyes adjusting from the bright outdoors, Durward was there, enveloping me in a warm hug. He whispered, "Claire, great to see you. Glad you're here. Thanks for coming."

I felt eyes of other mourners on us as we found seats near the back. They probably wondered who we were, come to pay respects to Durward's mother. And first wife of Elmer Hall—for one year. Elmer and I had been married twenty-one years.

By that time, the preacher had launched into reading the obituary, naming the survivors, and finally, that Florence ". . . was the widow of Elmer Hall, who predeceased her in 1951 . . ."

I didn't hear anything after that.

The mourners had been ushered out. Head bowed and my entire body in a tremor and encased in perspiration, I made for the exit. How could Durward allow such a lie to go unchallenged? I had to find him—quick.

Wilma found me first. "Oh, Claire, Claire." Arms extended like a farmer's hayfork, she scooped me into her arms, whispering apologies. "Oh, Claire, we had no idea. Florence's preacher put us off when we asked to see that obituary. Said he had it all put together."

I dabbed my face and honked into my hankie—two or three times. "I was shocked. Totally shocked. The few occasions I saw Florence . . . I never expected anything like that from her. You know what that would make me—an adulteress? And Elmer, a bigamist? Our children, illegitimate?" I stopped to catch my breath. "I've got that divorce certificate at home. I'm sending a letter to that preacher, telling him—"

"Not necessary, Claire. Durward knows you're Elmer's widow—no one else. I can't, for the life of me, I cannot understand . . . why Florence had to keep up that fiction that she was still married to Elmer to the day of his death. You've been through—"

"Claire!" It was Durward, his handsome face contorted as if in pain, bending down to enclose me with his presence. "I can't explain Mom's stubbornness, just cussed pigheadedness. Thought I talked her through it, that she'd put that aside six, seven, years ago. Now, you come out eighty-five miles to her funeral because it was the decent thing to do. And that preacher connived with her . . ." Both hands on my shoulders, he drew back and faced me. "I had—"

"I already explained, honey." Wilma stood between us, one hand caressing my back.

"It's okay. I'm getting over it," I really hadn't, but allowed my shoulder to sag against Durward's chest. "You've got to attend to other folks. I'll be all right. It just caught me by surprise." A big sigh. "We'll be going home. Stop by and see us, if you have time on your way back to Texas."

He gave my shoulder a squeeze. Bending down again, Durward whispered, "You sure you're okay?"

Pinching his jaw between thumb and forefinger, I chuckled. "Takes more than that to put me down, buster."

Wilma dismissed her husband. "Shoo. I'll take over repairs from here." Leaning toward me, she murmured, "Don't tell him I said this, but with his mother gone, we might be able to stay for one of your chicken-and-noodles dinners next time."

I gave her a healthy squeeze, and then turned to the boys, who'd been sitting back watching the fireworks. "Boys, let's head for the farm."

On our way home from Elkhart, Dickie asked why I was driving so fast. I told him I was upset over what happened at the funeral, and I didn't want to talk about it. There were no more questions about my driving or the funeral. The boys knew I was in no mood for such.

What I didn't tell them was that incident had so rattled my mind I wasn't about to introduce more change into our lives. I thought of Floyd, innocently trying to influence me toward a major change. He was coming down from Anthony next weekend. Not what I needed just then.

I'd have to tell him my true feelings, something I avoided doing most of my life, it seemed. Floyd was a wonderful man, but it wasn't the right time. It might never be. We had to save the farm in order to save ourselves, from my perspective. He saw us together, but he didn't see the bigger picture—that the farm represented hopes and dreams, a major fulfillment of life's purpose for me and the boys.

I must have been going a good clip when we came into Guymon. Jerry said, "Mama, there's the sheriff."

Dickie chimed in, "He's turned from that side street. He's coming right behind us."

My breath caught. "Oh, my goodness. I've never had a traffic ticket in my life, and I sure can't afford one now." Trying not to be obvious, I slowed the car to a crawl while watching the patrol car from the rearview mirror. "Turn around, boys. Don't stare back at him . . . Jerry! I said to turn around."

All was quiet in the car as the deputy followed us all the way out of town, and another two miles beyond on Highway 54. When he finally pulled over and headed back to Guymon, I allowed myself to breathe.

To celebrate my narrow escape, and make up to the boys for my grouchiness, I stopped in Hooker and bought us all ice cream cones. Seemed like it had been way too long since we'd simply enjoyed ourselves. Maybe Avis was right, that I needed to give myself some grace after three years of pressure, uncertainty, and grief. I was flummoxed at how my emotions could go from zero to ninety in nothing flat.

I still had one more important thing to do—have my lawyer send a letter to that preacher, certifying Elmer's divorce. Maybe he could make me a carbon copy for Durward and Wilma, just to remove all doubt in their minds, if any did exist.

My emotions went into high gear again. I'd better meet with Lansden, just to make sure he had that certificate of Elmer's divorce from Florence. I'd call his office for an appointment the minute we got home.

✎✎

Lansden's receptionist, Eileen, seemed reluctant to grant an appointment. "He's awfully busy. They've asked him to go down to Oklahoma City to testify again on petroleum waste disposal regulations. Can I tell him what this is about?"

I balled my fists, a headache threatening. "It's personal. I'd rather not discuss it over the phone. I want to . . . I need to see Mr. Lansden. It's very important to me." I vented a big sigh. "I'm on a party line."

At that, she quickly scheduled me for midweek.

✎✎

Waiting outside my attorney's office, I granted that a face-to-face meeting probably wasn't necessary. On the other hand, I wanted to be sure. Trusting other people's instincts and assurances had given me unwelcome surprises over the past several years—everything from Elmer's purchase of wild cows to the reading of Pop's will to dozens of disappointments from Elmer's side of the family. I thought how nice it would be to have someone else handle all my problems, which I knew Floyd wanted to do. But what if Floyd turned out to bring more problems than he solved? Right now, it was up to me. I'd better keep it that way.

The buzzer sounded on Eileen's desk, and I went in to Lansden's office. I must have looked like trouble, because he got right down to business. "Didn't expect to see you this soon, Claire, but how can I help you today?"

I explained what happened at the funeral. "I was ready to let the matter drop, even mad as I was, but I need you to show me there isn't something that might jeopardize our ownership of the farm. The claim by this Doolittle yahoo, taking a quarter of our mineral rights, has already put my teeth on edge. When's all this going to stop?" I smacked his desktop with my open hand.

Holding his fountain pen like a scepter, he jabbed the note pad laying before him. "You're right, Claire. You've got enough

299

cause to be upset, when outrages and claims—all unreasonable and unwarranted—never seem to end." He paused. "How are you doing?"

I drew a hand to my throat and stared at him. "Well, I'm still angry . . . about that preacher. Such disrespect, and an outright lie about Elmer, me, actually, about Florence, too."

"Let me put your mind at ease. I've got that certificate in my files. Elmer's divorce was legal. Neither she nor any of her heirs have any claim on your estate. Your stepson, Durward, has inheritance rights, based on his relationship to Elmer—not to her. But for the public record, I'd be happy to send a letter to the reverend, if you wish."

"Yes, I wish. Thank you. I'll get you the address."

"There is still the matter of this, this Nebraska Doolittle, as you call him. I may have to file a lawsuit to shake his grasping hand off your property. We simply have to wait and see if Standard Oil determines the Kizer well to the east of you is viable. Bob Phelps is the pumper. He'll tell me if and when they declare it a dry hole, which looks very likely, from what he's already said. If they plug it, we still may have to sue to terminate Doolittle's claim on your mineral rights. I'll let you know as soon as I hear."

ဆာ

Two months later, I received a letter from Lansden. His letter was brief and to the point:

> Doolittle refuses to accept your standing pertaining to the mineral rights on your farm and indicates he will file a counter claim retaining 25% ownership of those rights. Please contact my office to schedule a meeting regarding this matter.
> Merle Lansden
> Attorney at Law

I felt better. Lansden had to be ready to go; I sure was. This guy Doolittle wanted what wasn't his, and he obviously didn't care that I was a widow just scraping by.

ဆာ

I went into my attorney's office determined to do something about that.

Lansden leaned back in his chair, eyes directed upward, as if the answer to my trouble registered somewhere on his ceiling. "Doolittle has retained an attorney out of Omaha, big office occupying two floors in the Omaha National Bank Building. I expect they're licking their chops at the idea of taking on a hick lawyer from a Panhandle town no one's heard of."

He pursed his lips in a tight smile. "This might be fun."

45 True Grit

Claire

Elmer and Pop both had the opinion that lawyers and bankers created more pressure and anxiety than the problems they were supposed to solve. Necessary experts, they created systems that only they fully understood, which ground us producers of corn and wheat into finer dust.

I was a small-time operator, yet the boys and I couldn't bend our shoulders to long-term endeavors without attending to those necktied professionals who oiled and levered the gears of commerce. While we shivered breaking six-inch-thick ice in the stock tank so our cattle could drink and hauled eight-foot-high loads of bundled cane from snow-covered fields to feed the beasts, we watched leaden skies for signs of storms that could wipe out our herd in a matter of hours. Meanwhile, my attorney plotted strategy against an opportunist who planned to take a big part of what we'd worked for over the past fifteen years.

The next time I went to Merle Lansden's office, he said, "We've passed the critical fifteen-year mark of Doolittle's claim for a quarter of your mineral rights. He's banking on one of two things. First, Standard Oil—the driller of the well in Section Twenty-two—will determine that it's a bona fide producer of oil or gas, which would continue his rights as long as there is production. His second hope is that—out of ignorance, neglect, or simply being overwhelmed by it all—you will fail to contest the division order. Then he collects twenty-five percent of all future earnings from your mineral rights, just by doing nothing."

He drummed the top of his desk with a yellow pencil. "You'd be surprised how many landowners fail to contest a division order. In Doolittle's case, if he knows you're a widow, his attorney will probably try to bluff you out of keeping what's rightfully yours."

I slapped my gloves into my hand. "I read through those contract and lease forms from A to izzard. I believe I understand them, and I'm not going to let that skinner get the best of us."

"You're doing right, Claire." He looked up, a smile crinkling the corners of his eyes. "Doolittle and his attorney miscalculated you. I'll prepare the necessary papers and see if we can shake up the third floor of Omaha National Bank.

"If his bigshot attorney persists, I'll threaten him with harassment—or something. Probably the last thing he expects from a tumbleweed hick lawyer."

As I rose to leave, Lansden had a broad smile across his face. "Claire, your spunk does my heart good."

༄

Spunk. Telling it like it is, backbone, fortitude, grit. Never easy. Seemed like something showed up on my doorstep every other week, demanding a shovelful of pluck, as Pop would've called it.

The latest was when I said to Avis, "I broke his heart. Told him I couldn't marry him."

Avis had asked. I told her. Hadn't even told Sammy. She looked up at me from the same ladder-back chair the boys sat in when I cut their hair. "What'd you tell Floyd? I thought you liked him."

"I do like him. That's why it was so hard. I told Floyd it wasn't about him. It's where my life is. That didn't make anything easier. I enjoy his company. Told him what a wonderful man he showed himself to be.

"He told me how much he loved me, something any woman yearns to hear. But only if she can respond in kind. I couldn't. All along, I hadn't let myself go there."

By this time, I'd pulled up another chair, so I could sit beside Avis and unburden my soul. "Yes, it broke his heart. Knew it would."

Avis leaned back. "I can imagine what he asked next—another man?"

"I put that aside . . . which may have made it harder for him to accept. I told Floyd I can't even think of anything permanent now, that it's not the right time for me."

"To which he probably said he could wait. A few months, maybe a year . . ."

I laid my scissors on the table and sighed. "Yes. Then I had to further destroy his hopes. I told him the lives of my boys had been disrupted enough, with grief, uncertainty, knowing they'd never see their father again this side of heaven. They've had to deal with more than the loss of a father. If Elmer could've been in their lives,

303

watching them grow up, he could enjoy their successes, help them fight through defeats and struggles. He would've shown each one how to be a man—what's required for a boy or man to establish himself, hold his own, how to fix things, earn his place wherever he stood."

"I hear what you're saying, Claire. Having all girls, I can't speculate much on what that means. But wouldn't bringing a man into their lives do that for your boys?"

"Maybe the right man, but Floyd wasn't really what you'd call . . . a man's man. He was an office type, sold insurance most of his life. Doubt if he's ever milked a cow or ridden a horse." I dropped my head, massaging my temples. "Ray taught the boys lots about livestock—how to recognize a dangerous or fearful animal, diagnosing ailments—but what they need is a man to be a companion to them. That's how a boy learns to respond to challenges. Even how to relate to other men. So much of life is figuring out who you are, what you can and should do."

Her eyes widened. "You're quite the philosopher, Claire. I didn't realize you'd given that much thought to—"

I gave a short laugh. "When you've just got yourself to converse with, you say many things. And not having another adult around, I talk with my kids a lot. Probably more than most people do. Got to prepare my boys for whatever's out there.

"I believe in my sons. I tell them they can be anything they set out to be. I tell them that, nearly every day. Encouragement from Pop meant the world to me." A sigh. "When I can't give them anything else, I encourage. A mother will bandage their wounds and cheer them on. But sometimes, they need a man to tell them they're as good as the next guy, so when the chips are down, they can stand up to a loudmouth, a bully. That, I don't always know how to do. It worries me sometimes."

Avis settled back into the chair, and I stood to resume snipping. She said, "I can see how moving might affect your kids. I suppose they like church?"

"That and school is their social life."

She didn't say anything. For a while, neither of us spoke. I felt better, having told her about Floyd. That chapter in my life was behind me now. Later, I'd tell Ethel too.

I took a deep breath. "One thing I didn't tell Floyd—about our place. He sees it as a burden on me. I don't. Our farm is property, something the boys and I can always go back to. To others, it might be just a two-bit spread. Floyd promised he could take me to a secure life with him in Kansas. It would've been nice, having pretty things, no worries about sick livestock, getting a pregnant cow out of a blizzard to save her calf . . . watching for rain clouds when your crops are withering in the field . . . being out on the tractor in hundred-degree heat for days on end.

"But that would mean leaving this farm, land that Elmer and I fought and scraped to keep. I guess I was tied to that as much as anything. Floyd couldn't—maybe no one could—understand all this place means to my boys and me. Marrying him right now would jeopardize all we poured out our sweat and tears to keep this farm."

I must have said lots of other things that day. Avis was patient. Listened to all I had to say. She knew I needed to talk. I guess that's what friends are for.

§∼

Merle Lansden sent me several letters on his fine stationery over the next few months. The last one verified what we'd hoped for all along—Standard Oil had given up on making anything out of the Kizer well. They were plugging it.

That gave us all we needed to end Doolittle's claim on my mineral rights. However, I had to give Lansden the go-ahead to petition the Office of State Lands for a new division order. I still owed him fifty bucks for my last two visits.

It took five weeks for State Lands to act. Right after that, I received a letter from E. J. Bergenthal advising me that Texaco Oil planned to commence drilling on Section Twenty-one of our farm. Our farm! He said to expect a letter from Texaco within the next two weeks, and that I should have my attorney review it and all attached exhibits.

I stopped where I was and simply stared at each word, my heart beating a mile a minute. If only Elmer could have been there. He always believed someday the place would really amount to something.

The Texaco letter arrived by certified mail ten days later, dry as dust. It laid out the well location, access road, and droned on about my rights as landowner, state requirements for things I never thought of, compensation for damages to my land, and an overview of drilling operations and cleanup. I tried not to get my hopes up, but the boys and I couldn't help but be excited.

For what seemed like the tenth time in the previous two months, I went to Lansden's office. This time, it was to leave the Texaco letter with the packet of information. He came out of his office when he heard me speak to Eileen. "Claire, I imagine you'll want this reviewed right away. Frankly, I'd feel better to wait until the Office of State Lands approves our division order request. We want to assure Doolittle's rights have been terminated. Done. Ended. Otherwise, should your new well come into production, he'd lay claim to a quarter of the proceeds."

I shook my head. Would we ever get anything without a struggle?

৵৶

The day I received notice of State Lands approval of the division accord, I called Lansden. No more Doolittle.

In mid-December, five giant flatbed trucks, plus an assortment of semis, bobtail trucks and pickups arrived west of the big pond over a three-day period. That was after a survey rig, road grader, and a lowboy with dozer put in the access road and laid out the well location.

I hadn't told anyone outside of family about the operation, but Blanche was on the telephone the very morning Texaco staked out the well. "Claire, what's going on over on your farm?"

"What are you talking about, Blanche?" I decided to have some fun with her.

"Those trucks, Claire. There's trucks out on your field, west of the house. Ain't you seen them?"

Better be nice. "Yes, I saw them. Texaco is setting up to drill a well on the farm . . ."

Silence, then the clatter of the phone handset. In the background, I could hear Blanche hollering, "Henry! Henry, they's going to drill on Clair-ie's farm." More silence, followed by sounds of shuffling feet, then Blanche back at the phone, out of breath. "Oh . . . I'm so glad for you. I know it ain't for sure, but you been through so much, Clair-ie . . . Claire. The good Lord is looking out for you and them boys. I'll put out the word. Everybody in the neighborhood will be tickled to hear about this . . ."

Indeed, Blanche would make sure everybody knew about the drilling operation.

I enjoyed the attention for a while but didn't hold my breath the entire drilling period. People and trucks going in and out, I

306

couldn't keep track if the well was going to be a dandy or a dud. Ray and Edith kept me informed as best they could. One morning, Ray stopped by with the news that they'd hit gas, and the tool pusher said it looked to be a good well.

I read about it in the Southwest Daily Times, which had better ways of getting accurate information than I did . . . Forty-four million cubic feet of natural gas, and the paper proclaimed it to be one of the best gas wells in the area. The front-page article said that was enough natural gas to heat 30–40,000 homes a year. Sounded good, but we wouldn't let it change our lives.

The boys listening in, I tried to call Durward right away, as he'd worked in the oil fields all his life. Before I got through, and explained everything to him, he began laughing. "Claire, you got a darn good well." Except he didn't say "darn." He went on to explain the production would drop over time, but that it should pay for groceries, and then some.

He said I could tell the banker I could pay off every nickel I'd borrowed against the farm. He started laughing again. "Claire, if I was there, I'd give you the biggest hug you ever had."

I began crying then. My boys gathered around me, we hugged one another, not worrying about long-distance phone charges.

Epilogue

Claire and the boys stayed out on the farm for the next several years, and Dickie (Richard Lee) made it his home when he married Beverly and took over the farm. In 1957, Claire was hired as Deputy County Assessor, a job she enjoyed the remainder of her working life.

She remarried a year later, but in 1969, she was widowed again. Always active, Claire was getting ready to go dancing at the Senior Center when she was stricken with a stroke that would take her life at the age of ninety-four.

For her funeral, the Forgan Baptist Church was packed beyond its capacity of 200. Friends and family came from all over Beaver County to honor the little lady whose tenacity and faith sustained her and the boys beyond what anyone could have imagined.

Merle Lansden, her attorney, said what everyone else in the community was thinking. "Claire, I don't know how you did it."

Claire did: "By the grace and mercy of God, who never stopped loving us."

Acknowledgments

A Place to Stand continues the account of our family, begun in *Daughter of the Cimarron*. I determined that this memoir could best be presented primarily in the words of my mother, as she was the voice and burden-bearer of my brothers and me through those uncertain years after Dad died. Several scenes are given from the point of view of Elmer, my father, and others in my voice as a child. While I tried to be reasonably accurate in these accounts, any errors of omission or mistaken details of events are my own.

I give sincere thanks to my family, especially my wife Gloria who read chapters, gave encouragement and input into my descriptions of family interactions and relationships, and tolerated the inevitable seclusion that is the lot of every writer. Thanks to my brothers, Dick and Jerry, ready sources to confirm dates and events, as well as to laugh over surprises that colored what would have otherwise been forgettable, even sad, times.

My critique partners in Willamette Writers and Salem Christian Writers were unsparingly candid, yet gracious and encouraging as they relived this account with me—Frank Yates, Sandy McDow, Robert Pauls, Jerry Buss, Jean Rover, Mark McIntire, Char Kardokus, Rose Ricci—I thank you. Thanks to Nicole Miller for another outstanding cover, and to Roger Shipman and Jay Pritchard of Reify Press for all that goes into bringing a manuscript to fruition.